"In *Beyond the Cosmos*, Dr. Ross has shown that the tools scientists have used to deal with paradoxes in the physical world can also be applied to gain important insight into various paradoxes in Scriptures. Difficulties that have plagued the Christian community for centuries are not only clarified when 'seen' from the point of view of one living in a higher dimension, but those same difficulties also become the basis for strong proof of the supernatural inspiration of the Bible. This book will provide food for thought for any student of the Word, and will, no doubt, begin a new area of biblical research to which others can contribute."

–David Rogstad, physicist, Jet Propulsion Laboratory

"In *Beyond the Cosmos*, Dr. Hugh Ross considers application to theology of current scientific research suggesting that our universe may be more than four-dimensional. He suggests that we can use the general concept of extra-spatial and temporal dimensions to further our understanding of God and the nature of existence outside the universe. *Beyond the Cosmos* is a thought-provoking book, sure to inspire much discussion and contemplation."

–Gerald B. Cleaver, associate professor, department of physics,
Baylor University

"Not since the decade before the First World War has a Christian thinker given so much attention to the dimensional distinctions and boundaries that have been opened up in scientific discovery of a multi-dimensional universe, and reflected on what that demands of us in biblical and evangelical faith today. Hugh Ross offers readers a fresh and illuminating approach to thinking about God and divine revelation in open-structured and extradimensional ways that will be a great help to many people today."

–Thomas F. Torrance (1913–2007), author, theologian, and professor,
the University of Edinburgh

HUGH ROSS

BEYOND
the
COSMOS

THIRD EDITION

THE TRANSDIMENSIONALITY
OF GOD

Covina, CA

Cover design: 789, Inc.

Some of the anecdotal illustrations in this book are true to life and are included with the permission of the persons involved. All other illustrations are composites of real situations, and any resemblance to people living or dead is coincidental.

Unless otherwise identified, all Scripture quotations taken from the Holy Bible, New International Version ®, NIV®. Copyright ©1973, 1978, 1984, 2011 by Biblica, Inc.™ Used by permission of Zondervan. All rights reserved worldwide. www.zondervan.com The "NIV" and "New International Version" are trademarks registered in the United States Patent and Trademark Office by Biblica, Inc. ™ Other versions used include the New American Standard Bible® (NASB), Copyright ©1960, 1962, 1963, 1968, 1971, 1972, 1973, 1975, 1977 by The Lockman Foundation. Used by permission. www.Lockman.org; and the King James Version (KJV).

Ross, Hugh (Hugh Norman), 1945- author.
      Beyond the cosmos : the transdimensionality of God /
Hugh Ross. -- Third edition.
      pages cm
      Includes bibliographical references and indexes.
      "Revised and updated"--Cover.
      Originally published: Orlando, Fla.: Signalman
Publishing, ©2010.
      ISBN 978-1-886653-22-1

      1. God (Christianity) 2. Time--Religious aspects--
Christianity. 3. Astronomy--Religious aspects.
4. Physics--Religious aspects--Christianity.   I. Title.

BT103.R667 2017   261.5'5
                         QBI16-900029

Printed in the United States of America

For more information about Reasons to Believe contact (855) REASONS / (855) 732-7667 or visit www.reasons.org.

Contents

Illustrations

List of Figures

List of Tables

Acknowledgments

Thank God for a team of editors willing to suffer under my tendency to set unrealistic deadlines. Sandra Dimas, Marj Harman, Linda Kloth, Jocelyn King, Amanda Warner, and Colleen Wingenbach, I'm grateful for your grace under pressure, as well as for your skills and attention to detail. Your efforts have made a bigger difference than anyone can know. Thank you, Sean Platt, for greatly enhancing the graphics. And without your help, Diana Carrée, the manuscript would never have been assembled or delivered.

Thank God for all of you who shared personal stories about how this book, in its earlier editions, impacted your life and the life of someone close to you. No story has moved me more profoundly than that of a husband who studied these pages night by night with his beloved wife as together they prepared for her passage through death into eternal life. He said the insight to God's nearness and the preview of the new creation brought unspeakable joy and lifted them above the dark shadow cast by her cancer. Kathy and I wept as we heard these words.

Thank God for John Moore, who took meticulous care in reviewing the mathematics and physics on which this book's premises rest. Now that you've gone to be with the Savior, John, you know how vastly short my limited imagination falls of the actual splendors of his presence.

Thank God for John McClure and Signalman Publishing, who first brought this book back into print. Your efforts revived and expanded the book's audience, and we're grateful. That possibility seemed utterly remote until Kathy and I met you, John. We're eternally grateful.

Thank God for Kathy, my wife, who helped me (as always) find words to convey my thoughts. Your words and thoughts intermingle with mine on every line. Together we hope every individual who reads this book will experience the deepening of faith and joy that became ours day after day as we wrote and rewrote each chapter. What we prepared as an offering to the Lord became his gift to us.

Hugh Ross
2017

Preface to the Third Edition

Since the publication of *Beyond the Cosmos*, first and second editions, scientists have made even more discoveries substantially strengthening the evidence for general relativity (hence, for a transcendent Creator) and for string theory (hence, for a 10-dimensional cosmos). This new edition builds on the new data and adds more evidence for the biblical account of origins.

Readers of the first two editions asked for a fuller definition and explanation of dimensions, historical background on the development of extradimensional physics, and an idea of what the 10 dimensions of the universe look like today. I trust this third edition makes significant headway toward meeting these requests.

Dozens of suggestions offered by readers of the second edition were incorporated to make my theological points clearer and more specific and the text more readable. But my greatest goal is to create an edition that more effectively imparts a vision of God's awesome magnificence, a vision that expands readers' capacity to worship and serve our Creator and Savior.

Chapter 1

Invitation to Soar

Can we really know God in a relational sort of way? Christians often say that spiritual life is not about religion but about a relationship with our Creator and Savior. This declaration has a nice ring to it—especially to those who recognize relationships as not just interesting electives but life's core curriculum.

But how successful can we be in developing a relationship with someone we cannot physically see, hear, or touch? The relationships we are most familiar with and continually strive to learn more about are the ones with fellow human beings. We are especially eager—some would say desperate—to fulfill our longing for intimate, lasting relationships that allow us to know and be known, accept and be accepted, cherish and be cherished, all with a depth and breadth that grows over time.

If God is a personal Being, as the Bible says, then what we have learned from human relationships should allow us to make some applications to building a relationship with him. And what could be more desirable than an experiential connection with unlimited love, life, and truth? We want it; and according to the Bible, so does he. We follow through on the commitment he asks of us and the journey begins. Soon we learn why he promises to be faithful when we are faithless.[1] And we learn to say to the Lord, "I do believe; help me overcome my unbelief!"[2] We are glad for the encouragement of others who embarked on this relationship before we did, and we look to them for reassurance. Many distinguished theologians have offered useful assistance. They have focused our attention on God's character qualities and divine attributes, exhorting us to fix our minds on these things. They have reminded us to talk with him, to acknowledge his presence in and around us daily, moment by moment. They have given us practical instruction in worship. I value the work of these godly men and women, and I have seen its positive impact in my own life and in others' lives. And yet we still have much room to grow.

Because we cannot use any of our five senses to detect God's presence, his voice, or the feelings and attitudes behind his words, we often struggle with doubts and misgivings. And because many of his characteristics and doctrines seem contradictory, we do not know how to hold him in our mind's eye. We cannot picture him in his totality. Even when we invent pictures and ways to visualize him, we are cautiously aware of our tendency to distort.

If we are anything like the people portrayed in the Bible, we wish "God with us" would be tangible. Which of us does not sometimes question, as the first disciples did, why it is better for us if Christ (our physical proof of God's reality, power, and love) returns to heaven and sends the invisible Comforter, Counselor, Holy Spirit in his stead? Since Jesus said it, we accept it. Nonetheless, we wrestle with it. If only we could get a better grip on *how* it is better!

I believe God is enabling us to tighten our grip. He has proven, again, his willingness to disclose himself for the sake of strengthening and deepening our relationship with him and of drawing others to join us in that venture. In the pages that follow, I describe a remarkable set of scientific discoveries made in the 1990s and early twenty-first century that may open our understanding to some of the greatest mysteries of the ages, such as:

- How can my choices be totally "free" if God is in control of all things at all times and if he knows the end from the beginning?
- How can he hear my words and thoughts while listening to billions of others around the world at exactly the same moment?
- How can God be forever alive and still suffer death (in the person of Christ) on the cross?
- How can God be all-powerful and all-loving and yet allow so much suffering and evil?
- How can God be both three *and* one?
- How can Jesus claim that in a few hours on the cross he suffered the equivalent of eternal, unimaginable torment for billions of people?
- How can God subject someone to eternal torment and call that an act of his love?

For centuries, these "How can it be?" mysteries have tested the faith and love of those who believe in the biblical, personal God and have often served as stumbling blocks for those who do not.

These mysteries present Christians with an opportunity to honor him as the Truth, whose name is also Teacher, and to respect each other as students.

Still, though we know our assignment is to study, dialogue, and discern, we often dispute and divide. I hope we will use these breakthrough discoveries to help us resolve our differences.

These discoveries offer new insights into God's mind-boggling capacities both within and beyond the 10 (newly demonstrated *minimum*) dimensions of reality. Whatever mental pictures we hold of him will have to be expanded enormously. Though never complete in this life, these mental pictures will be more complete than before. We will know how God can be nearer to us than our own breath, nearer even than the person with whom we are most intimate. We will understand why it is better for Jesus to be where he is than to remain physically present with us. We will gain a clearer picture of where he is now and what heaven will be like. Comprehension of these capacities can launch us into greater heights of rejoicing and new depths of appreciation, individually and collectively, for the immeasurable gift of eternity with him.

For those who have not yet begun such a relationship, I hope that an exploration of these capacities will inspire not only awe but also a vision and desire for the possibilities of such a relationship.

Let's soar together through these newly charted regions beyond the matter, energy, and familiar space-time boundaries of the cosmos.

Chapter 2

Takeoff from Ground Zero

We are about to explore God's wonder and glory in and beyond all the cosmic space-time dimensions physicists have shown must exist. But before we burst through the space-time surface of the universe for a glimpse at God's extradimensional and transdimensional realm (throughout and beyond the cosmic surface), let's review what dimensionality is all about. (Readers with little scientific and math training may find chapters 2 and 3 more challenging than other chapters. Some may choose to skip ahead to chapter 4. From that point on, the material is readily accessible to all readers.)

Most people never think about dimensions, except in geometry and architecture classes, for the simple reason that our dimensional realm never changes. Since birth we have lived in the four dimensions of length, width, height, and time. We will continue to reside there until the day of our physical death. The laws of physics God designed for physical life require that all cosmic matter and energy be situated on (and confined to) the cosmic surface, or "envelope," where these four dimensions reside.[1]

Informal Definitions of Dimensions

Each of the four space-time dimensions of the physical universe is independent of the others. For example, in the length dimension we can extend a line as long or as short as we like without affecting any measures in the width, height, or time dimensions. Similarly, lines can be extended as far as we want, even infinitely far, along each of the dimensions of width, height, and time without affecting measurements in the other three dimensions. This independence means that each dimension must always be exactly perpendicular—exactly at a 90-degree angle—to all the other dimensions (in Euclidean geometries).

We cannot picture in our minds how the time dimension intersects our three space dimensions, yet we experience the effects of time and we can

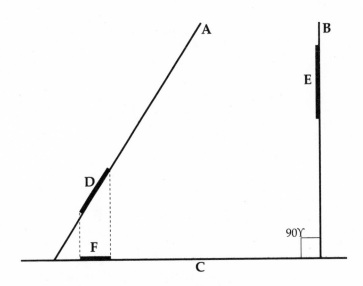

Figure 2.1: Dependent vs. Independent Dimensions
Dimension **A** is not independent from dimension **C** because a projection from dimension **A** (such as **D**) will cast a shadow (**F**) on dimension **C**. Dimension **B** is independent from dimension **C** because a projection from dimension **B** (such as **E**) will create a point rather than a shadow on dimension **C**.

measure its reality as an independent dimension. *What we must keep in mind is that our capacity to visualize things will be limited to the three space dimensions that our five senses can directly detect.*

The difference between a dependent and an independent dimension is shown in figure 2.1. Lines drawn along the dependent dimension (A) project (as in casting a shadow) on the alternate dimension (C). All lines drawn along the independent dimension (B) make no such projection. They will show up only as infinitesimally small points.

Adding Dimensions
A one-dimensional realm is a single line. That realm includes only points and lines fixed along that one-dimensional line. Let's call that line "length." A two-dimensional realm is a plane. It is described by two lines that are always at right angles (90 degrees) to each other (assuming Euclidean geometry). Let's call these lines "length" and "width." In such a realm, points, lines, and two-dimensional figures—polygons, circles, ellipses, and countless other shapes residing in the plane—are possible.

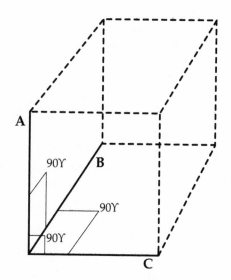

Figure 2.2: A Two-Dimensional Depiction of a Three-Dimensional Realm
This illustration of a box shows three-dimension-defining lines: **A** (height), **B** (length), and **C** (width) each at right angles to the other two, as 90-degree angle markers on the box's sides indicate.

A three-dimensional realm is a volume defined by three dimensions. Each line defining one of the dimensions is at right angles to both of the other two lines (see figure 2.2). Let's call these lines "length," "width," and "height." In this realm, points, lines, two-dimensional figures, and three-dimensional solids or volumes are possible.

To construct a four-dimensional realm, we need four dimension-defining lines, each line lying at right angles to the other dimension-defining lines. Let's call these dimensions "length," "width," "height," and "time." Such a dimensional frame is the realm of our existence. But because we cannot place ourselves beyond the four dimensions—say, in a fifth dimension where we could gain some perspective—we cannot picture all four simultaneously. We are limited to picturing only three. This limitation struck me and my fellow students forcibly one day in a college course on complex algebra.

The professor described how in four dimensions of space, a three-dimensional basketball could be turned inside out without making any breaks in its surface. None of us could picture how. But, given the mathematics of four independent dimensions of space, we could, without too much difficulty, demonstrate that the professor was right. Such a phenomenon could indeed occur. We had proved it, but we could not visualize it, and we felt uncomfortable with that limitation.

Then our professor referred us to a film. By animating two dimensions at a time, the filmmaker actually depicted a basketball turning inside out without breaking its surface. This film frustrated us even more. We could see from different perspectives (various "top," "bottom," "side," etc., views) how the transformation progressed, yet we could not unify in our minds the various two-dimensional images into one four-dimensional picture. In the end, we were forced to let go of the frustration and be satisfied with our equations. That step was a big lesson, and an important one for the sake of ongoing research.

Subtracting Dimensions

Architects use the same technique the filmmaker used with the basketball phenomenon. The big difference, however, is that the architects' clients are not asked to cross a dimensional threshold. A three-dimensional building is portrayed to three-space-dimension people by showing them various two-dimensional cross sections. A plane view (from above) and side views from the east, west, north, south (and possibly other angles as well) suffice to give clients a detailed mental picture of how the building will look.

This technique works because the architects' clients live in three dimensions of space. But what if the clients were deprived of just one dimension of space? If they were confined to the length and width dimensions alone, with no visual access to the dimension of height, they would experience the same frustration in trying to visualize buildings as my class did in trying to picture a basketball turning inside out in four space dimensions.

These two-space-dimension creatures would, however, be capable of determining the properties of the three-dimensional building. Once convinced that three space dimensions are possible, they could mathematically add an extra space dimension to the two-dimensional mathematics they normally work with. They could then establish which attributes and descriptions of the building could be true and which could not. Ultimately, they, too, would have to deal with visual limitations and accept the equations.

Other Perspectives on Dimensions

A more rigorous but still nontechnical way of looking at dimensions is to describe them as different orders of infinity. A single-order infinity would permit an infinite number of specific items. For example, counting to infinity means

Rescuing the Cosmological Argument for God's Existence

Viewing dimensions as different orders of infinity explains why what most philosophers describe as the strongest argument for God's existence, namely, the cosmological argument of Augustine, Aquinas, and Kalam, has had little impact on modern-day educated skeptics. The argument rested on the unproved assumption that an infinite regress of cause-and-effect events is impossible. (Hence, there must exist an ultimate First Cause or Causer for the cosmos.) So, the argument holds only if one can prove that the natural realm is limited to a first-order infinity of cause-and-effect events. Fortunately, as chapter 3 explains, scientific discoveries of the past few decades now provide such evidence.

counting through an infinity of different numbers. Experiencing forever is having the capacity to enjoy an infinite number of events. A single dimension has room for an infinite number of different points.

A second-order infinity permits an infinity times infinity (∞^2) of specific items. In two dimensions there is room for an infinity multiplied by infinity of different points. This is because in an infinitely extended two-dimensional plane, one can draw an infinite number of spatially separated parallel lines. Each infinity of lines can contain an infinite number of different points.

In three dimensions, room exists for infinity to the third power (∞^3) of different points. Four dimensions permit infinity to the fourth power (∞^4) of different points. Thus, a 10-dimensional universe could possibly contain ∞^{10} of different points.

The most consistent way, scientifically, to consider dimensions would be to frame them according to the behavior of the laws of physics. For example, the forces of electromagnetism and gravity permit stable orbits of electrons about atomic nuclei and planets about stars because they obey an inverse square law. This means a doubling of the distance between two masses reduces the gravitational tug they exert upon one another by two squared (or four times); a tripling, by three squared (or nine times); a quadrupling, by four squared (or 16 times); and so on. To physicists, a three-dimensional spatial manifold is the realm where gravity and electromagnetism obey an inverse square law. In two spatial dimensions, gravity and electromagnetism would follow an inverse law.

In four spatial dimensions, they would obey an inverse cube law; in five spatial dimensions, an inverse fourth-power law; and so on. One of the evidences examined in chapter 3 for the creation of 10 space-time dimensions at the cosmic origin moment is the existence, at that time, of inverse eighth-power laws.

Beyond the Fourth Dimension

The method that complex algebra students use to mathematically construct a realm of four space dimensions can also be used to build realms of virtually any number of dimensions. With five dimension-defining lines, and with each line at right angles to the other four, we can describe, in mathematical terms, a five-dimensional world. With six such lines, we can describe a six-dimensional realm. And so on. For each of these n-dimensional worlds we formulate geometrically, we can design algebraic expressions to describe what shapes, functions, and behaviors are possible for physical entities existing in those n dimensions.

With the help of supercomputers, mathematicians have designed realms with as many as a million dimensions of space. Their n-dimensional equations can predict what phenomena are possible in each of these n-dimensional worlds. One of the patterns they observe is that the more dimensions in a realm, the closer certain odd-shaped objects, such as 3-D spheres, can be packed together.

This higher dimensional mathematics makes for some fun exercises, but does it have any *practical* significance if extra dimensions beyond length, width, height, and time (what mathematicians typically call D5, D6, D7, etc., or De, Df, Dg, etc.) do not exist? Not really, but the exciting news is that these mathematical exercises have prepared us to grapple with new scientific discoveries about physical reality.

What physicists have discovered in the past few decades can be neither understood nor appreciated without such mathematical tools. I cannot help but say the timing is perfect. Physicists have uncovered strong evidence that extra dimensions do indeed exist.

Yet predating these physics discoveries by more than 1,900 years are the words of the prophets and apostles who penned the 66 books of the Bible. These ancient authors, under the inspiration of the One who exists both in and beyond the universe and the universe's 10 space-time dimensions, described phenomena—such as the creation event, miracles, Jesus's post-resurrection capacities, as well as paradoxical doctrines—that *require* the existence of extra dimensions, or the functional equivalent of extra dimensions. These writers assured their readers that God's ways and thoughts are beyond our human limits, but that "eternity," some unknown reality beyond this universe, is somehow inscribed within us.

Now we have the opportunity and the privilege to see from a new perspective—and to integrate—what yesterday's Bible authors and today's physicists affirm about reality beyond the cosmos.

Chapter 3

Physics Breaks through to New Realms

The first hint at the existence of extra dimensions (beyond length, width, height, and time) came from Einstein's theory of general relativity. Almost at a glance, the set of 10 general relativity equations indicates an ultimate origin for matter and energy. Even without the detailed calculations, a picture emerges from those equations, a picture of continual expansion from a cosmic beginning. A closer study of the general relativity equations reveals that the entire universe burst forth and is still expanding outward from an infinitely (or nearly infinite) dense state.[1]

This cosmic creation event, often called the big bang, has been confirmed in several ways through the past few decades of research.[2] The most direct evidence comes from measurements of the distances and motions of galaxies[3] and of the temperature and characteristics of the radiation remaining from the cosmic creation event at varying distances from us.[4] The first measurements allow us to watch the galaxies continuously moving away from one another, while the latter measurements allow us to observe the universe getting cooler and cooler as it gets older and older, or larger and larger. This bursting forth of the cosmos from an infinitely small volume, or essentially an infinitely small volume (a few cosmological models predict an initial maximum volume of 10^{-100} cubic centimeters), implies that the universe has a beginning, a starting point in the finite past. Einstein recognized this implication[5] and dared to say that it affirms the necessity of "a superior reasoning power."[6]

Space-Time Theorems Emerge

Einstein's conclusion went against the grain of astronomers and physicists trained to presume an infinitely old universe and an irrelevant, if any, cosmic Initiator. The simplicity and obvious nature of Einstein's conclusion made it all the more irritating.[7] Several attempts were made to prove that this beginning in the finite past arose from incorrect assumptions about the universe's homogeneity and symmetry.[8] Critics tried introducing all manner of inhomogeneities, asymmetries, and rotations into Einstein's theory, but to their amazement, these machinations backfired. If correct, these machinations would have actually slightly shortened the timescale back to the beginning.[9] No matter how astrophysicists manipulated the theory, this stubborn singularity (the infinitesimally small volume threshold at which matter and energy began) would not go away.

It was left to the next generation of astrophysicists to figure out why it would not, and could not, go away. Over a four-year period, starting in 1966, George Ellis, Stephen Hawking, and Roger Penrose affirmed that any expanding universe governed by general relativity that also contains at least some matter and energy must possess a singular origin in the finite past.[10] But they went further. In fact, they carried the solution of Einstein's equations further than anyone else had. In doing so, they discovered that the operation of general relativity guarantees a singular boundary not just for matter and energy but also for space and time. In other words, if the universe contains matter and/or energy and if general relativity accurately describes the dynamics (movements of matter and energy) of the universe, both the stuff that makes up the universe and the dimensions in which that stuff exists share a common origin, a finite beginning. Physicists call this finding the space-time theorem of general relativity, and it carries profound philosophical and theological significance.

As it turns out, the theorem developed by George Ellis, Stephen Hawking, and Roger Penrose was simply the first of the space-time theorems. Its proof was developed in the context of general relativity where it was presumed that the cosmic expansion rate did not vary much throughout its history. Since then, theoretical physicists have produced a whole family of space-time theorems. These extensions of the first space-time theorem apply to all possible inflationary big bang models (models where the universe experiences a brief, hyperfast expansion when it is less than 10^{-32} seconds old). In all these possible cosmic scenarios, the space-time theorems apply. Space and time had a beginning. Therefore, space and time must be created entities.

Reliability of General Relativity

During the 1970s and 1980s, a crucial *if* hung over the space-time theorems. Expansion was no longer in doubt; the existence of matter and energy had never been in doubt. And though the operation of general relativity had been affirmed to 1 percent precision (two decimal places),[11] it had not yet been established with adequate certainty to put theoreticians' doubts to rest.[12] By 1980, the level of certainty had improved to better than 0.01 percent precision (four decimal places)[13]—impressive, and yet still not quite enough to satisfy the most skeptical theoretician.[14] But in 1993, that lingering shred of uncertainty was finally vanquished.

The Nobel Prize in physics that year went to Russell A. Hulse and Joseph H. Taylor Jr. for their study of the binary pulsar PSR 1913+16. This stellar system consists of two neutron stars (one of which is also a pulsar) orbiting closely about one another. Through a 20-year-long study of this system—in which gravitational forces exceed those seen in our solar system by hundreds of thousands of times—a team led by Taylor was able to affirm the accuracy of general relativity to better than a trillionth percent precision (that is, to 14 decimal places).[15] In Penrose's words, this set of measurements "makes Einstein's general relativity, in this particular sense, the most accurately tested theory known to science!"[16]

Ten years later, a team of astronomers using the Parkes radio telescope in Australia discovered the first known binary pulsar (PSR J0737-3039) in which *both* neutron stars are pulsars.[17] This pair also stands out as possessing the shortest orbital period for any known binary pulsar—just 2.4 hours. The unique characteristics of PSR J0737-3039 have enabled astronomers to produce "the most precise confirmation yet of the theory of general relativity."[18]

One of the ways PSR J0737-3039 verifies general relativity is by testing one of general relativity's unique predictions, specifically the prediction that the orbits of binary pulsars will shrink over time.[19] Measurements of PSR J0737-3039 show that its orbit is shrinking by seven millimeters per day, a measure in perfect accord with general relativity. By this means, astronomers have established the certainty of general relativity "a hundred billion times better than current Solar System tests."[20]

General Relativity Confirmed in All Contexts

While Hulse and Taylor's measurements plus the observations on PSR J0737-3039 convinced the physics and astronomy community of general relativity's reliability, a few doubters remain, primarily among theologians and philosophers. Philosopher J. P. Moreland, for example, seems unimpressed by the predictive and explanatory successes of general relativity.[21] He and others are waiting for general relativity to be proved in *all* relative contexts.

Previous to Hulse and Taylor's work, general relativity had passed 11 independent experimental tests. These experiments are described in some detail

Figure 3.1: The First Image of a Complete Einstein Ring at Optical Wavelengths
Credit: NASA/ESA/STScI

in two of my previous books (*The Fingerprint of God* and *The Creator and the Cosmos*).[22] A few of the tests include:

- the bending of distant star and quasar light by the gravity of the sun or of distant quasar light by the gravity of a galaxy;
- small adjustments in the orbits of planets and asteroids about the sun;
- gravitational red shifts in the wavelengths of certain spectral lines;
- the retardation of radar and laser signals bouncing off various solar system bodies; and
- the orbital characteristics of binary star systems containing pulsars.

What astronomers lacked at the time was the detection of near-perfect (and therefore unambiguous) "Einstein rings," as well as confirmation of the predicted but elusive "Lense-Thirring effect." Recent observations, however, have supplied these evidences.

Einstein Rings: General relativity predicts that gravity will bend light. In fact, the first confirmation of general relativity came during a solar eclipse in 1919 when the stars in the Hyades star cluster were observed to be slightly out of place. A much more dramatic and definitive test of general relativity can be had when a massive galaxy lies exactly on the line of sight between the observer's telescope and a distant quasar. In this case, general relativity predicts the appearance of an Einstein ring centered on the image of the quasar. A complete Einstein ring, designated B1938+666, was observed for the first time in 1998.

Figure 3.2: Einstein Rings Imaged by the Hubble Space Telescope
Credit: NASA/ESA/STScI/SLACS Team

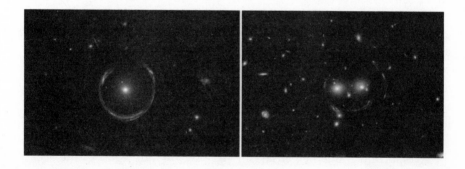

Figure 3.3: Double Einstein Ring Imaged by the Hubble Space Telescope
Credit: NASA/ESA/STScI/SLACS Team

It was seen at both optical and infrared wavelengths.[23] The accompanying image (see figure 3.1) was sent to Earth by the Hubble Space Telescope. Physicist Andrew Watson termed it a "dazzling demonstration of Einstein's theory at work."[24]

Since 1998, astronomers have discovered more than a dozen complete Einstein rings. Figure 3.2 shows eight such rings. In 2008 NASA announced the discovery of a double Einstein ring (see figure 3.3). In this case, a foreground galaxy 3 billion light-years away served as a gravitational lens for two distant galaxies, one of them 6 billion light-years away and the other 11 billion light-years distant. Both were perfectly aligned with the foreground galaxy and Earth. This double Einstein ring, designated SDSS J0946+1006, provides the most spectacular visual proof to date of the reliability and accuracy of general relativity theory.

Lense-Thirring Effect: The last major prediction of general relativity to be observationally confirmed was the Lense-Thirring effect. This prediction says that the spin of a massive body will generate space-time curvature in its vicinity and therefore will alter slightly, in a predictable manner, the path of a smaller body or a disk of material orbiting about it.

For bodies within the solar system the predicted effect is extremely small, and until the late 1990s no instruments existed with the necessary sensitivity to either confirm or deny general relativity in this context. What apparently did the trick was a four-year long study on two laser-ranged, Earth-orbiting satellites, LAGEOS I and LAGEOS II.[25] With data from these satellites, five physicists from Italy and Spain established that the Lense-Thirring effect does indeed exist, and its value is within 10 percent of general relativity's prediction, with a plus or minus probable error of about 20 percent.[26]

In 2010, the LARES satellite will be launched to overcome at least some of the limitations of the LAGEOS project. However, physicists are putting their *real* hope for a definitive confirmation of the Lense-Thirring effect in the Gravity Probe B.

NASA launched the Gravity Probe B into orbit on April 20, 2004, with the goal of confirming the Lense-Thirring effect to four places of the decimal. Data was collected for more than a year. Then began the long process of data analysis. Alas, even by August 2008 the confirmation attained a level barely superior to that produced by the LAGEOS satellites.[27] Refined measurements await completion.

Fortunately, astronomers are not limited to searching for the Lense-Thirring effect only in the dynamics of solar system bodies. If a disk of material orbits a very dense body (such as a neutron star or black hole) at an angle to the plane of the star or hole's spin axis, the dragging or twisting of space-time that the Lense-Thirring effect predicts will cause the disk to wobble like a toy top. In turn, the wobble will generate oscillations in the intensity of the x-ray radiation emitted from the gas in the disk. The theory even predicts the rate at which the oscillations should occur, given the spin characteristics of the particular neutron star or black hole.

A team of Italian astronomers pointed out a way to use existing telescope instrumentation to detect the Lense-Thirring precession of orbiting material about identified black holes within our own galaxy.[28] The first such detection of the predicted quasi-periodic x-ray brightness oscillations (QPOs) was made in 1998.[29] Since then, astronomers have succeeded in detecting the Lense-Thirring effect for a number of black hole and neutron star binaries, as well as for the Sagittarius A supermassive black hole at the center of our galaxy and the gamma ray blazar/quasar PKS 1510-089.[30]

Today it can be said that no theory of physics has ever been tested as rigorously and in so many different contexts as general relativity. The fact that general relativity has withstood all these tests implies that no basis remains for doubting the conclusions of the space-time theorems of general relativity.

An Even More Powerful Theorem

Many scientists were deeply troubled by the philosophical implication of the space-time theorems, specifically its indication that a causal Agent beyond space and time must have created our universe of matter, energy, space, and time. In an attempt to eliminate the need for a transcendent Creator, several theorists proposed cosmic models without a space-time beginning. However, these models would not permit the existence of physical life. They typically negated the second law of thermodynamics. But without heat consistently flowing from hot to cold sources, as the second thermodynamic law demands, life molecules cannot be assembled nor can metabolic reactions proceed.

Theoretical physicists Arvind Borde and Alexander Vilenkin spent 10 years exploring the limits of the space-time theorems. Their research led them to discover powerful extensions to the theorems. These extensions established that regardless of the universe's homogeneity, isotropy, uniformity, or lack thereof, and regardless of its energy conditions, the universe indeed must have had a beginning.[31] Together with Alan Guth, Borde and Vilenkin concluded that any cosmic model in which the universe expands (on average) can be traced back in finite time to an actual beginning, or creation, of space and time.[32] As Vilenkin later wrote in his book *Many Worlds in One*, "With the proof now in place, cosmologists can no longer hide behind the possibility of a past eternal universe. There is no escape, they have to face the problem of a cosmic beginning."[33]

Second Dimension of Time

The space-time theorems are no longer in question. Nor is their corollary that the cause (Causer) of the universe operates in a dimension of time or its equivalent (that is, maintains some attribute, capacity, super-dimensionality, or supra-dimensionality that permits the equivalent of cause-and-effect operations) completely independent of ours. The law of causality (or the law of statistical correlation in which quantum or statistical mechanical effects are significant) says that effects emanate from causes and not the other way around. Thus, causes precede their effects. Time, then, can be defined as a dimension along which cause-and-effect phenomena occur.

While a few philosophers might object to this causal definition of time,[34] it is a definition that allows all time-dependent phenomena in all the sciences to be treated consistently. It is also the most common definition of time employed by the popular media and in society at large. Since no living human transcends the space-time manifold of the universe (and, therefore, cannot observe time from outside or beyond time), no living human can boast a correct, absolute, or complete definition of time. But such a definition is not necessary. We simply need a consistent definition, and we need to use that definition consistently. So, whenever I refer to time in this book, I mean physical time—time as defined by the operation of cause-and-effect phenomena where effects follow after their causes.

The creation event—the origin of the universe's matter, energy, and total dimensionality—is an event that *includes* our time dimension. Whoever caused the universe, then, must possess at least one more time dimension (or some attribute, capacity, super-dimension, or supra-dimension that encompasses all the properties of time). To put it another way, God is able to interact with us in ways we interpret (through our time-bound experience of cause and effect) as the result of time-like capacities in the person or essence of God or the existence of other time-like dimensions or properties through which God operates.

In this space-time theorem and its corollary, we find confirmation of the biblical revelation of a Creator who exists and operates beyond our time dimension and who is in no way confined to it or by it. In other words, the Creator's capacities include the equivalent of at least two, and perhaps more, time dimensions. Just imagine for a moment what his time capacities, thus cause-and-effect capacities, must be. No wonder he calls himself the "I AM," the Alpha and the Omega. (We'll delve into the deeper theological implications of God's time-fullness in later chapters.)

Unified Field Theories

Still more scientific breakthroughs have come and are coming. Physicists can now demonstrate that the Causer exists and operates in multiple spatial dimensions (or their functional equivalent) beyond our three, in addition to the one time dimension (or the equivalent).

This rapidly unfolding drama started more than a half century ago in the quest for a single elegant theory that would explain the relationship of all four forces of physics, a "unified field theory." Einstein devoted the last 25 years of his life to this ambitious quest. He failed to achieve his goal, not for lack of brilliance, but for lack of technological tools: (1) particle accelerators powerful enough to produce the extended family of fundamental particles and to probe unification energies, (2) supercomputers capable of generating various solutions to sets of complex nonlinear differential equations, and (3) ground- and space-based telescopes capable of penetrating the farthest reaches of the cosmos to its earliest moments of existence. (The more distant a galaxy, the longer it took that light to reach us and, therefore, the farther back in time we are peering.)

Einstein succeeded in his goal in one significant sense: He paved the way toward development of that magnificent theory. In developing special relativity, he showed how matter and energy are interchangeable under certain conditions. In general relativity, he showed how space and time, as well as matter and energy, are interchangeable under certain conditions. The key to this interchangeability, or "unification," was the addition of a dimension. When the traditional three-dimensional approach led to a dead end, Einstein proposed a four-dimensional system requiring calculations in 4-D, rather than 3-D, geometry. He treated time as a fourth dimension, virtually equivalent to length, width, and height. And his approach worked.

Einstein's addition of a dimension to unify matter and energy (special relativity) and eventually matter, energy, length, width, height, and time (general relativity) set today's generation of physicists on the right track. By adding not just one but several dimensions of space to our three, these researchers may well have accomplished what once seemed impossible. The latest findings demonstrate that electromagnetism, the weak and strong nuclear forces, and gravity—the four fundamental forces of physics—can be unified in a 10-dimensional realm.

The first observational indication came in the 1970s and early 1980s when newly available 100 billion-electron-volt particle accelerators brought physicists success in unifying electromagnetism and the weak nuclear force into one force, called the electroweak force.[35] Their efforts showed, at least to some extent, that force unification is possible.

A series of 1990s experiments using much more powerful particle accelerators aided in the discovery of several dozen fundamental particles, including the six quarks predicted by theories explaining the unification of the strong and weak nuclear forces with the electromagnetic force.[36] Based on these findings, researchers are confident that the strong nuclear force, too, must be unifiable with the electroweak force. Exactly *how* has yet to be observed, but particle physicists have theoretically established that such unification will occur at energy levels of about a trillion trillion electron volts (a trillion times more energy than the highest levels achieved to date in particle accelerator experiments).

Resolving the Gravity-Quantum Mechanics Impasse

What emerged from these physics experiments was a theoretical construct called supersymmetry, the conclusion that electromagnetism and the weak and strong nuclear forces are indeed unifiable. The next step was to fit gravity into the scheme.

The first to attempt the integration of gravity and supersymmetry was California Institute of Technology's John Schwarz in the mid-1980s. What Schwarz soon discovered was that the dimensions of length, width, height, and time did not provide enough room for all the symmetries demanded by both gravity and quantum mechanics (the subatomic world where energy is not infinitely divisible). In other words, in four space-time dimensions all possible formulations of gravity predict that quantum mechanics must be false, and all possible formulations of quantum mechanics predict that gravity must be false. Since overwhelming physical evidence establishes that both gravity and quantum mechanics are true—in fact, human life is impossible unless both are true[37]—the universe in some context must be composed of more than four dimensions.

For the 10 years that followed Schwarz's discovery, he and his growing team of theoreticians built models of creation that ran the gamut from 8 to 26 dimensions of space and time. What emerged were millions of possible solutions with little hope of discerning which of the possibilities might be correct.

Strings

The theoretical and observational success of supersymmetry convinced researchers that extra space dimensions must exist. This new perspective on reality became possible only because researchers would not give up in the face of a seemingly intractable problem. As long as they treated fundamental particles as points, all attempts at finding the correct solution for unification failed. Worse yet, their equations yielded absurd conditions for the universe at ultra-high temperatures.

Something was wrong, but what? Fundamental particles look like points and behave like points, but because models treating them as points developed problems under extremely high temperature conditions that must have existed very near the beginning of the cosmos, obviously the models were incorrect. What if fundamental particles looked and behaved like something other than points in the newborn universe? Through painstaking effort John Schwarz's team and others found that if fundamental particles function as loops of energy, what physicists call "strings," unification theories and the entire array of physics theories—even special and general relativity, gravity, and quantum mechanics—could work together.

A Close-up on Strings

Strings are less like strings than they are like vibrating, rotating elastic bands. They are greatly stretched at the extremely high temperature of the first split second of the universe's existence. At the lower temperatures since then, they are contracted to such a degree that they behave like points. (Typically they are a hundred billion billion times smaller than a proton.)

String theories do not work in three space dimensions. They need much more room to operate. However, they need that room—six extra space dimensions—only for a moment, just a split second after the initial creative burst. From that moment on, these six extra dimensions are no longer necessary to the universe's development. So, if they existed, what happened to the six?

For many months, scientists grappled with literally thousands of possible answers to the question. Because of the enormous complexity of the string theory equations, more than a hundred million possible mathematical solutions existed; and, because our knowledge of conditions in the earliest moments of the universe lacks necessary precision, determining which of these solutions correctly described reality posed a daunting challenge.

Math Breakthrough Solves String Problem

In the latter weeks of 1994, while people around the world prepared to celebrate Christmas, physicists Ed Witten and Nathan Seiberg gave their own special gift to humanity. They reduced an entire field of mathematics to a single short explanation. For decades, mathematicians were stymied in their attempts to describe with precision certain physics phenomena requiring four-dimensional space. Their equations seemed impossible to solve, even with supercomputers. But a pair of super human brains did it. Witten and Seiberg transformed these extremely complex equations into simple ones,[38] almost as simple as the

Gallery of Strings

Though strings are just one-dimensional line elements, they can behave in exotic ways in multiple space dimensions. Heterotic strings, for example, are closed loops with two types of vibrations. The clockwise vibration operates in 10 dimensions of space, the counterclockwise in 26 dimensions (16 of which have been compacted). In a six-dimensional realm, a five-dimensional analog to the one-dimensional string appears, namely, a five-brane (a five-dimensional super-membrane). Type II strings also appear. In the dimensional realm where these strings operate, electrical charges disappear. In four dimensions of space, "solitons" appear. These particle-like objects include magnets with only one pole (i.e., magnetic monopoles).

calculus equations so familiar to undergraduates.

While string theorists recognized almost immediately that they had just received a tremendous boost toward success, even the optimists assumed that producing a workable theory would take at least a few more years of hard work. To their surprise and joy, the crucial breakthrough came in a matter of months.

Witten and Seiberg helped eliminate an annoying physical absurdity from supersymmetry theory. When Witten and Seiberg introduced a hypothetical particle with mass that has the potential to become massless, the absurdity vanished.[39] Taking a clue from this approach, physicist Andrew Strominger proposed a certain type of black hole, a charged extremal black hole, as the possible solution to a similar problem encountered in string theory.[40] Strominger later teamed up with physicists Brian Greene, Juan Maldacena, and Cumrun Vafa and mathematician David Morrison to demonstrate that charged extremal black holes can transform into fundamental particles, and vice versa, in a manner similar to ice turning into liquid water and liquid water into ice.[41]

As an unexpected bonus, Strominger and his team found that by introducing such transformations, the hundred million plus different string models operating in 4, 5, 6, and 10 space dimensions could all be united with perfect consistency into just one theory, the 10-dimensional one. To put it another way, theories formerly thought to be competing descriptions of reality—theories invoking "magnetic monopoles," "ordinary strings," "five branes," "solitons," "type II strings," and "heterotic strings" (see box on page 36)—can all be integrated into a single, overarching theory.[42]

Massless Black Holes?

As most students of science and viewers of *Star Trek* realize, a black hole has so much mass that its gravity pulls in anything that comes close enough to it, even light. But for Strominger's black holes to fit neatly into string theory, black holes must become massless at critical moments. This necessity raises an obvious question: How can a black hole have zero mass without violating the definition of a black hole? Or, more difficult yet, without violating the principles of gravity? Simply put, how can there be gravity without mass?

The answer was found in the spatial configuration of a black hole in extra dimensions. Strominger discovered that in six space dimensions, the mass of a particular black hole (an "extremal" black hole, one with a mass and charge so tiny as to be comparable to one of the fundamental particles) is proportional to its surface area. By making this area small enough, eventually the mass becomes zero. To answer the question another way, special relativity ($E = mc^2$) tells us that mass and energy are interchangeable. General relativity extends this principle to space and time. When spatial lines are curled up tightly enough, mass and space become interchangeable. For the tiny black holes Strominger describes, the space curvature is certainly tight enough to accomplish this interchangeability. As if this finding weren't exciting enough, Strominger also discovered that his extremal black holes become massless in precisely those circumstances—and only those circumstances—necessary to eliminate the remaining physical absurdities of string theory. Black holes, which never fit into string theory before, now do fit. And they fit in a way that actually solves string theory's most perplexing problems.

Experimental Evidences for Strings

Unquestionably, strings yield an amazingly elegant set of physical principles. They beautifully unite the physics of the very small with the physics of the very large. But do string theorists have any experimental or observational evidences to support their gorgeous equations? This claim that the universe began with a single time dimension and nine space dimensions, in which during the first split second all nine space dimensions rapidly expanded in such a manner that enabled unification of physics forces, is undoubtedly dramatic and elegant. However, what verification, besides workable equations, can we see?

Evidences come from six specific areas of research, including those made

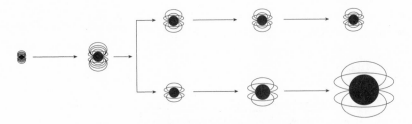

Figure 3.4: The Growth and "Splitting" of the 10-Dimensional Universe
In the beginning (T = 0) the Creator brought into existence 10 infinitely compressed dimensions. These 10 dimensions uncurled, forming a larger and larger volume of 10-D space. At T = 10^{-43} seconds, the emerging universe splits into a 6-D piece and a 4-D piece. The six dimensions stop growing while the other four dimensions continue to expand, forming the universe in which we now reside. (It is not possible to depict in this illustration that the six dimensions remain curled up around the other four.)

possible by development of particle accelerator technology, such as the Large Hadron Collider. For those who want a detailed account of these findings, see the appendix. For those who prefer a brief summary, here are the six specific areas of research:

1. Observation of partial unification of physical forces
2. Discovery of both fermions and bosons
3. Further confirmation of general relativity
4. Reconciliation of quantum mechanics and gravity
5. Resolution of the black hole entropy-information problem
6. Observation of the spin rate of black holes

To say that string theory represents a monumental development in physics, helping us to understand the natural realm and the awesome capacities of the God who created it, is to state the case mildly.

Dimensional Partition
At the very heart of string theory is the proposal that the cosmos experienced a dimensional "split" at 10^{-43} seconds (a 10 millionth of a trillionth of a trillionth of a trillionth of a second) after the creation event began. At that instant, the 10-dimensional expanding universe split in two: a six-dimensional piece that permanently ceased expanding and never produced matter, and a four-dimensional piece that became our dimensions of length, width, height, and time. That four-dimensional system continued to expand and eventually produced

matter and stars (see figure 3.4).

A better way of picturing this dimensional partition is to see all the spatial dimensions of the universe originally curled up in a very tiny "superball." In the beginning, these spatial dimensions began to uncurl as the universe expanded. At 10^{-43} seconds after the creation event, six of these dimensions stopped uncurling (that is, stopped growing) and the rest became our observable universe of gas, dust, galaxies, solar systems, etc. To this day, the six other dimensions remain curled up everywhere, at every location within or around our four still-expanding dimensions of length, width, height, and time.

An analogy for what happened would be to picture a sheet of paper so tightly curled up around one of its edges that it now appears to be a string or line. What was once a two-dimensional sheet of paper, a plane, would now look like a one-dimensional line since the second dimension is so tightly curled up around the first dimension as to disappear. For the present-day universe, the curl for the other six dimensions is very tight indeed. Their spatial cross sections are only 10^{-35} meters. This is much less than a millionth of a trillionth of the classical radius for an electron. Since no instrument even comes close to resolving such small measurements, we humans sense the existence of only the four large, still-expanding dimensions of length, width, height, and time.

String Models Galore

Physicists' demonstration that the universe is defined by nine space dimensions and one time dimension leaves room for a wide range of cosmic models. In fact, room exists for 10,500 different models. Trying to sift through such an enormous number of possible cosmic configurations to determine which are more viable is not only daunting but depressing for theoretical physicists to contemplate.

However, hope is not lost. Exotic objects in the universe, such as the double pulsar binary PKS J0737-3039, already have placed strong constraints on specific families of string theory models.[43]

Extra Space Dimensions and God

The space-time theorems establish not only the Creator's extra time dimension(s) or their equivalent, but also his capacity to operate in all the space dimensions the universe has ever possessed (or their equivalent). What follows, then, from string theory and from all these recent findings in particle physics and astrophysics, is that God must be operating in a *minimum* of 11 dimensions of space and time (or their practical equivalent).

Why So Few Dimensions for Us?

We may be inclined to wonder why God limited our existence to just three space dimensions when we could have enjoyed some spectacular "advantages" by living in a few more. The Bible suggests that we will one day live with him in something resembling those dimensions (see chapter 17); but as it turns out, human life—our physical, carbon-based life—could not exist in a universe composed of any more (or fewer) than three expanding large dimensions of space. The gravity that makes stable planetary systems possible, including the system that gives us the necessary temperature, atmosphere, day-night cycle, and other life-essential conditions, would render such systems impossible in a four-or more-dimensional system (also in a two-or-less-dimensional system). Stable, approximately circular orbits are possible only if gravity obeys an inverse square law, as it does in three space dimensions.

Electromagnetism provides another reason we need three space dimensions. In a system with anything other than three space dimensions, electrons would either spiral away from or into the nuclei they orbit. In anything other than a large three-spatial-dimensional universe, neutral atoms (atoms with no charge) and molecules could never exist. Stable stars are possible because the electromagnetic forces in stars balance the gravitational forces, a condition met only in a large, three-dimensional system. Thus, atomic-based physical life—subject to gravity, thermodynamics, and electromagnetism—would be impossible in any universe but a three-space-dimensional one.

A home fit for our physical bodies can exist only in a space-time region composed of one large, uncurled dimension of time, three large, uncurled dimensions of space, and six very tightly curled-up dimensions of space. The universe's dimensional makeup constitutes one of dozens of tangible evidences for purposeful cosmic design for the benefit of life (a concept popularly known as the anthropic principle).[44] By definition, design implies the involvement of a personal, intelligent, intentional, and powerful Designer.

A Privileged Generation

Life in the twenty-first century may present us with some dreadful liabilities— social, political, economic, and environmental crises, to mention a few. And yet, from a scientific and spiritual perspective, we can consider ourselves privileged.

We are the only people ever to see (or need) direct scientific evidence not only for God's existence, but also for his transcendent capacity to create space and time dimensions, as well as to operate in dimensions independent from our own four. The remarkable advances of research reveal a God who lives and operates in the equivalent of at least 11 dimensions of space and time. They show that God can create space-time dimensions at will and is not limited by any of his created dimensions. Such transdimensional and extradimensional capacities are more than adequate to resolve the doctrinal conflicts and paradoxical concepts that have divided the church and perplexed both believers and nonbelievers for centuries.

To loosely paraphrase a verse of Scripture, "Where division, arrogance, and unbelief abound, humbling evidences abound all the more." That is God's grace.

Chapter 4

Science's Tethers

Breakthroughs revealing a 10-dimensional universe and pointing to a realm beyond the cosmos gave scientists an indescribable thrill. Some went so far as to hope to find a "theory of everything," even "the mind of God."[1]

Such bold endeavors can arouse disdain and distrust among God-fearing people who might, in turn, be tempted to discount, if not utterly reject, these researchers' valuable achievements. Let us not make that mistake. While we can allow scientists some appropriate pride of accomplishment and heartily congratulate them, we can rest assured that their hope is futile—the Bible says so and so does science. Another, less heralded set of discoveries securely tethers our flights of fancy and our Babel-like inclinations.

While pushing past old boundaries, researchers have proven, ironically, that the theoretical limits on our ability to measure and understand are much more circumscribed than they had imagined. Rather than elevating human beings and demoting God, scientific discoveries do just the opposite. Reality allows less room than ever for glorifying humans and more than ever for glorifying God.

Unknowable Center

Through special relativity theory, scientists learned that no absolute reference system exists for measuring motions in space.[2] Through general relativity, we learned one reason for that impossibility: The universe's matter and energy reside on the three-dimensional surface of a four-dimensional system.[3] These findings mean that we humans can never locate the center of the universe. We can only make measurements along its space-time surface.[4]

Our situation is analogous to two-dimensional beings residing on the surface of a three-dimensional sphere (see figure 4). Their bodies extend over two dimensions only—length and width, or longitude and latitude. They have no thickness, no radius dimension. They can make length and width measurements only. Even though they may be able, through careful study, to determine

Figure 4: Two-Dimensional Creatures Residing on a Three-Dimensional Sphere
The three dimensions of the sphere are longitude, latitude, and radius. The creatures have no radius, only longitude and latitude. Living on the surface of the sphere, they can make measurements of "longitude and latitude" anywhere along the surface, but would be unaware that their measurements arose from a three-dimensional Euclidean sphere defined by a specified radius. Neither could they ever detect or measure anything in the radius dimension. Though they could determine that their world has a center in the third dimension, they would never be able to locate that center.

that their physical environment is a three-dimensional globe, they would never be able to determine where they are relative to the center of the globe. Likewise, we cannot determine where we are relative to the center of the universe. The only advantage we have over the 2-D creatures on a 3-D globe is that our 4-D universe is growing, and we 3-D creatures can measure that growth. Thus, we can determine more easily that our system has some kind of center. But the actual location remains hidden from us. Only a being transcending our 4-D cosmos would be able to see it.

Uncertainty Principle

Researchers always have acknowledged that the uncertainty of their measurements is limited by the precision (or imprecision) of their measuring tools. In 1925, Werner Heisenberg discovered that even with perfect instruments, a fundamental limitation remains. According to Heisenberg's uncertainty principle, we cannot accurately measure all of a particle's properties (such as its energy, position, and momentum). We know a particle is really a wave. But this particle-wave (identified by a particular wave function) cannot be measured directly or completely. So we are stuck measuring just one of the particle's various properties. Unfortunately, whenever we measure one of these properties, we devastate the particle's wave function and force the particle, in an uncontrollable way, into a new wave function. Thus, the measurement yields information about the new wave function and says nothing about the original one. This results in serious limitations to our accuracy. For example, if we were to measure the position of an electron to within a millionth of an inch, we could determine that electron's position one second later to an accuracy no more precise than 1,500 miles!

A very large amount of ignorance for the human observer is fundamentally built into the sub-microscopic world of quantum mechanics (the realm in which energy is not infinitely divisible). God, on the other hand, does not need to measure a particle to know its properties. He already knows the shape of the wave function.

Since the 1920s, the measuring limits implied by Heisenberg's uncertainty principle have been confirmed by countless experiments.[5] These experiments demonstrate that the degree of uncertainty is just right for the sustaining of life. Since certain metabolic reactions sensitively depend on the degree of quantum uncertainty,[6] if the degree of uncertainty were any greater or smaller, physical life would be impossible.

Thermodynamic Limitations

One corollary of the big bang model and of general relativity says that the universe is "thermodynamically closed." No energy or matter from any other thermodynamic system can flow into ours, nor can energy or matter from ours flow into it, at least not during the universe's knowable history. All the universe's matter and energy remain confined to the universe's space-time dimensions. Thus we humans are confined in our measuring and detecting abilities to our universe's space-time "envelope." If any other universe exists, we cannot make contact with it or detect its existence. Its space-time envelope cannot overlap ours.

Built into the inflationary hot big bang model[7] is yet another knowledge boundary. If the universe did indeed undergo a brief period of hyper-expansion roughly 10^{-35} (0.00000000000000000000000000000000001) seconds after the initial creation event, this hyper-rapid expansion effectively washed out much, if not all, information about what was happening in the universe before that moment.

A practical limitation on our ability to probe the early cosmos also exists. As the universe expands, it cools. The closer we get to the creation event, the higher the universe's temperature. The only way to directly test early conditions is to recreate extremely high temperatures with the help of particle accelerators.[8] But to duplicate the conditions present at 10^{-35} seconds would require a particle accelerator more than 40 trillion miles long. Since our resources for building instruments will always be limited, there will always be at least a tiny time period about which we must remain at least partly ignorant. Again, God knows, but we cannot.

Incompleteness Theorem

In 1931, Austrian mathematician Kurt Gödel established that mathematical "truths" exist for which we can develop no absolutely rigorous proofs. No set of axioms can be proven totally consistent. No set of axioms, then, is provably complete.

Gödel's discovery became known as the incompleteness theorem, for it meant that mathematicians must accept a minimum level of incompleteness in their "facts." The ramifications of Gödel's theorem reach beyond mathematics. The theorem also imposes a minimum incompleteness on our theories of physics and our knowledge of the universe.

This principle of incompleteness will be reflected in whatever model proves most accurate in describing our universe's origin and characteristics. Since we humans are confined to the universe's space-time dimensions and are constrained by the laws of physics, we can never get outside the universe to observe all its properties. We can never discover and state all the truths about the universe or demonstrate the totality of its consistency. Perfect, complete insight into the physics of the cosmos will always remain beyond our capability. However much we come to know about the universe, we will not be able to discover a "theory of everything" because no rational models of the universe can be proven totally consistent and complete. As God chooses what to reveal to us through the Bible, so also he chooses what to reveal to us through his creation, the "words" he declares through the heavens and the earth.[9] In the words of Moses, "The secret things belong to the Lord our God, but the things revealed belong to us and to our children forever."[10] Deut. 29:29

Plenty of "Things Revealed"

The "things revealed" deserve our attention and our probing to the maximum extent of human capability. What thrills and challenges researchers in virtually every discipline is that every discovery opens yet another door for exploration. What we learn shows us how much more there is to learn.

The limits on our abilities to know truth and visualize truth merely remind us that we are the creatures, not the Creator. But the limits do not stop us from seeking to gain a clearer picture of who he is through studying both his inspired Word and his creative work. Each will reveal his glory in its own way. Even if the windows through which we gaze on his realm have a few ripples and dark spots in them, we will be awed at the majestic beauty we see. He has left the curtains open. He invites us to look in.

Chapter 5

Extra Dimensions in the Bible

A few thousand years before physicists conceived of general relativity, space-time theorems, quarks, supersymmetry, unified field theories, and vibrating strings, a written document described both transdimensional and extradimensional reality. That document is the Bible. While discovery of the existence of dimensions beyond length, width, height, and time may rank as one of humanity's greatest achievements, far more amazing is the fact that the Bible writers depicted phenomena beyond their capacity to experience or envision. Mere imagination would be incapable of such a feat; and indeed, no other book previous to the modern era describes phenomena in dimensions (or their equivalent) beyond or independent of our four.

Beginning of Time

The first scholars to speak about the beginning of time were not Stephen Hawking and Roger Penrose, but rather Moses, the apostle Paul, and the author of Hebrews. Genesis 1:1 boldly declares, "In the beginning God created the heavens and the earth." The phrase, "heavens and the earth," is translated from a combination of Hebrew nouns that together refer to the totality of the physical creation, that is, to the entire physical universe.[1] The Hebrew verb for "created" suggests the origin of something totally new, something that did not previously exist or that was previously undetectable.[2] The book of Hebrews provides this clarification: "By faith we understand that the universe was formed at God's command, so that what is seen was not made out of what was visible."[3] To paraphrase, the cosmos we *can* detect came from that which lies *beyond* our ability to detect. These biblical statements declare that a transcendent Being created the cosmos, One who operates in a reality beyond our matter, energy, space, and time.

Specific mention of God's transcendent time dimension appears in the

New Testament epistles:

> This grace was given us in Christ Jesus before the beginning of time.[4]

> God, who does not lie, promised [the hope of eternal life] before the beginning of time.[5]

The text states here that our time dimension had a beginning and implies that God created our time dimension. These verses also tell us that God engaged in cause-and-effect action before our time dimension existed. Thus, there must be at least the equivalent of a second dimension of time in God's realm.

Other biblical passages refer to God's activities before he created the universe (or "the world"):

> The Lord brought me [Wisdom] forth as the first of his works, before his deeds of old; I was formed long ages ago, at the very beginning, when the world came to be.[6]

> "And now, Father, glorify me in your presence with the glory I had with you before the world began. . . . You loved me before the creation of the world."[7]

> He chose us . . . before the creation of the world.[8] He was chosen before the creation of the world.[9]

Most Bible scholars agree that "world" in these contexts refers to the totality of God's physical creation.[10] Again the Bible claims that God caused certain effects—he appointed, glorified, and made choices—before bringing the cosmos, including our time dimension, into existence.

The beginning of matter, energy, and even nonphysical entities is declared in these two passages:

> Through him all things were made; without him nothing was made that has been made.[11]

For in him all things were created: things in heaven and on earth, visible and invisible, whether thrones or powers or rulers or authorities; all things have been created by him and for him. He is before all things, and in him all things hold together.[12]

More than 75 Bible verses affirm that the universe had a beginning and that God created the universe.[13]

Contrasting Time Frames

According to the Bible, God can operate both apart from our time frame and within it. But God's time-full realm gives him a different perspective on time and a different experience of it:

> A thousand years in your sight are like a day that has just gone by, or like a watch in the night.[14] *Ps. 90:4*

In past centuries some scholars interpreted this verse concretely, concluding that God's clock runs precisely 365,242 times slower than our earthly clocks.[15] In fact, whole theological systems have been built on this interpretation. One group insists that God created the heavens and the earth in six consecutive thousand-year "days" and that the return of Jesus Christ must occur exactly 6,000 years after the creation of Adam.

However, the metaphoric intent of this verse (Psalm 90:4) seems obvious from the context. The verse also compares a thousand years to a "watch in the night," which means four hours in Old Testament times and three in New Testament times. In other words, what seems a long time to us can be an arbitrarily short time to God.

Peter suggests an even broader interpretation of this verse when he writes, "With the Lord a day is like a thousand years, and a thousand years are like a day."[16] Peter means here that God can experience the passing of time more quickly or more slowly than we humans do. He has the capacity to experience time at any rate he chooses.

This biblical claim makes sense if God operates along the equivalent of one or more time dimensions independent of cosmic time (see figure 5.1).

Extra Space Dimensionality·

In many biblical passages God manifests himself in earthly dimensions in ways that seem strange to human observers. He speaks to Moses from a burning bush that does not burn up. The Israelites see him in a pillar of cloud by day and of fire by night. His voice hits their ears like thunderclaps. God's "finger" inscribes the Ten Commandments in stone.

As astonishing as these encounters must have been, imagine the disciples' amazement when Jesus came to them bodily, after being crucified, without

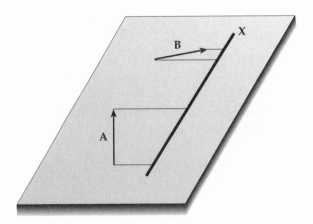

Figure 5.1: God's Time vs. Our Time
In the equivalent of two or more time dimensions, God can choose to operate along a variety of timelines, such as **A** and **B**. Though **A** and **B** have equal length, if we superimpose them on our timeline (**X**), we would experience **A** as much longer than **B**.

opening the locked doors or windows of their hideout. Both John and Luke record the event:

> On the evening of that first day of the week, when the disciples were together, with the doors locked for fear of the Jewish leaders, Jesus came and stood among them and said, "Peace be with you!"[17]

> They were startled and frightened, thinking they saw a ghost. He said to them, "Why are you troubled, and why do doubts rise in your minds? Look at my hands and my feet. It is I myself! Touch me and see; a ghost does not have flesh and bones, as you see I have."

> When he had said this, he showed them his hands and feet. And while they still did not believe it because of joy and amazement, he asked them, "Do you have anything here to eat?" They gave him a piece of broiled fish, and he took it and ate it in their presence.[18]

The disciples' shock arises not only from their inability to comprehend how Jesus could be alive and present but also from their knowledge that physical objects cannot pass through physical barriers without damage to either the object or the barrier. No wonder they concluded that Jesus must be a ghost!

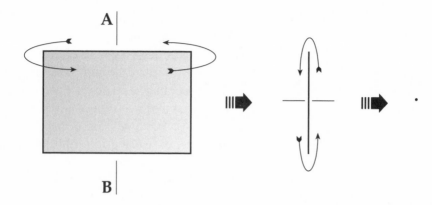

Figure 5.2: Transforming a Rectangle into a Point
The two-dimensional rectangle on the left rotates about an axis (**AB**) into a third dimension of depth. It now appears to us three-dimensional observers as a line only. If the rectangle were to rotate again into a fourth space dimension, that line would appear to us as a point only.

What they saw made no sense to them.

Jesus responded to their perplexity by demonstrating his physicality. He invited their touch, confirming that he had the solidity of flesh and bones.[19] He ate food from their table, further affirming his physical reality.[20]

The disciples could not know at that moment they had seen an example of what is possible for someone who has access to extra space dimensions or their equivalent. They had not seen a film depicting how in four spatial dimensions a ball can turn inside out without breaking its surface. They did not understand that when an object can rotate into extra space dimensions, what seem to be barriers no longer are barriers. That's because each rotation can reduce, by one, the number of dimensions presented to the object as a barrier.

Figure 5.2 demonstrates this principle of dimensionality reduction. A two-dimensional rectangle can be rotated from its position in the dimensions of length and width into a third dimension of depth. A three-dimensional observer facing the axis of rotation from far away in the depth dimension would see the rectangle shrink in its length dimension until it becomes a line. If a fourth dimension of space existed, the rectangle could be rotated about another axis from its position in the width and depth dimensions into a new position located in the depth dimension plus a fourth dimension. The same observer would see the "line" transform into a "point." From his or her perspective, the rectangle has lost both its length and width dimensions.

Jesus would have had no problem passing through the walls of that locked room with his physical body if he were simply to rotate his body into extra dimensions of space or their equivalent. For example, he could have rotated the first dimension of his physical body from spatial dimension one into spatial dimension four. He could have rotated the second dimension of his physical body from spatial dimension two into spatial dimension five. And he could have rotated the third dimension of his physical body from spatial dimension three into spatial dimension six. His physical body would then have been present in dimensions four, five, and six and absent from the disciples' dimensions one, two, and three. Since the walls of the upper room were in dimensions one, two, and three, they would no longer pose a barrier to Jesus's physical body. He would have had no trouble moving into the upper room without disturbing the walls or doors. Once inside the upper room, he could have rotated his physical body from spatial dimensions four, five, and six back into dimensions one, two, and three, where the disciples could see, hear, and touch him.

This six-dimension rotation scenario may explain how Jesus entered the upper room to meet with his disciples after rising from the dead, or he may have chosen a different approach entirely. The point is not to assert one explanation above others but rather to suggest that his transdimensional and extradimensional capabilities offer him countless ways to accomplish the feat—and the feat itself more than hints at his extradimensionality.

Other Transdimensional/Extradimensional Miracles

Miracles described in the Bible seem to fit into one of two categories. The first category includes natural events occurring with supernatural timing or supernatural placement or both. The event itself is not unnatural, but when and where it occurs is unexpected. The second encompasses transcendent supernatural events, phenomena that defy the physical laws of the universe.

As an example of the first type of miracle, God fulfilled his promise to deliver Jerusalem from Assyria's siege when thousands of King Sennacherib's soldiers fell ill and died in one night.[21] We are familiar with people dying of an ailment; but when several thousand previously healthy soldiers die overnight from an illness at a critical moment in the siege, we are astonished.

The second type of miracle represents the biblical revelation of a transcendent, extradimensional God, and Scripture offers many examples of such miracles, including "transportation" phenomena among them:

- Elijah's ministry ends with a gravity-defying ride to heaven in what appears to Elisha as a chariot of fire.[22] *2 Kings 2:1-18*
- Philip is sent by an angel to explain the gospel to an Ethiopian eunuch in Gaza and immediately afterward arrives in Azotus.[23] *Acts 8:26-40*
- Jesus glows with blinding light as he converses on a mountaintop with Moses and Elijah, who had left Earth many centuries earlier.[24] *Luke 9:28-36*

Miracles such as the backward movement of the shadow on Hezekiah's sundial also describe transdimensional/extradimensional phenomena. Since the miracle was witnessed in Jerusalem and acknowledged in far-flung regions,[25] neither local atmospheric conditions nor misreading nor malfunctions of sundials offer reasonable explanations. Nor does reversal of the earth's rotation or the Sun's sudden leap from its position, for both events would be sufficiently wrenching to destroy all life on Earth. The more reasonable conclusion is that God intervened from beyond our space-time dimensions.

In the account of Jesus and Peter walking on water, we see a violation of gravity, among other physical laws. Some force from beyond matter, energy, and our space-time dimensions held the two men above the waves.

Though self-declared seers have always been around seeking to make a name and a fortune by their supposed powers of prognostication, none has proved reliable even to 50 percent accuracy. Even that percentage is bumped up by the tendency toward ambiguity and short-range prediction. But what more can be expected of humans restricted to a single timeline where time proceeds forward only? That God's spokesmen can precisely describe all manner of future events, both scientific and historical,[26] demonstrates that his time capabilities extend beyond the linear.

The book of Revelation goes so far as to predict the eventual replacement of the entire universe and all its physical laws and space-time structures. The apostle John's description of the new heavens and earth requires the operation of new physical laws—distinct from gravity, thermodynamics, and electromagnetism—and a different dimensional matrix (see chapter 17). And, since all spirit beings survive the elimination and replacement of the familiar dimensional domain, these beings must reside—at that moment—in a transdimensional/extradimensional realm.

Christ's Dimensional Sacrifice

Jesus Christ's incarnation and resurrection represent the most dramatic and significant expressions of God's transdimensional/extradimensional capacities. A succinct description appears in Philippians.[27]

In coming to Earth as an embryo in the virgin's womb, Christ "made himself nothing" and "humbled himself." While losing none of his divine attributes or access to his divine powers, Jesus (with rare exceptions) chose to put aside the transdimensional/extradimensional realm and capacities he shared with God the Father and God the Holy Spirit. When he had completed the work he set out to do, the work of redemption, he returned to the place and the powers he had left behind. The magnitude of this dimensional (or equivalent) sacrifice ⌣ staggers human imagination (see chapters 9 and 10).

Though the illustration pales by comparison, consider what it would be like for us to put aside temporarily just one dimension and thus enter a two-dimensional realm, even for an hour. Imagine what it would be like to tell two-dimensional "beings" about our three-dimensional realm of shapes, colors, sounds, tastes, and countless experiences—and *truths*—unimaginable to them. If we cared for them as God cares for us, we would gently invite them to come with us and remind them that help is available to get them to this new world. A special tutor—the Holy Spirit—is available at every moment to guide them in understanding, trusting, and applying the promises and truths of that three-dimensional reality so they can experience it directly if they so choose.

Chapter 6

Extradimensional Doctrines

.

In addition to the direct biblical evidences of God's transdimensional/extradimensional intervention in our four-dimensional realm, the Bible presents doctrines that can make sense only if extra dimensions, or their equivalent, exist. Such doctrines represent one of the Bible's great distinctive features. They provide evidence of divine inspiration in that they defy human imagination and visualization. Other holy books include contradictions that cannot be resolved in extra dimensions, or they attempt to explain all God's attributes and activities in a four-dimensional context. Cultic sects of Christianity insist on interpreting all biblical doctrines within the constraints of four dimensions. These books and sects reflect human thinking, which both the Bible and the record of nature tell us will always fall short of God's thinking.

The Rut of the Familiar
Extradimensional thinking is difficult for most people, especially for adults. Age seems to lock our minds in a four-dimensional rut. One reason may be that the older we become, the farther removed we are from the transition we made in infancy from two-dimensional perception to three-dimensional. Until we are at least a few months old, we have difficulty distinguishing between life-sized photographs and real people or objects. Our brains need some practice at transforming two-dimensional images into three-dimensional forms and distinguishing which is which. The older we get, the more difficult we may find the transition to the further steps of 4-D, 5-D, and more-D thinking.

Contradictions, Antinomies, and Paradoxes
Because physicists work with paradoxes and dimensionality all the time, they have ready access to terms and concepts that are needed in applying the new cosmological findings to issues beyond science. Unfortunately, these terms and

concepts are rarely, if ever, taught in seminaries, where theologians, pastors, and other Christian leaders receive professional training.

Here is a brief overview of some key terms and their definitions (see box on page 59 for more complete definitions):

Contradiction: a direct and unresolvable opposition between two statements, laws, or principles

Paradox: a direct but resolvable opposition between two true statements, laws, or principles

Antinomy: a direct contradiction between two statements, laws, or principles that seem equally true and necessary

Recognizing the apparent contradictory nature of certain biblical doctrines, Bible students often struggle to find some way to adjust the texts, the terms, or the concepts, and end up with the discomfort of accepting what does not make sense. Some give up their complete trust in the accuracy and authority of God's Word, choosing which parts to accept and which to reject, while others simply redefine biblical "inspiration" and "inerrancy."

Those who hold fast to their view of Scripture as the true and trustworthy Word of God often resort to treating these problematic doctrines as "antinomies," and the results are painful. Christians' approach to the doctrine of humanity's free will (or choice) versus God's sovereignty provides an example. The Bible teaches that God has total control over everything, including all our decisions, actions, words, and thoughts. It also teaches that we have moment-by-moment freedom—and responsibility—in making decisions and taking action. As J. I. Packer points out, the Puritan tradition acknowledges both statements as undeniably true and yet undeniably contradictory.[1] Since a hallmark of the Christian faith is its freedom from contradiction,[2] traditional Puritans and others inevitably chose sides, some upholding divine predestination and denying human free will, and others upholding human free will and denying divine predestination. The church splintered over the issue. Tragically, people even killed others over it.

If only Christian leaders had recognized certain biblical "contradictions" for what they are, as paradoxes, the church could have avoided untold damage and heartache. If only they had trusted God's "higher ways" and "higher thoughts" while awaiting further research and insight, wasted energies and lives could have been profitably invested in the advance of God's kingdom.

What's the Difference?

Many people confuse or equate paradoxes with contradictions or antinomies. Yet important distinctions exist among the three terms.

Contradiction: direct opposition between statements, conclusions, laws, or principles so that it remains impossible for the statements, conclusions, laws, or principles being compared to be true at the same time, in the same location, and in the same context. An example would be the people of Jerusalem at one instant concluding that Jesus was not the Messiah because they knew where he came from and at another instant concluding he was not the Messiah because they did not know where he came from.[3]

Antinomy: opposition or a contradiction between statements, conclusions, laws, or principles that seem equally logical, reasonable, or necessary. An example would be the Puritan conclusion that both human free will and divine predestination are undeniably true and yet undeniably contradictory.[4]

Paradox: an apparent contradiction; something that seems contradictory but has at least the possibility of resolution when examined in all possibly existing time, space, and contextual frames of reference. An example would be a man aging only about 30 years as he makes a round trip to the Andromeda Galaxy at relativistic velocity while back home his friends on Earth would experience the passing of 4 million years.[5]

Tools for Resolving Paradoxes

One wonderful advantage of being alive today is that astronomers and physicists have given us both the faith-supporting verification of God's supernatural capacities and the methods for using this new information to resolve faith-shattering conflicts. Their investigation of the physical realm has enabled them to distinguish paradoxes from contradictions and to discover what works and what doesn't in the task of unraveling paradoxes. The eight basic tools they have developed work as well on biblical and philosophical problems as they do on physical ones. Applied either singly or in combination, these tools always succeed:

1. Establish the correct frame(s) of reference or point(s) of view for measuring or observing the phenomena in question.

2. Establish the correct definition(s) and context(s) of the system(s) under investigation.
3. Identify correctly and completely the initial and final conditions of the phenomena in question.
4. Gather more information about the circumstances in which the phenomena occur.
5. Make more precise measurements.
6. Make measurements over a larger or smaller range of magnitude (e.g., over a longer or shorter time span or distance).
7. Make measurements over different dimensions.
8. Calculate or discern effects of dimensions or "realms" beyond dimensions, or realms in which human measurements cannot yet be made.

Though these precepts sound more scientific and mathematical than theological, they are equally effective when applied to biblical paradoxes; it just takes some practice. Before we begin making these applications, though, I must add one more tool to the list.

God's capacities may supersede cause-and-effect endeavors along dimensional lines, even along an infinite number of dimensional lines. Since God has demonstrated the capacity to create space-time dimensions, he may have at his disposal super-dimensions that encompass space-time capacities and much more, or he may possess transdimensional attributes that somehow permit cause-and-effect endeavors independent of space-time-type dimensions. Such speculations as yet lie beyond human discovery. So, we will continue to explore what has been discovered and what such discoveries can do to strengthen the faith and enhance the oneness of Christians around the world.

Triangles and Circles

Resolution of most biblical paradoxes requires application of more than one of the eight tools listed starting on page 59. To prepare for tackling such complex cases, we can practice on some simple, physical paradoxes, ones that a single tool can fix.

For example, we can resolve this seemingly contradictory set of statements: Triangles cannot be circles, and triangles can be circles. Given two dimensions of space, we take it as an obvious fact that triangles are never circles, and circles are never triangles. After all, triangles always have corners and circles never do. From this perspective, the second of the two statements seems blatantly incorrect. But in reality—three-dimensional reality—the second statement is

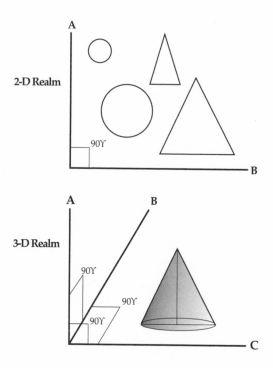

Figure 6.1: Triangles and Circles in Two and Three Dimensions of Space
In a two-dimensional realm, triangles cannot be equivalent to circles in any context. But in a three-dimensional realm, an isosceles triangle (for example) could be rotated about its axis to form a cone. This triangle could be described as a series of concentric circles with progressively smaller diameters rising from the base of the triangle to its vertex.

as correct and rational as the first. In three space dimensions we can stand the triangle up on its base, bringing its length into the height dimension, spin the triangle around on its height axis, and thereby transcribe a cone (see figure 6.1). Since a cone is a series of concentric circles with progressively smaller diameters rising from the base to the vertex, a triangle can be equal to a circle in a three-dimensional context. There, the truth of both statements about triangles and circles can be recognized.

From a two-dimensional perspective, all we can perceive is one side of the paradox, namely that triangles are not circles, whereas from our three-spatial-dimensional perspective we can visualize both sides of the paradox. Plane dwellers, or flatlanders, could use higher dimensional mathematics to demonstrate that the paradox is resolvable in three spatial dimensions, but without

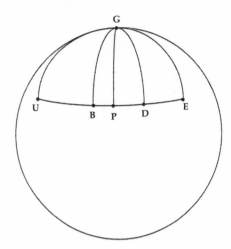

Figure 6.2: God's Operations in a Sphere of Time
In three dimensions of time, or the equivalent, God could generate causes anywhere within, on, or outside of the sphere. The line segment **UE could** represent the time dimension for the universe. At point **U** the universe comes into existence. At point **E** its existence ends. **B** is the birth date for an individual human. **D** is his or her time of death, and **P** the present moment. God, from a single point or instant of time, say **G**, could simultaneously generate causes at points **U, B, P, D,** and **E** along our timeline.

some evidence for the existence of the extra dimension, they would probably not think to approach the problem that way, nor could they gain a visual grasp of the different contexts that make the paradox resolvable.

Do Logic Rules Change in Extra Dimensions?

The rules of logic do not change as one travels from one specific dimensional system to another. They do, however, become more difficult or complicated to apply and test.

The law of causality can be used as an illustration. This law says that every effect must have a cause, and that effects emanate from their causes. For beings experiencing one time dimension only, cause-and-effect phenomena will always proceed along that single timeline. If time cannot stop or reverse, causes must always precede their effects. If the arrow of time could be reversed, however, causes could either precede or follow their effects.

In two dimensions of time, a particular cause-and-effect process that would take a fixed period to transpire in one time dimension could occur over an arbitrarily long or brief period (including infinitely long and infinitely brief) along other timelines in the time plane (see figure 5.1).

A being in three time dimensions could simultaneously generate effects in the past, present, and future of a being in one time dimension (see figure 6.2). Though the law of causality remains the same in all four of these dimensional situations, its application can produce radically different results.

Basic arithmetic provides another illustration. Switching geometric systems may seem to change the rules, but it does not. In Euclidean (plane) geometry, the shortest distance between two points is a straight line. In non-Euclidean (curved) geometry, the shortest distance may be an arc. San Francisco and Tokyo, for example, are measured to be about 5,225 miles apart in non-Euclidean geometry (measured along the earth's surface) but only 4,853 miles apart in Euclidean geometry (cutting a straight line through the interior of the earth). When we present the two statements side by side, San Francisco and Tokyo are 5,225 miles apart and 4,853 miles apart, the arithmetic value of the mile appears to have changed, but it has not. Only our geometric perspective has changed.

In extra dimensions of time and space, rules of logic—including rules of morality—remain consistent. They do not change or bend or twist. Yet the geometric axioms we use and the capacities available to accomplish certain tasks surely do.

Paradox Avoidance and Heresy
Some Bible scholars express concern that approaching biblical difficulties as paradoxes opens a door to heresy. It can lead to error if we mistake a non-paradoxical problem for a paradoxical one or if we misapply the tools for paradox resolution. In either case, careful scholarship, meticulously reviewed, offers a vital safeguard. So does training and practice in identifying and resolving paradoxes. The more experience we gain in working with paradoxes, the more easily and accurately we will be able to identify them and the more adept we will become at resolving them.

Must We Think So Hard?
For many of us, perhaps the greatest resistance to exploring extradimensional doctrines and employing the tools of paradox resolution comes from our hesitancy to exercise our minds. Though none of the thinking processes required for extradimensional forays requires a high IQ, their complexity and our inability to make concrete mental pictures demands greater mental focus and mental discipline than we may typically practice. But the rewards are also greater.

Worshiping the Lord with more of our mind can only enhance our capacity to worship him with our heart, soul, and strength (Deuteronomy 6:5 and Matthew 22:37). In that spirit, let's now take a look at some of the paradoxical biblical doctrines that have mystified Christians and non-Christians for centuries.

Chapter 7

God and Extra Time Dimensions

If God does operate in the equivalent of at least one extra dimension of time, what does this tell us about God's capabilities *beyond* creating the universe and us? What we have discussed in preceding chapters lays a foundation to answer some mystifying questions about God, questions raised by children and scholars alike.

Whatever campus I visit, from grade school to graduate school, two questions come up more frequently than any others. The first is this: If God created us, who created God? Children ask this question with obvious sincerity as they seek to affirm their emerging comprehension of time and cause and effect. Skeptical scholars sometimes ask without listening for an answer. They raise the question as an impossible stumper, as justification for their agnostic stance.

For anyone willing to stretch his or her mind a little, an answer is available, one that represents both the truth of Scripture and the facts of nature. Both sources affirm that the universe, with everything it contains, is confined to a single timeline (or dimension) and is further confined to moving in one direction along that line. Even if we were to experience the stretching or dilation of time by moving at velocities approaching the speed of light, we could neither stop nor reverse time's arrow. The question of God's beginning reflects our understanding of these principles: Whatever exists has a starting point along the line of time and was caused by something or someone with an earlier starting point. In other words, any entity confined to a single line of time in which time cannot be stopped or reversed must have a moment of beginning or causation.

An uncaused effect, a beginning-less anything or anyone, contradicts our experiential knowledge of reality—but not reality itself. For both the Bible and scientific investigation present us with the reality of a Being who has the capacity to create our time dimension and fix its direction, a Being who possesses apparently unlimited time-full capacities.

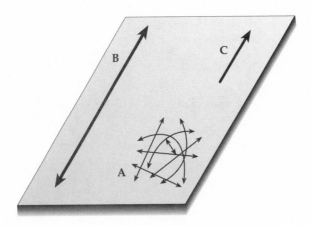

Figure 7.1: An Uncreated God in Two Time Dimensions
If time were two-dimensional rather than one-dimensional, it would be described as some kind of plane rather than a line. If this were the case, one could have an infinite number of timelines (see **A**) that run in an infinite number of directions. This, according to the space-time theorems and the Bible, is the situation with the Creator. If the Creator were to so choose, he could move and operate for infinite time, on a timeline **B** that never intersects or touches the timeline of our universe (line **C**). As such, he would have no beginning and no end. He would not be caused or created.

For our limited imagination's sake, however, we can consider what is possible for him in a two-dimensional time frame, which would constitute a time plane. Just how many time dimensions, or their equivalent, God accesses we do not know, but we do have theoretical, observational, and theological proofs for these two dimensions or their equivalent.

As figure 7.1 shows, a plane of time offers the possibility of an infinite number of timelines running in an infinite number of directions. God has the capacity, thus, to move and operate along an infinitely long timeline, or along as many timelines, infinite or otherwise, as he chooses. He can operate, if he desires, on a timeline parallel to our timeline or on one intersecting our timeline, but he is not compelled to do either. Thus, God has the capacity to cause effects for infinite time on innumerable timelines that never intersect or touch our timeline. As such, we could point to no beginning and no end for him. Since beginnings only make sense where time is linear in some way, God must be a beginning-less Being. He has always existed and will always remain. He never required a causation, or creation, event.

This illustration helps us to picture more clearly how the words of John 1:3 and Colossians 1:16–17 can be true. Just this one extra time dimension

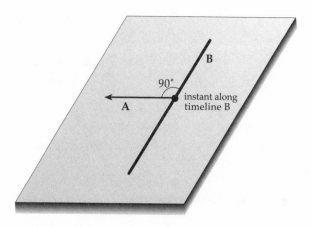

Figure 7.2: Infinite Time at an Instant of Time
In a plane of time, timeline **A** can proceed indefinitely from the point at which it intersects another timeline, such as timeline **B**. The intersection point is a mere moment on timeline B. The first timeline, **A**, simply needs to be perpendicular, or at a right angle (in Euclidean geometries), to the second line, **B**.

removes the necessity of a beginning—and an ending, for that matter. As these verses declare, he and he alone is not created.

Among the world's "holy" books, these statements are unique to the Bible. They could only be true of a Being with access to the equivalent of two or more time dimensions. They could only be inspired by a Being whose experience is not limited to a single dimension of time.

Tuning in to Simultaneous Prayers

Anyone who has tried to listen to two or three conversations at once will guess what the second question is: How can God hear and respond to my prayers while millions or even billions of other people are praying at the same moment around the world? Again, our experience with time and attention tells us that no one can tune in to billions of voices at the same moment, much less respond to them all. As one third-grader stated the situation, a billion simultaneous calls would jam up God's phone line.

Because of our confinement to a single, unidirectional, unstoppable timeline, we humans are forced to communicate with other individuals (or groups) sequentially. But God is not. In a two-dimensional time plane (or its functional

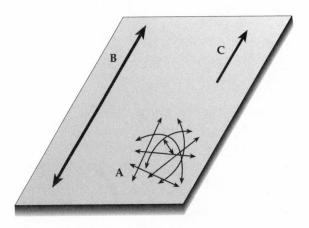

Figure 7.3: Listening to 6 Billion Simultaneous Prayers
In a timeline perpendicular to ours, such as line **A**, God could divide up 2 billion hours into 6 billion 20-minute segments, for example. A mere instant for us (on timeline **B**) can become 2 billion hours, or even an infinite amount of time on line **A**. Thus, God can easily pay attention and respond to the entire human race's prayers to him simultaneously.

equivalent), such as the one shown in figure 7.2, his capacity to communicate with any number of individuals simultaneously can be demonstrated.

In this plane, God can extend a timeline perpendicularly, or at a right angle, to our timeline at any given moment along our timeline. On this perpendicular line, God can give individual, undivided attention to any number of prayers simultaneously. None of us have any need to worry that our communication with him will be drowned out by the communication of others (see figure 7.3).

Operating in a time plane is one provable way God could give individual attention to 6 billion simultaneous prayers. But, as the Master and Creator of at least 10 space-time dimensions, he obviously would have many more options. This simple illustration goes far in reassuring us that God really is attentive to us at every moment, in every situation. It gives new meaning to King David's expression of joy and wonder:

> How precious to me are your thoughts, O God! How vast is the sum of them!

Were I to count them, they would outnumber the grains of sand.[1]

"Timefulness" vs. Timelessness

My choice of the word *timeful* to describe God's time-related capacities deliberately contradicts a notion that much of Christendom has held and taught for many centuries, the notion of a "timeless" eternity as the realm where God lives and where we will live someday also. Timelessness seems to contradict both biblical and scientific evidences for the reality beyond our universe.

Plato first introduced the concept.[2] He reasoned that since all time-dependent phenomena are temporal, then to some degree they must be illusory and valueless, for only what is timeless, unchanging, and eternal retains ultimate reality and value.

Eight hundred years later, Saint Augustine incorporated Plato's concept into his interpretation of Christian doctrine.[3] Augustine noted that the Bible teaches God's independent, transcendent existence; that is, God lives apart from and beyond the limits of his creation. Since time is a component of the physical universe (the creation), Augustine correctly positioned the Creator outside the universe's time frame. To Augustine, this positioning meant God lives outside of time altogether, that is, in timelessness.

Eight centuries later, Saint Thomas Aquinas expanded on Augustine's interpretation of God's transcendence.[4] Aquinas claimed that God's transcendence demanded the attributes of perfection, omnipotence, omniscience, omnipresence, spacelessness, and timelessness.

In the centuries since, Augustine's and Aquinas's teachings have so dominated centers of theological scholarship that rare indeed is the student or professor who dares to challenge the doctrine of God's dwelling in a timeless eternity. Ironically, the notion of spacelessness is rarely, if ever, mentioned. Some scholars see this doctrine of God's timelessness as an essential element of orthodoxy. What many of these scholars have failed to grasp is that time, or its equivalent, as understood by most people today could exist in some way other than the time dimension of the cosmos.

The difficulty arose, and still arises, from a limited perspective on what time in the scientific age means. Time and causality are inextricably intertwined. Time typically is defined by the operation of cause-and-effect phenomena. It does not necessarily follow, however, that all causation occurs within the arena of the cosmic time coordinate as we humans experience it. Again, God may possess super-dimensions, capacities, or attributes that permit causation just as a time coordinate does. To most modern-day people, attributing complete timelessness to God means that God exists where causes and effects do not happen, and this idea contradicts biblical teachings. To be fair, Augustine and

Aquinas probably did not see the connection between time and cause and effect to the degree that people in contemporary society do. These philosophers probably would be shocked to discover that for many today, timelessness connotes total inactivity and complete boredom. Perhaps we can see from this connotation why so many people, both children and adults, have difficulty not only picturing but also anticipating heaven. That God is there and that we will dwell with him in person helps stir our desire to be there, but beyond that, timelessness suggests a kind of motionlessness that strikes us as less than compelling or inviting.

We all like to be in "neutral" once in a while, but only to refuel our engines for jumping back into action. Personally, I can hardly wait to discover what multidimensional activities God has in store for our unendingly timeful life with him in the equivalent of multiple time dimensions.

Chapter 8

Extradimensionality and God's Proximity

God's nearness to us, his constant awareness of everything about us, is a comforting thread woven throughout the biblical tapestry. The reminders are pervasive, from Genesis to Revelation, as the following abbreviated list of references shows:

You are the God who sees me.[1] *Genesis 16:13*

Surely the Lord is in this place.[2] *Genesis 28:16*

The Lord searches every heart and understands every desire and every thought.[3] *1 Chron 28:9*

You [God] alone know the human heart.[4] *2 Chron 6:30*

He [God] knows the way that I take.[5] *Job 23:10*

His [God's] eyes are on their ways.[6] *Job 24:23*

Does he [God] not see my ways and count my every step?[7] *Job 31:4*

His eyes are on the ways of mortals; he sees their every step. There is no deep shadow, no utter darkness, where evildoers can hide. God has no need to examine people further, that they should come before him for judgment. . . . He takes note of their deeds.[8] *Job 34:21-23, 25*

The Lord looks down and sees all mankind; from his dwelling place he watches all who live on earth—he who forms the hearts of all, who considers everything they do.[9] *Ps 33:13-15*

The Lord is close.[10] *Ps. 34:18*

He [God] knows the secrets of the heart.[11] *Ps. 44:21*

The Lord knows the thoughts of man.[12] *Ps 94:11*

Yet you are near, O Lord. . . . All my ways are known to you.[13] *Ps. 119: 151, 168*

You have searched me, Lord, and you know me. You know when I sit and when I rise; you perceive my thoughts from afar. You discern my going out and my lying down; you are familiar with all my ways. Before a word is on my tongue you, Lord, know it completely. . . . Where can I go from your Spirit? Where can I flee from your presence? If I go up to the heavens, you are there; if I make my bed in the depths, you are there. If I rise on the wings of the dawn, if I settle on the far side of the sea, even there your hand will guide me, your right hand will hold me fast.[14] *Ps 139 1-4; 7-10*

The Lord is near.[15] *Ps 145:18*

For your ways are in full view of the Lord, and he examines all your paths.[16] *Prov 5: 21*

"Who can hide in secret places so that I cannot see them?" declares the Lord. "Do not I fill heaven and earth?"[17] *Jer 23:24*

Your [God's] eyes are open to the ways of all mankind.[18] *Jer 32:19*

The very hairs of your head are all numbered. So don't be afraid. [19]

Surely I [Jesus] am with you always, to the very end of the age.[20]

He [God] is not far from any one of us.[21]

Never will I [God] leave you; never will I forsake you. [22]

These verses represent but a fraction of the total. Any message repeated so often must be important. And it must be one we will have some difficulty grasping. To believe that God sees, knows, and understands everything about every human being; that he sees us individually, not as a generic group; that he stays closer to each one of us than we can stay to each other; that he sees our actions, hears our words, and knows our thoughts—all require faith. At times, it even seems we must simply take his word for it. And we do, but not always. Sometimes we forget. Sometimes we doubt. Sometimes we wish he were not scrutinizing our lives so closely, and then a moment later we fear that he has stopped seeing and hearing us—or worse yet, stopped accepting us as we are, with all our foolishness and weakness.

God really is omnipresent. His omnipresence, of course, applies to all dimensions and realms: those we live in (four space-time dimensions), those we can discover (10 space-time dimensions), and those beyond what we can discover (heaven, hell, etc.).

God, Invisible and Untouchable
While no one could be more attentive to us, more loving, more understanding, more steadfast, and more aware of our innermost being than God, neither could anyone be more invisible and untouchable. The Bible emphasizes that God is Spirit[23] and describes him as utterly unapproachable—through our five physical senses, that is.

God's invisibility and intangibility are just as clearly affirmed in the Bible as are any of his other attributes, including his nearness. Jacob adds an important note to his acknowledgment of God's presence: "Surely the Lord is in this place, and I was not aware of it."[24] God explains to Moses: "No one may see me and live."[25]

As Job, Elihu, Eliphaz, Bildad, and Zophar debate, they make statements about God's invisibility:

> When he passes me, I cannot see him; when he goes by, I cannot perceive him.[26]
> If I go to the east, he is not there; if I go to the west, I do not find him.
> When he is at work in the north, I do not see him; when he turns to the south, I catch no glimpse of him.[27]
> The Almighty is beyond our reach.[28]

Isaiah gives this description of God: "Truly you are a God who has been hiding himself."[29]

Paul refers to God as "the blessed and only Ruler, the King of kings and Lord of lords, who alone is immortal"[30] and as one "whom no one has seen or can see."[31]

John the apostle proclaims the following:

No one has ever seen God.[32]
You have never heard his voice nor seen his form.[33]
No one has seen the Father.[34]

These Scriptures teach not only that no human being has ever seen God but also that it is impossible in any earthly situation for us humans to see God in his totality. God is hidden from us in the sense that we cannot make contact with him through our five senses. We do not appreciate this intangibility. We cannot help but think that the disciples had an easier time knowing him, believing him, understanding him, trusting him, and loving him than we do. How often have we heard ourselves or someone else express the wish that God were right here in person, physically present on Earth?

Jesus's longest recorded conversation addresses this very concern (see John 13–17). During his last evening alone with his twelve disciples, the One whom the twelve had finally recognized as "God with us" reminded them, "I will be with you only a little longer. You will look for me, and just as I told the Jews, so I tell you now: Where I am going, you cannot come."[35]

These words cut right to the heart. The most wondrous, joyous, and hope-giving season in these men's lives was the time they spent in Jesus's company, eating, sleeping, talking, walking, laughing, crying, loving, learning, and ministering side by side. Now he said it was over. He was going away, and they could not come with him.

The disciples, of course, wanted to know where Jesus was going. Jesus replied, "Where I am going, you cannot follow now, but you will follow later."[36] This answer did not satisfy their curiosity or their longings. They wanted to know why they could not go with him. Surely their years of service with him qualified them for better treatment. As Peter pleaded, "Lord, why can't I follow you now? I will lay down my life for you."[37] Peter did not understand that no human being, not even such a fervent friend as he, could yet enter the realm Jesus was about to enter.[38] Jesus replied by telling them plainly that he was going to his Father's house, and that one reason for his soon departure and their later arrival was his desire to prepare a special dwelling place in his Father's house for each one of them.[39]

Jesus's explanation helped some, but the disciples' apprehension and grief still held sway. They did not know anything tangible about the house of which Jesus spoke. They had no idea where this house could be found or what the special dwelling place would be like. Worse yet, they were unsure about how they would get there and about how long they would have to wait before reuniting with him. And how on earth would they get along without him? Jesus anticipated their concerns with these words:

> Rather, you are filled with grief because I have said these things. But very truly I tell you; it is for your good that I am going away. Unless I go away, the Advocate will not come to you; but if I go, I will send him to you.[40]

The disciples heard his promise: He definitely would not abandon them and leave them to their own resources. But they still did not understand. From their perspective, Jesus answered one mystery with another. While they were puzzling over this second mystery, Jesus presented them with a third. He told them what they were about to experience would be something like giving birth:

> You will grieve, but your grief will turn to joy. A woman giving birth to a child has pain because her time has come; but when her baby is born she forgets the anguish because of her joy that a child is born into the world. So with you: Now is your time of grief, but I will see you again and you will rejoice.[41]

With this analogy, Jesus prepared them for great pain and anguish with a promise that this suffering would later seem very brief and completely worthwhile. The joy and help they were about to receive would heal their pain and enable them to cope with his physical departure. And they would be carried along by an increasingly confident hope of reunion with him, not in familiar surroundings, but in better ones.

The Dimensional Barrier

Accepting the benefits of that departure was not easy for them, especially at first,[42] and it still presents difficulties for us. But we can receive (for the asking), as those who knew Jesus face-to-face did, both the joy and help of his indwelling Spirit, who will always remain. The awesome benefits of his internal "nearness" will be discussed in a later chapter. What we can begin to address here, through an exercise of our imagination, is the benefit of his physical "distance," which in his case makes possible greater nearness and greater intimacy than we may have imagined.

Imagine the kind of relationship we could develop with two characters we design on a computer screen (see figure 8). These screen people would occupy only two dimensions while we reside in three. Given the right software,

Figure 8: A Three-Dimensional Being in Proximity to the Screen People
Mr. and Mrs. Screen are two-dimensional beings confined to the plane of length and width on a computer screen. A three-dimensional being can approach their plane from the depth dimension and extend a hand to a hundredth of a millimeter from the body of either one of them. Despite this proximity, the Screens would be unable to detect the hand's presence, much less understand and describe its physical characteristics.

we could give them color and animation, and we could create splendid scenes for them to move around in, all the while sending electronic signals to let them know of our presence. In reality, these two-dimensional beings would not possess the capacity to think, feel, and know anything in a physical sense like we do because atoms, molecules, brains, nerves, and so on require three large space dimensions. But, for the sake of the analogy, we can pretend they have the ability to physically think, feel, and know.

As their designers, we know everything about them. Whatever capacities they possess, we gave them. If we enable them to move about the screen, we know the possibilities and the limits of their mobility. Whether they come to recognize the fact or not, their existence depends entirely on us. They have no control over the power supply, or the "on" switch, that keeps electricity flowing into the system that is their universe.

We can imagine the difficulty these screen people would have in comprehending us and relating to us (see figure 8). Could they be certain of our existence? Perhaps reasonably so, if they came to recognize their incapacity to create themselves or anything else in their screen environment, and if they discern that their power source is located outside their realm. Could they perceive our three-dimensionality and how it compares with their two-dimensionality? Given adequate research, they may discover enough about themselves and their environment to recognize that a third dimension must exist to make their existence possible, but they will never fully comprehend what a difference that third dimension makes, nor will they be able to visualize more than two dimensions at a time. Visiting them in person (screen-person, that is) would bridge the gap; but who, then, would stay outside the screen to handle the controls? For us, this is not an option.

As close as these characters may come to each other on the screen, they will remain unable to detect certain things about themselves, characteristics that we can easily observe from our three-dimensional vantage point. Because we experience depth, we can stand back from them and instantly see their complete outline or shape. All they can perceive of one another are various lines. If they are round, they may figure out that their bodies are circular by carefully moving around one another, but they will not see each other's circles as we who look on from outside the screen see them. We can program them to rebound off each other and to make a certain sound when they do, but they have only growing or shrinking lines to indicate movement.

Even if we put our hands or faces right up to the screen, perhaps covering them up completely, they cannot see or hear or feel our nearness through the glass barrier. Sending strong vibrations through the glass might only confuse or frighten them—given, of course, that we have endowed them with emotions as well as sense receptors and minds.

We observe something else about the screen people that they can never see. We can see what is inside them. The details and workings of their interior body parts, for example, are fully exposed to us. The amount of information we have about them is at least an order of magnitude (that is, at least a factor of 10 times) greater than what any of them possesses even about himself or herself.

In this simple analogy, just one dimension separates the screen people from us humans. And yet, the advantage of that one extra dimension suffices to explain how we could be closer to the screen people than they are to each other, fully comprehending them inside and out, while remaining invisible and untouchable to them. Knowing the value of seeing and touching, we could give them the capacity to detect and contact each other, but they would be unable to understand how much more limited these senses are for them than they are for us. They can only detect and contact outer edges, whereas we can see and electronically "touch" every part of them.

God's dimensional advantage over us goes far beyond this one-dimensional difference. He can operate in at least the 11 dimensions established by the space-time theorems and string theory (see chapter 3)—and beyond. His capacity to maintain close and comprehensive contact with us—despite our incapacity to experience him physically through our space-bound dimensions—becomes a comprehensible reality. We cannot begin to picture it, except perhaps by analogy, but it does make sense.

Making sense of his nearness is more important, for now, than physically sensing his nearness. Pleasure is something our senses can give us, and it is temporary; but joy comes from a source beyond the senses, and it lasts. It comes from discovering and grasping truth, among other things. Pleasure and physical nearness are good, but the pleasures and nearness available to us in his extra dimensions go immeasurably beyond what we can think or imagine, as his written Word declares. In one sense, God's invisibility and untouchability keep our yearnings focused where they rightly belong, on the supernatural realm that awaits us. His written Word combines with evidences in this spectacular but limited physical realm to communicate that his desire and plan involve transporting us, at some future moment along our timeline, across our dimensional barriers into his super-dimensional realm.

Below are just a few of the verses in which he expresses his knowability, the benefits of embracing him through faith, this extra "sense" he has given us. Faith, as defined in Scripture,[43] integrates all the information and evidences we accumulate in our pursuit of truth, and faith takes us beyond mental acceptance of facts to "belief in action," to trust.

> If you seek him, he will be found by you.[44]

> Come near to God and he will come near to you.[45]

> The Lord is near to all who call on him, to all who call on him in truth.[46]

> The Lord is close to the brokenhearted.[47]

> I [the Lord] live in a high and holy place, but also with the one who is contrite and lowly in spirit.[48]

> Anyone who comes to him [God] must believe that he exists and that he rewards those who earnestly seek him.[49]

This last verse appears to state necessary conditions for finding him—believing in his existence and in his desire to reward our search for him. Another way to look at this verse is to focus on the promise it holds. This promise is that an earnest search for him will always be rewarded and never disappointed.

These verses and our research into every aspect of God's creation, including the creation's miraculous, transdimensional origin, point to a God who wants to be found, to be known, and to be near, not just in the limited ways possible here and now—as essential and wonderful as they are—but in the imagination-stretching ways our three-dimensional, time-bound bodies cannot experience or even survive.

That future crossover into the resurrected and ascended Christ's tangible presence and into his new creation will require some radical alterations in our physical being. Both the Bible and science tell us that these mortal bodies must first be transformed. After all, our bodies are meticulously designed to function in this particular four-dimensional universe with its particular thermodynamics, electromagnetism, and gravity.

> Flesh and blood cannot inherit the kingdom of God, nor does the perishable inherit the imperishable.[50]

> In a flash . . . the dead will be raised imperishable, and we will be changed. For the perishable must clothe itself with the imperishable, and the mortal with immortality.[51]

> The body that is sown is perishable, it is raised imperishable; it is sown in dishonor, it is raised in glory; it is sown in weakness, it is raised in power; it is sown a natural body, it is raised a spiritual body.[52]

These verses suggest we will still have "bodies," or individual identities, in the realm to which we are headed, but these bodies will no longer experience fatigue, disease, or decay. Clearly, the laws governing their operation will be different from the laws governing our operation today. Our new bodies will be suited to our new environment. Imagine the screen people's two-dimensional bodies trying to support the screen people anywhere but on the computer monitor's surface. Such bodies would simply be too unstable, too limited and limiting. The same could be said of our present bodies in whatever dimensional realm he intends to place us.

In the words of the apostle John,

> Dear friends, now we are children of God, and what we will be has
> not yet been made known. But we know that when Christ appears,
> we shall be like him, for we shall see him as he is.[53]

As we will describe more fully in chapter 17, when we see him with our own "eyes," we will be seeing him with a new and indescribable sight capacity. All our other capacities will be new, too. In fact, they will in several ways be capacities like his, capacities beyond our comprehension, capacities that enable us to participate fully in what he describes as "married life" at home with him.

Chapter 9

Extradimensionality and God's Triunity

One distinctive, transdimensional/extradimensional doctrine of the Christian faith is God's triunity. This doctrinal cornerstone, which we can neither adequately picture nor explain, has proved a stumbling block throughout the ages to many people's belief in the God of the Bible. The inability to form a mental picture or to develop a complete explanation has caused many to wrongly conclude that the doctrine is contradictory or, at best, logically and rationally incoherent.

Jews reject God's triunity, or the Trinity, as a violation of God's oneness. Muslims mock its "mathematical absurdity" as proof that their beliefs make much more sense than do those of Christians. Cults have emerged around various four-dimensional redefinitions of it. America's famed orator, Daniel Webster, received public ridicule for his acceptance of it: "How can a man of your mental caliber believe that three equals one?"[1]

Biblical Statements on the Trinity

More than 500 Old and New Testament verses refer to God as both singular and plural (see table 9). Genesis opens with a reference to God the Creator and God the Spirit. When the narrative zooms in on the creation of humans, the writer assigns both singular and plural pronouns to God: "Let us make man in our image, in our likeness."[2] "So God created man in his own image."[3] Several other Bible verses refer to God with both singular and plural pronouns.[4]

One of God's names in Scripture, 'ĕlōhîm, is the Hebrew plural form for God. El is the word for God, or god, in the widest possible sense.[5] 'Ĕlōhîm used as a plural in Scripture can denote pagan images and the imaginary (or demonic) deities they represent (Deuteronomy 4:28 and 12:2), and yet in verses such as Genesis 1:1, the plural form denotes the singular supreme deity.[6]

The Bible declares emphatically that there is only one Savior,[7] one Creator,[8] one Redeemer,[9] and one Resurrector,[10] and yet it identifies two or three members of the Godhead as that one Savior, Redeemer,[11] Creator,[12] and Resurrector.[13] The one name God assigns to himself is the unpronounceable *YHWH*. In one paragraph of Scripture, both God the Father and God the Son lay claim to this name.[14]

When Jesus commissions his disciples for ministry, he instructs them to baptize new believers "in the name of the Father and of the Son and of the Holy Spirit."[15] One name somehow identifies the one and the three. Many other passages imply that our salvation rests on the deity of God the Father, God the Son, and God the Holy Spirit—together, in some unfathomable way, the one and only God.

The charge that "Trinitarians" accept a mathematical absurdity would seem appropriate in light of these and other verses—*if* the biblical God were confined to the same dimensional realm as humans. Fortunately, he has shown us abundant evidence that he is not. Unfortunately, many of the illustrations Christians use to explain the Trinity are only three-dimensional and may serve to muddy the water more than to clarify it.

One popular illustration compares the Trinity to an individual's simultaneous multiple identity as, for example, a father, a son, and a grandson. In this illustration we have one being with three different relationship labels that can be applied simultaneously. But we do not have three persons who are capable of relating to one another in any self-distinctive way.

Another illustration likens the Trinity to water at its "triple point" (32°F or 0.01°C), the temperature at which it can be ice or liquid or vapor. Water can take all three forms and still retain its distinctive molecular makeup, but any particular quantity of water will typically take one form and not the others. Or some fraction of it will take one form, say liquid, while another fraction takes another form, say ice, and perhaps another fraction, the other form, vapor. It cannot be 100 percent liquid, 100 percent ice, and 100 percent steam at the same time.

The Sun provides another familiar illustration of oneness and threeness—the Sun is simultaneously a star, a light source, and a heat source. We see the Sun's light and feel its heat without having tangible contact with the Sun. The light and heat manifest the Sun's properties to us, as God manifests his properties through the Son and the Holy Spirit. This illustration seems helpful at first glance, but it falters on two important points. First, the Sun's heat is not an individual entity in any way but rather a portion of the Sun's light spectrum. Second, the light and heat energy coming from the Sun cannot be considered

Table 9: Bible Verses Expounding God's Triunity

Genesis 1:1–3, 26–27	Matthew 11:27	Ephesians 4:3–6
Genesis 3:22	Matthew 12:28	Philippians 1:2
Genesis 11:7, 9	Matthew 22:41–46	Philippians 2:5–11
Genesis 16:7–13	Matthew 28:18–20	Colossians 1:15–17
Genesis 18:1–32	Mark 1:10–11	Colossians 2:9–10
Genesis 22:11–16	Luke 1:35	1 Thessalonians 1:1–5
Exodus 23:20–23	Luke 3:21–22	2 Thessalonians 1:2
Deuteronomy 4:35, 39	Luke 10:22	2 Thessalonians 2:13–17
Deuteronomy 5:7–11	John 1:1–3, 32–34	1 Timothy 1:2, 17
Deuteronomy 6:4, 13	John 5:17–23, 37	1 Timothy 2:5
Deuteronomy 32:39	John 6:27	1 Timothy 6:13–16
2 Samuel 22:32	John 8:58	2 Timothy 3:15–4:1
Nehemiah 9:6	John 10:17–18, 30–39	Titus 1:2–4
Job 33:4	John 14:6–11, 16–26	Titus 2:11–14
Psalm 2:2–12	John 15:26	Titus 3:4–6
Psalm 110	John 16:7–15	Philippians 3
Psalms 139:7–10	John 17:1–11, 21–24	Hebrews 1:1–8
Proverbs 30:2–4	John 20:28	Hebrews 9:14
Isaiah 6:8	Acts 2:30–36	James 2:19
Isaiah 7:14	Acts 5:3–4	1 Peter 1:2
Isaiah 9:6–7	Acts 17:29–30	1 Peter 2:4
Isaiah 37:20	Acts 20:28	1 Peter 3:18
Isaiah 41:4	Romans 1:4, 7	1 Peter 4:14
Isaiah 43:10–11	Romans 3:30	2 Peter 1:1–2, 16–17
Isaiah 44:6–8	Romans 8:9–11, 26–29	1 John 1:2–3
Isaiah 45:5, 14	Romans 9:1–5	1 John 4:2–3
Isaiah 45:21–23	Romans 16:25–27	1 John 4:9–15
Isaiah 46:9	1 Corinthians 1:3	2 John 3–4, 9
Isaiah 48:12–17	1 Corinthians 2:10–16	Jude 1–4, 20–21, 25
Isaiah 59:15–20	1 Corinthians 8:4–6	Revelation 1:1, 4–5
Isaiah 61:1–3	1 Corinthians 12:3–6	Revelation 2:27–29
Jeremiah 23:5–6	2 Corinthians 1:2, 21–22	Revelation 4:8–11
Hosea 12:3–5	2 Corinthians 13:14	Revelation 5:2–7, 12–13
Micah 5:2–5	Galatians 1:3	Revelation 6:16–17
Zechariah 6:12–13	Galatians 3:20, 26	Revelation 15:3–8
Matthew 3:16–17	Ephesians 1:2, 13–14, 17	Revelation 19:15–16

from any perspective as equivalent to the Sun itself.

Some Bible scholars have proposed the picture of a cake, which simultaneously can be thought of as ingredients, layers, and slices. The ingredients would represent the Father; the layers, the Son; and the slices, the Holy Spirit distributed to individual believers. To paraphrase a cliché, the problem here is that we cannot have our cake and eat it too. Once the slices are all distributed or eaten, neither the layers nor the cake would remain intact.

Another illustration uses light, heat, and air to represent the Trinity.[16] Each has its individual properties and obeys different sets of physical laws, yet all three are essential to life. This illustration shares a weakness with the Sun analogy. Heat is but a subset of light. It also falls short in reflecting the Trinity's oneness, for light (including heat) and air have totally distinct properties.

The famous Princeton seminary theologian Benjamin B. Warfield viewed the human being as the best analogy for the Trinity. Humans represent the expressed "image of God."[17] Humans are body, soul, and spirit, three components performing distinct functions yet unified, as may be said of the Trinity. One drawback to this illustration is its cultural and theological bias. Only some cultural, philosophical, and theological systems make a distinction between soul and spirit. Perhaps a more serious problem is the difference in limitations among these three aspects of a person. The body cannot live apart from the soul and spirit, but the soul and spirit do continue to exist when the body dies.

While each of these Trinity illustrations is helpful, one significant weakness hampers all of them (and many others). They attempt to explain a supernatural, extradimensional being in the frame of reference we four-dimensional beings occupy. Thus, as well-meaning as their originators may be, each illustration is doomed to reflect some distortion of God's identity—distortions or partial truths often characterizing cults and other religious systems. One distortion portrays the Trinity as a plurality, characteristic of polytheistic systems: God is a divine triumvirate in total agreement to work cooperatively toward one purpose. Another distortion, built in defense of monotheism, presents a modalistic entity: a personal Being who manifests himself in one of three different modes—Father, Son, or Spirit—at different times and in different circumstances as he sees fit. Neither of these views aligns with biblical revelation. Indeed, they cannot. All naturalistic, four-dimensional representations of the Trinity must reflect either tritheism or modalism. Our human frame of reference holds no other options.

For that matter, all naturalistic, 10-dimensional representations of the Trinity will to a lesser extent fail too. The triune God, after all, has the power to create and remove space-time dimensions at will. The new physics tells us that he transcends the 10 space-time dimensions of the cosmos. Thus, the extra dimensions exposed by the new physics will not define the Trinity. Nevertheless, they will enhance our understanding and comprehension of a meaningful doctrine.

Creedal Statements of the Trinity Doctrine

The early church fathers, recognizing the importance of nipping heresies and cults in the bud, took painstaking care to explain in what sense God is plural and in what sense singular. They accomplished this task by convening councils to write creeds. Because few people of their time had access to education, even to basic literacy, these scholars labored to prepare accurate, brief, and easy-to-memorize statements of the faith. The most famous of such creeds expounding the doctrines of Christianity is the Nicene Creed, penned in the fourth century AD. The following excerpt focuses on the Trinity:

> We believe in one God, the Father almighty, maker of heaven and earth, of all things visible and invisible.
>
> And in one Lord Jesus Christ, the only Son of God, begotten from the Father before all ages, God from God, Light from Light, true God from true God, begotten, not made; of the same essence as the Father. Through him all things were made. . . .
>
> And we believe in the Holy Spirit, the Lord, the giver of life. He proceeds from the Father and the Son, and with the Father and the Son is worshiped and glorified.[18]

The Nicene Creed, while declaring there is but one God, specifically assigns deity to the Father, the Son, and the Holy Spirit. Each is declared to be the Creator. Their oneness is explained in terms of their being of "the same essence."

The Athanasian Creed, developed in the same era, focused more on defending the doctrine of Christ's deity, a significant aspect of the Trinity doctrine but with a narrower purpose. It was also much more detailed and philosophical than either the Apostles' Creed or the Nicene Creed.

Reformation Confessions of the Trinity

With the dawning of the Reformation and the spread of literacy, Bible scholars saw the need for more detailed written explanations of the Trinity. Two great confessions of the Christian faith were published. A committee of German Lutheran theologians prepared the first of these, entitled "A Confession of Faith," presented to Germany's King Charles V in Augsburg in 1530. The second came from the Assembly of the Divines, a consortium of English theologians commissioned by the British House of Commons and House of Lords. This group devoted five years to the writing of the Westminster Confession, adopted by the British parliament and the Churches of England and Scotland in 1648.

Both the Augsburg and Westminster Confessions are lengthy documents, but their statements on the Trinity are relatively brief. Article one of the Augsburg Confession reads as follows:

> Our churches teach with great unanimity that the decree of the Council of Nicaea concerning the unity of the divine essence and concerning the three persons is true and should be believed without any doubting. That is to say, there is one divine essence, which is called and which is God, eternal, incorporeal, indivisible, of infinite power, wisdom, and goodness, the maker and preserver of all things, visible and invisible. Yet there are three persons, of the same essence and power, who are also coeternal: the Father, the Son, and the Holy Spirit. And the term "person" is used, as the ancient Fathers employed it in this connection, to signify not a part or a quality in another but that which subsists of itself.
>
> Our churches condemn all heresies that have sprung up against this article, such as that of the Manichaeans who posited two principles, one good and the other evil, and also those of the Valentinians, Arians, Eunomians, Mohammedans, and all others like these. They also condemn the Samosatenes, old and new, who contend that there is only one person and craftily and impiously argue that the Word and the Holy Spirit are not distinct persons since "Word" signifies a spoken word and "Spirit" signifies a movement that is produced in things.[19]

The Westminster Confession, chapter 2, article 3, makes the following declaration:

> In the unity of the Godhead there be three persons, of one substance, power, and eternity; God the Father, God the Son, and God the Holy Ghost. The Father is of none, neither begotten nor proceeding; the Son is eternally begotten of the Father; the Holy Ghost eternally proceeding from the Father and the Son.[20]

The Augsburg Confession adds to the Nicene Creed an attempt to clarify what the word "Persons" means and does not mean with respect to the Godhead. This treatise specifies that each member of the Trinity exists or "subsists" on his own and is more than merely a part of the existence of the other members. To put it another way, the Augsburg Confession emphasizes that the divine Persons are not mere aspects or portions of God's Being, but are distinct, personal Entities who nonetheless manifest the unity of the divine Being.

The Westminster Confession declares the unity of the Godhead with full recognition of the three personal distinctions included within the Godhead. The confession also explains at length what God's eternality implies for each member of the Godhead in his dealings with individual human beings.

Lutherans quickly and universally adopted the Augsburg Confession, as Anglicans adopted the Westminster Confession. In fact, the scholarly excellence of these works still stands. Most Protestant, evangelical denominations and independent congregations have incorporated one or both in their own statements of faith.[21] Such incorporation has done much to blunt the attacks of cults upon the Christian church, cults that without exception deny the doctrine of the Trinity and base their denial upon the Trinity's paradoxical nature.

Modern Formulations of the Trinity

Some of the twentieth century's most distinguished Bible scholars have devoted themselves to updating the language of the church's doctrinal statements. They acknowledge that current culture demands not only more familiar vocabulary and syntax but also a return to brevity. James M. Boice offers the following summations:

- There is but one living and true God who exists in three persons: God the Father, God the Son, and God the Holy Spirit.
- The Lord Jesus Christ is fully divine, being the second person of the Godhead, who became man.
- The Holy Spirit is fully divine.
- While each is fully divine, the three Persons of the Godhead are related to each other in a way that implies some differences.
- In the work of God the members of the Godhead work together.[22]

Boice adds that the knowledge, feelings, and will of each person within the Godhead—Father, Son, and Holy Spirit—are identical.[23] Charles C. Ryrie condenses the Trinity doctrine into this brief declaration:

> There is one only and true God, but in the unity of the Godhead
> there are three eternal and coequal Persons, the same in substance
> and distinct in subsistence.[24]

Ryrie borrows the word *subsistence* from John Calvin to distinguish independent "sustenance" from "independent personalities," a confusion sometimes arising from the use of the word *Persons*. Geoffrey Bromiley states the doctrine this way:

> Within the one essence of the Godhead we have to distinguish three
> "persons" who are neither three gods on the one side, nor three parts
> or modes of God on the other, but coequally and coeternally God.[25]

Recognizing that "essence" and "persons" may be misunderstood terms for the Trinity, Bromiley's statement seeks to distinguish what orthodox Christian scholars imply and do not imply about the application of these terms to God.[26]

R. A. Finlayson offers these operational definitions of the Godhead:

1. The Trinity expresses unity in diversity. There are not three individuals, but three personal self-distinctions . . . Each person is self-conscious and self-directing, yet never acting independently [that is, expressing independence of will, actions, or feelings].
2. The Trinity expresses equality in dignity. All three Persons of the Trinity are perfectly equal in nature, honor, and dignity.
3. The Trinity expresses diversity in operation. Each Person of the Godhead performs different functions that involve certain degrees of subordination (in relation, though not in nature).[27]

Finlayson describes how the nature, operation, and expression of the Trinity enable God to reveal Himself to humans and commune with them. He explains how the Trinity provides for humanity's redemption and for all true fellowship among his spirit creatures.[28]

One immeasurable value of all these doctrinal creeds, confessions, and statements lies in their uncompromising preservation of the paradoxical nature of the Trinity. They present a doctrine that can be true only in a realm beyond what we humans experience. Also, in view of how rampant experiential theologies have become in many of today's churches, the creeds provide an exactness of language and solid doctrinal parameters for protecting lay Christians from theological aberration and heresy.

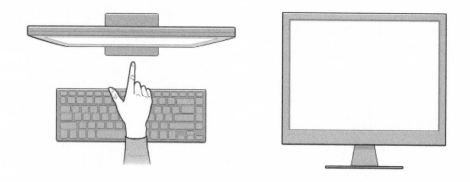

Figure 9.1: Screen People's Perception of a 3-D Hand Near Their Plane
View A: Looking edge-on to the screen people's plane, the 3-D hand is near but makes no contact with it. View B: Looking straight onto the plane, no part of the hand is present on the plane, and, therefore, the hand remains invisible to the screen people.

Illustrating the Trinity's Extra/Transdimensionality

Given that our attempts to illustrate the Trinity may distort and damage people's understanding of God more than they help, we may feel inclined to abandon all attempts at illustration and stick solely to our creeds and confessions. But this abandonment poses an equally serious risk: the loss of an important communication tool—if not more.

For Christians to offer only the hard-to-comprehend and abstract words of our creeds, doctrines, and confessions suggests to many people that God is distant and incomprehensible—perhaps merely a reflection of humanity's weaknesses, fears, and larger-than-life imagination. Though we know God cannot be understood completely by human beings, he does give ample evidence that he desires to be known and is knowable.

What may prove most helpful to believers and nonbelievers alike would be the development of illustrations of the Trinity that cross the dimensional limitations of human experience without doing undue damage to biblical definitions and doctrine. Better yet, we may simply find ways to portray the difficulties we four-dimensional creatures face in our attempts to comprehend our super-transdimensional God. The difficulty, of course, lies in our inability to visualize phenomena in a realm beyond our experience. In other words, an illustration involving more than our familiar four dimensions may not be helpful.

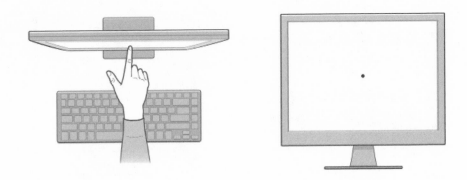

Figure 9.2: Screen People's Perception of a Fingertip of the 3-D Hand Just Touching or Grazing Their Plane
View A: Looking edge-on to the screen people's plane, a fingertip of the 3-D hand barely makes contact with the plane. View B: In the plane itself, the hand shows up only as a single point that would disappear and reappear as the fingertip is pushed into and pulled away from the screen.

So, what illustrative options do we have? One possibility involves a crossover from the four dimensions we experience to a realm with fewer dimensions. Such an illustration, while not completely analogous, may help us make some sense of our struggle to understand how God can possibly be one and three at the same time without violating the rules of logic and reason, including basic arithmetic.

Let us revisit the illustration of the screen people presented in chapter 8. We can try to imagine (and this calls for plenty of imagination!) what would happen if we brought one of our three-dimensional hands into contact with the two-dimensional screen people. Remember, since our hand exists in a third dimension perpendicular to the plane of the screen people, its position outside the screen will always be defined by them as "above" or "below" them, though we see its position as "beside" the screen.

Now, as long as our hand remains above the plane of the screen people, they cannot observe or detect anything at all about our existence, our characteristics, our powers, or our modes of operation (see figure 9.1). If we were to touch their plane with the very tip of one finger, however, they would see us as a single point, a point that can, as the finger touches and withdraws from the plane, appear and disappear at any time (see figure 9.2). If we were to touch their plane with the side of an extended finger, they would see us as a line (see figure 9.3). If instead of a finger extended straight out, we were to touch their plane with the side of a curled up finger, they would see us as a curved line.

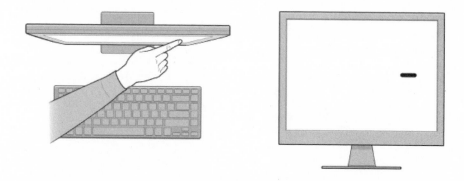

Figure 9.3: Screen People's Perception of the Side of an Extended Finger of a 3-D Hand Just Touching Their Plane

View A: With the side of an extended finger of the 3-D hand just touching the screen people's plane, the screen people observe it as a thick line. View B: If that finger is curled a little, the screen people would see the hand transform from a straight line into a curved line.

If the screen were not a solid barrier to us, we could push a finger vertically (that is, perpendicularly) into their plane (see figure 9.4). This time the screen people would see us as a small, slightly irregular circle.

If we were to push it deeper, the screen people would observe our extended finger as an enlarging irregular circle. If, instead of penetrating their plane with one finger exactly perpendicular to their plane, we were to penetrate it at some other angle to their plane (see figure 9.5), the screen people would now behold our extended finger as an elongated ellipse, which could enlarge depending on the degree of penetration.

From the screen people's perspective, the finger could appear at different times as a point, a straight line, a curved or angled line, a small irregular circle, a larger irregular circle, an elongated ellipse of variable size, or not even appear at all. They could easily conclude that the same finger is six or more different entities, each manifesting some distinct characteristics. They might never discern that the six-plus manifestations were all governed by one entity and one source of operation.

The analogy illustrates at least to some degree how we can misunderstand God's contact with our world. Because he manifests himself to the human race at different times and in different ways, we may conclude that God is not one but several deities or that he is one totally changeable, unpredictable, and undefinable deity. Consider people's confusion over Christ's manifestations of himself as the Creator, as the Angel of the Lord, as Jesus of Nazareth, as the

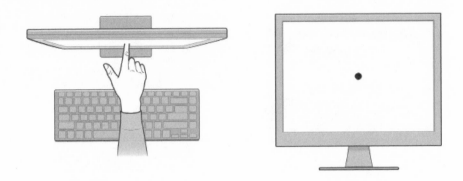

Figure 9.4: Screen People's Perception of a Finger of a 3-D Hand Poking through Their Plane
View A: As the finger pokes farther through the plane, the screen people would see first the fingertip, then, eventually, a cross section of the first knuckle of the finger. The finger would appear to them to transform from a point into progressively larger circles. View B: With the finger penetrating their plane, the screen people now see the 3-D hand as a small circle.

sacrificial Lamb of God, as Judge, and much more. Some sects, for instance, insist that the Angel of the Lord cannot be Christ. Others refuse to acknowledge Christ's authority and action as either the Creator or the Judge.

Let us take this illustration of the screen people and the human hand further. Instead of penetrating the plane of the screen people with just one finger, we could penetrate it with two, three, or more fingers, and each of these would enter at a slightly different angle from the others. We could bend our pointer finger so that the fingertip just touches, making a small dot, while our thumb passes into the plane sideways, making an elongated ellipse, and our middle finger passes straight through the plane perpendicularly, making an irregular circle. If we move these fingers, they may appear to the screen people to be functioning in complete independence of each other.

In this extension of the illustration, the screen people would be tempted to conclude that this higher being contacting their realm might be three different and independently operating beings. They would see the hand as at least something like themselves, a number of independently functioning, closed line segments. In fact, from the screen people's perspective, these closed surfaces (each circle or ellipse closes off a specific area) could not possibly constitute one closed surface, for the screen people would be unable to see how closed surfaces could be anything other than closed line segments.

In three spatial dimensions, however, the fingers and thumb belong to the single closed surface that encompasses our body. What the screen people could

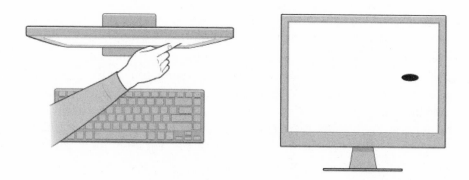

Figure 9.5: Screen People's Perception of a Finger of a 3-D Hand Penetrating Their Plane at a Non-Perpendicular Angle
View A: The finger appears to change shape again as it pokes through their plane at an angle other than perpendicular. View B: The screen people now see the 3-D hand as an elongated ellipse.

not see, nor even comprehend, is how the various circles and ellipses can be united into the surface, that is, the skin, that encloses a body (or even a part of it, the hand). Though they see segments of the fingers, they would not be able to visualize the totality of the fingers, and they would have no concept of the hand. They could imagine the twoness, threeness, or moreness of the hand (or one aspect of that plurality), but not the oneness. In fact, their concept of the hand's oneness would be so unfathomable as to appear impossible and thus "incorrect."

The reverse difficulty could just as easily occur. If we were to pass our outstretched hand, fingers and thumb pressed tightly together, through the plane right up to the wrist, the screen people would attest to the oneness of our hand while remaining ignorant of, and perhaps arguing against, the plurality manifest by our separate fingers.

Screen People Theologians
In response to the revelation of various cross sections of our fingers, one group of screen people might become the equivalent of convinced polytheists, certain that multiple higher beings exist who can never be treated in any context as one. In response to the revelation of the wrist cross section, another group of screen people might become the equivalent of a category of monotheists who insist that the one higher being can never, in any context, be two or more. We can also imagine both groups decrying the absurdity of a simultaneous plural

and singular higher being.

Taking the illustration still further, we can imagine a plethora of debates among screen people who saw dots, lines (of different configurations), circles and ellipses (of different sizes), staying still or moving, appearing or disappearing, enlarging or shrinking. At some point, one group might band together to found the Church of the Three Circles, while another group launches the Ellipsoid Society; another, the Two Circle Fellowship; another, the Science of Lines; and yet another, the Church of the One True Ellipse. These groups might divide up through time, of course, and new groups begin as new interpretations of the revelations arise.

The teachings of each group might be similar in some points, but for the most part sharply divergent. We can imagine the ensuing conflicts that might arise should attempts be made to overlook differences and to unite against big social problems. We can even imagine the cynicism of some screen people who say all this talk of higher beings means nothing; all that has appeared is some amazing but explicable (with enough research) screen phenomenon that, once understood, will usher in a new age of screen people consciousness.

The great irony of the disagreement about the higher being is that none of these groups and individuals has more than a tiny clue about who that being is and what that being can do. They all have an incredibly limited perspective on the attributes of the being, especially on the powers available to this being.

What if one bold group of the screen people dared to acknowledge both the plural and singular manifestations of the higher being as possibly connected? Some of the screen people may have studied our contacts closely enough to watch our fingers enter their plane from above and continue to move down through their plane until the fingers converged in a cross section of our palm (see figure 9.6). These screen people would see that we first appeared as dots, but then the dots enlarged to form slightly irregular circles, which then flared on one or two sides and eventually merged into one elongated sausage shape (see figure 9.7). The flares for each of the circles would become larger and eventually join together. This group of screen people might try to tell the others that the plurality somehow became a singularity.

If this group drew its conclusions too quickly, without waiting to see our hand change from sausage-shaped back to circles and dots, they might conclude that what was once four has become one and is no longer four.

We can imagine what would be possible if some members of this screen group had received and read some electronic code from the person to whom the hand belongs. Based on their confidence that the code came from outside

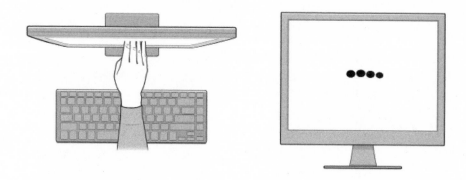

Figure 9.6: Screen People's Perception of Four Fingers of a 3-D Hand Poking through Their Plane

View A: With four fingers of the 3-D hand penetrating their plane, the screen people now see the hand as four slightly irregular circles. View B: As the fingers enter the plane, the screen people would see first a point, which grows into a small circle just as another point appears and begins to grow into a circle, then another and another until they see four slightly irregular circles.

and spoke of possibilities beyond their screen life, this group might be willing to accept what they cannot picture, that a three-dimensional being does exist and can exist as a fourness and oneness simultaneously, continuously, and permanently. They could, then, draw up a Quadrinity doctrinal statement.

They could affirm through review of their observations that the fourness they saw did not negate the oneness of the hand (though they would not really understand that word), nor did the oneness negate the fourness. Realizing they could observe only two of the hand's dimensions at a time but that the hand must exist in a higher realm, they could conclude that the revealed oneness neither detracts from nor contradicts the fourness and that the fourness neither detracts from nor contradicts the oneness. They would never, as part of the screen world, be able to picture these truths. But with some trust in the motivation of the higher being to make contact and explain him or herself truthfully (say through electronic messages), and perhaps by combining their observations with some research in higher-dimensional math problems, these screen people could determine the validity of their conclusions about the hand and the limited validity or downright invalidity of others' conclusions.

Even this group of screen people would possess, at best, an extremely limited view of the nature and capacities of the three-dimensional hand. Their view of the higher being would acknowledge significantly more, but nowhere near *all* of the hand's (or the whole higher being's) power and capability than

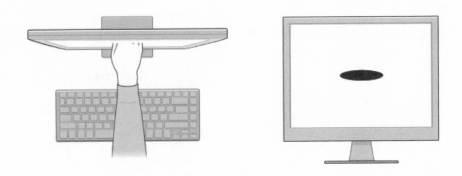

Figure 9.7: Screen People's Perception of Four Fingers of a 3-D Hand Penetrating Their Plane Almost up to the Palm
View A: As the hand pokes through the screen's plane almost up to the palm, the screen people would see the middle circles develop flares on two sides. View B: As the hand penetrates beyond the fingers and down to the palm, the screen people would observe the flaring circles fusing together to become one larger sausage-shaped object, with bumps where the knuckles are.

do the other screen people, the mistaken ones. But the Quadrinitarians' view of the hand's potential still falls enormously short of the hand's—and the whole higher being's—actual potential.

What we must not overlook in this illustration is that the dimensional difference between the screen people and ourselves, the "higher beings" in the analogy, adds up to just one. If we endow the screen people, imaginatively, with enough resources, they could calculate some of the possibilities, capacities, and characteristics of our extra dimension and determine by how much these possibilities, capacities, and characteristics exceed the limits of their two dimensions. Though such understanding would give them a genuine basis for awe and wonder, it would still fall far short of reality. Perhaps it would motivate them to ask the higher being for further assistance in believing and knowing what the hand can do.

Limits of the Extradimensional Illustrations
While the analogy of the hand in two and three spatial dimensions is more useful than the others for explaining the Trinity, it is still not complete, nor is it doctrinally accurate. Ultimately, the hand is bound to a set number of dimensions of space. God is not. Whereas the fingers are not individually the hand but only aspects or parts of it, Jesus Christ is, for example, fully God.

A more accurate, but still inadequate, illustration could be developed if we were to create an analogy in which we three-dimensional beings interact with individuals confined to only one dimension of space—linelanders, as opposed to the screen people. And, further, what we have illustrated with extra space dimensions should also be illustrated with extra time dimensions.

Even the best extradimensional analogies we humans could develop for God's triunity will fall short. We do not know the extent of God's attributes, capacities, and transdimensionality/extradimensionality. Though we certainly can expose more of God's threeness and oneness to human comprehension, ultimately there are limits to what we can discover.

The intent of this analogy of a 3-D hand visiting screen people is to stimulate our thinking about God's powers and attributes, including his triunity, from a transdimensional/extradimensional perspective. With the creativity God has given us, we can surely develop more and better analogies with which to build our own faith and spark the faith of others.

One important gap in our understanding and depiction of the Trinity has to do with the interrelationship of God's will and emotions. All of the modern formulations of the Trinity doctrine emphasize that the three Persons within the Godhead never respond with independent decisions, desires, or actions.

Though the Bible affirms that all of God's responses end up in total unity, the process toward these responses may be more complicated than we can grasp.

Jesus manifests some level of freedom and independence of will if his temptation by Satan in the desert represents anything more than just a formality.[29] At Gethsemane Jesus prays three times, "My Father, if it is possible, may this cup be taken from me. Yet not as I will, but as you will."[30] The Gospels record that Jesus's soul was overwhelmed with sorrow to the point of death, that his emotions were so intense he sweated drops of blood.[31] Obviously, some kind of interaction of the wills takes place between the Son and the Father.

Jesus prays for all of His followers to be one, just as He and the Father are one.[32] He defines this oneness as being a "complete unity."[33]

We see here, at the divine level, a hint of some aspect of the simultaneous operation of human free will or choice and divine predestination, a subject addressed in later chapters. God's unsearched treasures of wisdom and understanding challenge us to keep digging.

Enlarging Our View

How many of us are willing to admit that our view of God soars just slightly above the horizon of our four-dimensional realm? If we laughed at the Quadrinitarians' underestimations of the nature, powers, and capacities of the

3-D hand, what can we say for ourselves?

These hypothetical screen people made their gross underestimation in a realm just one dimension short of the hand's realm. Our human realm falls at least seven and possibly many more dimensions (or their equivalent) short of God's realm. This dimensional difference means that our underestimation of God is many geometric orders of magnitude greater than we can imagine even with the help of a dimension-crossing illustration.

This enormous degree of underestimation seems difficult, if not impossible, to grasp. The following numerical analogies may provide some tangibility to the gap we need to bridge.

Without question, the screen people with the most accurate vision of the nature, powers, and capacities of the 3-D hand underestimated its reality by at least a factor of a trillion (the number more likely approaches infinity). Since God possesses at least seven dimensions of advantage over us, rather than just one, we doctrinally orthodox Christians potentially underestimate God's nature, powers, and capacities by at least a factor of a trillion in one dimension, at least another factor of a trillion in the next dimension and additional factors of a trillion plus in the remainder of the seven plus extra dimensions. In mathematical notation this underestimation factor would be 10^{84+}.

To put this enormous underestimation factor into perspective, the total number of protons and neutrons in the universe adds up to only 10^{79}.

But, given that the underestimation factor is more like infinity than it is a mere trillion, the underestimating factor really would be more like infinity times seven plus, or in mathematical notation, (∞^{7+}) times.

Sometimes we Christians glibly declare our belief that God is infinitely greater than we can think or imagine, never realizing that the attributions of just a first order infinity (infinity not taken to any power in the index) to God absurdly underestimates him. We verbally acknowledge his immeasurable power, grace, wisdom, love, and so on, yet our prayers, concerns, actions, and attitudes treat him as One who is only an order of magnitude (if that) beyond us. The value of mathematically calculating a minimum limit to the superiority of God's powers and capabilities over ours lies in its potential to deliver us from such a tremendous underestimation of God. It should certainly sweep away doubts about God's capacity to manifest himself as a Triune Being.

And it may add some punch to the apostle Paul's prayer that we will be able, more and more through time, "to grasp how wide and long and high and deep is the love of Christ, and to know this love that surpasses knowledge."[34] A tiny speck of faith placed in his hand can accomplish far more than the relocation of a mountain. It can change our lives profoundly, giving us new courage to face our past, present, and future.

Chapter 10

Extradimensionality, the Incarnation, and the Atonement

By returning once again to the illustration of the screen people, we have the opportunity to develop some additional theological insights of enormous personal significance. These imaginary characters can carry us to a new depth, perhaps a new dimension, of appreciation for Jesus Christ's sacrifice for each of us.

Let's consider the question of how to let them know of our existence, our characteristics, and our motives toward them. Because of our dimensional differences, the face-to-face option would be available only if we had the capacity to alter our dimensionality. In reality we cannot gain an extra dimension through which to operate. Neither can we put aside a dimension in which we operate. But what if we could? What if we were to choose to become screen people? Consider for a moment what the loss of just one dimension would mean. It's virtually impossible to fathom. Given the costs involved in such a choice, what would compel someone to go through with it?

Far beyond whatever costs anyone can imagine stands the incarnation. We humans have barely begun to appreciate this choice to put aside not one but *many* dimensions. As our appreciation of his choice grows, so will our comprehension of what his love means.

Who Exactly Is the Incarnate Christ?

The incarnation—coming in the flesh[1]—refers to God entering human life in a human body. Jesus Christ, the second person of the triune God, the Creator of all angels and of the entire physical universe, actually became a man. He did this of his own free will, without external compulsion. The incarnation is possible—God on Earth, God with us and among us, and God in heaven—only because of God's transdimensional/extradimensional capacities.

Jesus's divine identity as God, his character, wisdom, purity, and motives, remained perfectly intact,[2] but he voluntarily relinquished (with only occasional exceptions) the independent use of his divine powers and his extradimensional capacities. He accepted all the functional limitations of a human brain and body, all the needs, weaknesses, desires, sufferings, and trials of human life, and yet did not sin.[3]

Many distinguished theologians have devoted their careers to exploring and expounding the mysteries of the incarnation, delineating what it means and what it does not mean. For example, some describe how Christ became fully human without inheriting or committing any sin. They cite Scripture passages indicating that he did not inherit his humanity from either Adam or Joseph. Scripture tells us that God supernaturally entered the womb of a virgin (Mary).[4] How God interacted with or modified Mary's egg is not made clear in Scripture, but he became a flesh-and-blood embryo. At that point, Christ received the physical and spiritual nature of a human being. But as deity, he was free, and could be kept free, from pollution by sin. We have much more to learn from discussions of a doctrine so central to the Christian faith, and I defer to the expertise of biblical expositors.

What we can achieve by an extradimensional-physics-eye view of the incarnation is a more complete understanding of what Christ willingly endured on behalf of those who would believe and embrace his message. And we can gain a new perspective on how he could be at once both God and man, in heaven and on earth, omnipotent and weary, working miracles and praying for miracles, fully God, yet acknowledging God the Father as "greater."

Both God and Man

We human beings have no control over the four dimensions we experience; we can neither gain nor lose a dimension. But God's control and mastery is complete. He created our four dimensions and several more. Obviously, if God can create and enter dimensions, he can remove and exit them. With such capacities, he has free rein in choosing which ones he will use in his interactions with us. Further, he can choose to be bound to, or to use, one set of dimensions for certain contexts while choosing other sets of dimensions or even realms of existence beyond dimensions for other contexts.

Examples of Jesus's control over dimensionality while he was with us in human form may be found throughout the four Gospels. One appears in the accounts of the temptation by Satan. Jesus, near death from starvation, was reminded of his supernatural capabilities. All Jesus had to do, Satan goaded, was to turn the stones scattered about him into bread.[5] Such a proposal would pose no temptation for any of us for the simple reason that we would be unable to act on it. The temptation might sharpen our hunger pangs when we heard mention of bread. It might tempt us to hurl some of those stones at our tempter. But to transform the stones into food would be impossible for us. Satan's approach in this temptation suggests that, though Jesus had imposed on himself the limitations common to humanity, he retained the capacity to deliver himself from those limitations at any time and any place he chose.

A more explicit demonstration of Jesus's total, uninterrupted (but not independent) authority over the dimensions and components of his creation may be seen in the story of Jesus calming the storm. While Jesus slept in the stern of the boat, a squall came up, threatening to capsize the vessel. Fearing for their lives, the disciples awakened Jesus. When he saw the men's panic, Jesus at once rebuked the wind and told the waves, "Be still!"[6] Immediately, the wind died down and the surface of the water became completely calm.

This incident shows Jesus's capacity to transition between contexts. First we see Jesus submitting to the wind and waves he created. In the next moment, however, Jesus exercises control and authority, as God the Father's agent, over the elements. In the first context, we see Jesus's humanity. In the second, we see his divinity. Jesus can be both God and man because he alone can choose when and where (and with what part of his being and essence) to operate in whatever form and over whatever dimensions or transdimensions he pleases.

An Atoning God

God's purpose in the incarnation goes far beyond breaking through the dimensional barrier to communicate with us face-to-face, to help us understand and believe his message, to show us his love, and to give us hope. He came to break the sin barrier, to repair the damage done in the Garden of Eden. Christ came in human flesh to be the second Adam, the Man who would resist the temptation to "do his own thing." In perfectly obeying the Father, even to the point of death, Christ would finalize God's victory over the original and most powerful insurrectionist, Satan. The author of Hebrews explains at length why our Redeemer, the Mediator between God and humankind, had to share in our humanity,[7] to be made like us in every way,[8] tempted in every way as we are,[9] and yet without committing sin.[10]

The cornerstone of the Christian faith is the doctrine of the atonement: We human beings—all born with a propensity to serve ourselves rather than God,[11] a propensity the Bible calls *sin*—can be "acquitted" because Christ stepped in and paid sin's full penalty. Jesus's perfect life and substitutionary death restores

to humanity the possibility of a personal, loving, shameless, never-ending relationship with our Creator. This relationship is available to anyone for the
asking—an asking that paradoxically costs us both nothing[12] and everything.[13]

Christ's death to save "whosoever believes in him"[14] is a doctrine on which
Christians generally agree. Disagreements typically arise over other atonement-
related doctrinal issues, such as the meaning of "believe in," the requirements
for receiving and keeping God's gift of salvation, and the freedom or predetermination of our decision to accept that gift. These topics will be discussed in
later chapters. For the moment we will focus on other atonement perplexities:
How could God be dead and alive at the same time? Does Christ's death pay for
all people's sin or just the sin of those who accept his pardon? How could one
man's suffering for several hours cover all the wickedness of all the people who
have ever lived or will live?

These questions, among many others, reflect our three-dimensional (plus
time) thinking about Christ's atonement. They cannot be answered self-consistently within the confines of that perspective. But answers can be found if
we look beyond our earthly context and consider what is possible in God's
transdimensional/extradimensional existence.

Simultaneous Death and Life?

When Jesus of Nazareth died on the cross, much more happened than a physical death. The book of Romans reminds us that sin entered the world through
one human's decision to disregard God's way and to act on his own authority.[15]
This first expression of sin did not cause Adam and Eve to immediately drop
dead physically. Physical death came to them some time later.[16] Neither did
they lose their capacity to hear God's voice. But sin's consequences were indeed
profound. Humanity tasted autonomy, a separation of self from the source of
all life, goodness, truth, and love. The branch disconnected itself from the vine
and sought sustenance elsewhere. The evils, pains, and sufferings that followed
in Adam and Eve's lives and in the lives of all their progeny demonstrate the
devastating results of that initial separation.

Adam and Eve were not the first creatures ever to taste autonomy. But they
were the first human beings to taste it, and in doing so they placed themselves,
their family, and all their descendants in the camp of God's enemy, the insti-
gator of all insubordination and evil: Satan. Who could repair such damage?
Adam was helpless to do so, however remorseful he may have been. No human after him could accomplish the repair, for each was born of that separated
branch. The angels, however magnificent and obedient, also lacked the capacity

to carry it out.[17]

Only God himself could make the mend. He alone could survive the journey across the gap and make possible the restoration. The Restorer had to be able to enter not just some, but all the dimensions and realms occupied by both man and God. Angels could be sent into contact with humanity's dimensions, but the sin gap could not be closed by them because they could not enter all of man's dimensions and realms and all of God's. Neither did they possess the attributes, resources, and transdimensional/extradimensional capacities to pay sin's penalty. One might also point out that the gap was closely guarded by Satan, whom no other angelic being could overpower.

In one moment—for him, what could be an eternal moment *and more* because of his access to the equivalent of extra dimension(s) of time—Christ crossed the divide caused by sin. The Bible says, "God made him who had no sin to be sin for us,"[18] taking into himself the wound of separation, the enmity or wrath of God against sin. In a human body, he proved his perfect obedience, his wisdom, and his power to live—and die—with the capacity for autonomy and yet wholly ("holy") attuned to the Father's will. He lived up to God's perfection and qualified himself to pay the ransom, namely his own death, for the penalty incurred by humanity's sin.

His death in the physical dimensions of time and space was real, not feigned, an experience he chose to undergo on our behalf. But he also experienced the indescribable spiritual torment of hell, of being shut out in some way we cannot picture, from his Father's approbation.

God Both Dead and Alive

Jesus Christ's payment for all of our sin through his death on the cross and his subsequent resurrection from the dead ranks as the most dramatic expression given to us of his control over all dimensional realms. Because he died, remained dead for "three days and three nights,"[19] and arose bodily from death to life, exactly as he predicted, this proves that he has the power to *limit* any portion of his capacities and powers to any degree he chooses, whenever and wherever he chooses, and along whatever space-time dimensions (or super-or supra-dimensions) he chooses. The converse is also true. Jesus can *expand* any portion of his capacities and powers to any degree he chooses, whenever and wherever he chooses, and along whatever space-time dimensions (or super- or supra-dimensions) he chooses.

Some skeptics and atheists have argued that if Jesus were God, he could not have died; and if he died, he could not have been God. They recognize, of course, the contradiction in saying that Jesus is both really dead and really alive. Several famous nonbelievers have used this line of reasoning to conclude that the Christian faith is irrational and, therefore, unworthy of consideration.

The simultaneity of Jesus's death and immortality would be a contradiction, however, only if the time, place, and context of his death were identical to the time, place, and dimensional context of his being alive (see the discussion of contradictions and paradoxes in chapter 6 on pages 57–64). Even with respect to human death, we recognize the role of an extradimensional realm, though we may not use those words. Death, for us, refers to a change, a transition, a cessation of some kind, but not an annihilation (see chapter 16). While our physical death involves a definite and significant loss, that loss does not negate the possibility of a far greater extradimensional gain. Ultimately, we know our existence continues when our physical bodies can no longer sustain us.

The apostle John implies that the Holy Spirit communicates this fact to all;[20] however, in their rebellion against God or practice in ignoring him, some people work very hard to deny it.[21] When we leave our familiar time and space abode and the physical bodies in which we were born, we enter some other realm or dimension(s), because our life extends beyond mere physical reality. While our physical body dies, our spirit continues to live. As the book of Ecclesiastes explains, eternity is "written" on our hearts.[22]

Because of Christ's identity as God and his access to all the dimensions or super- or supra-dimensions God encompasses, he could experience suffering and death in all the human-occupied dimensions and then transition into any of his other dimensions or realms once the atonement price had been paid. Evidencing his divine nature, Jesus resisted the temptation to escape from the agonies of a torturous death and finalized the payment for all our sin.

Limited or Unlimited Payment

The debate over whether Christ's atonement was "limited" or "unlimited" arises from two misperceptions. One equates sin (singular, universal) with sins (plural, individual) and thus quantifies that *something* for which atonement is required. The other, connected with it, applies God's foreknowledge to that quantitative assumption. The Bible declares God knows even before we are conceived or the universe was created whether we will reject his offer of forgiveness for our sin(s).[23] According to one line of reasoning, the penalty for which payment is needed must be the penalty for the sin of those and only those whom he knows will accept his payment made on their behalf. The rationale here is that for Christ to pay for all the offenses for all humanity, and yet have only some humans receive the benefit of the payment, is tantamount to saying that Christ's payment is at least partially without effect. And for Christ to be in any way ineffective would mean he is less than omnipotent.

This argument correctly affirms Christ's omnipotence but stumbles into contradiction with many other passages of Scripture. These three are typical:

> Christ died for the ungodly.[24]

> He [Jesus] suffered death, so that by the grace of God he might taste death for everyone.[25]

> Jesus Christ, the Righteous One. He is the atoning sacrifice for our sins, and not only for ours but also for the sins of the whole world.[26]

The debate can be resolved, at least to some degree of satisfaction, by reconsidering the logic or validity of labeling "unaccepted pardon" as "ineffectual payment." To use a human example, if the court accepts my offer to pay the traffic fines for four of my friends, knowing that I can cover the maximum amount charged for their violations, my bank account and generosity are not limited nor judged insufficient should any of my friends refuse to accept my offer to pay their fines.

A complete resolution may be had if we accept that God had an important purpose in dying for everyone regardless of anyone's decision to receive or reject his offer of forgiveness. Christ may have died and paid the penalty for all so that no one could ever, at any future point, rightly conclude that God did not express his love toward that person. In a later chapter on hell's torment, we will look at the proposition that God continuously expresses his perfect love to all for the rest of eternity.

Resolving the deeper issue of human free will and how it can operate without contradicting God's sovereign will, and vice versa, would offer a much more deeply satisfactory answer. This resolution, which can be accomplished in extradimensional reality, will be addressed in a later chapter.

Adding up the Price

A quantitative perspective on our atonement price and a four-dimensional view of what Christ endured on the cross have raised a target for secular skepticism and ridicule. The idea that one man's suffering for a little more than one afternoon on a Roman cross—a painful execution that many other men endured—could even approach equivalence to the eternal torment and suffering of the billions who have rejected or will reject his offer of redemption, seems absurd. Jesus's suffering on the cross lasted but six hours.[27] (The emotional and spiritual pain of knowing what he would endure began much earlier, of course, perhaps even before the angels and the universe were created. In this sense the agony of the atonement began much before the incarnation.) His suffering on the cross, though greater than what any other being has ever endured,[28] may at first glance seem finite and imaginable. How, then, could one imaginable experience of torment of apparently limited duration be equivalent to hell's unimaginable torment visited for an unimaginable duration on vast numbers of people?

Such reasoning overlooks the implications of Christ's simultaneous deity and humanity. His payment of our ransom price must be accounted for in a perspective that goes beyond our physical realm. The book of Hebrews offers this insight:

> He [Christ] went through the greater and more perfect tabernacle that is not made with human hands, that is to say, is not a part of this creation.[29]

> For Christ did not enter a sanctuary made with human hands that was only a copy of the true one; he entered heaven itself, now to appear for us in God's presence. Nor did he enter heaven to offer himself again and again. . . . Christ was sacrificed once to take away the sins of many.[30]

A significant part of what transpired in Christ's payment of all that our death warrants took place in God's transdimensional/extradimensional realm. While Scripture is clear that all of our sins have been completely atoned for by Christ's one sacrifice,[31] it does not explain every detail of how the atonement price was accounted. What matters is that Jesus Christ has the capacity to make full payment. Our confidence rests in his adequacy.

Given even a limited understanding of Christ's transdimensional/extradimensional characteristics and powers, however, we can suggest some possible approaches to that accounting. Perhaps the easiest for us to comprehend would be reckoning Jesus's payment of our atonement price in two extra dimensions of time.

The penalty for one person's sin—unimaginably painful torment and eternal isolation from God and everything and everyone good and righteous—would require that individual's existence (after physical death on earth) on at

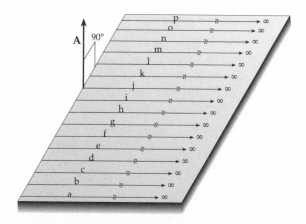

Figure 10: Paying the Atonement Price in Multiple Dimensions of Time
Line **A** represents the universe's timeline. One of many ways Christ could atone for all the sins of humanity would be to pay the redemption price in two dimensions of time, completely independent of our time dimension. In this time plane, Christ could suffer for infinite time on billions of different timelines: **a**, **b**, **c**, etc. Thus, in a few moments on the cross in our time dimension, Jesus Christ could experience the payment for the sins of every human who has ever lived or will ever live.

least one infinitely long timeline. If some 20 billion people incur sin's penalty, 20 billion infinite timelines would represent the cumulative total of sin's penalty. With a second time dimension, God could move along, that is, experience, these 20 billion timelines. He would possess a plane of time that could encompass all of them (see figure 10). Thus, while Jesus suffered on the cross for six hours on our timeline, he could have experienced the suffering of 20 billion infinite timelines in two other dimensions of time.

There are countless other ways, of course, that Jesus could have experienced the fullness of hellish torment. Jesus could have used his superior capacities to experience intensified torment on a limited timescale. In other words, he could choose to suffer to an infinite degree for a finite time rather than to suffer to a finite degree for infinite time. Either way, the sum total remains the same.

This minimal comprehension of what Christ endured to cover the consequences of all our sin can be mind-numbingly overwhelming. But as we allow time for this numbness to wear off, we can experience anew, perhaps much more deeply than ever, gratitude and amazement at the magnitude of his love. And we may better understand the basis for this question in Hebrews: "How shall we escape if we ignore so great a salvation?"[32]

Does the Atonement Demote Christ?

Some Christians also express concern that the notion of Christ's infinitely intense or infinitely enduring payment for sin's penalty somehow diminishes him in relation to God the Father and God the Holy Spirit. Their concern arises, perhaps, from our familiar, finite perspective. A finite supply of anything can be diminished by withdrawals or expenditures from that supply. However, even if the supply of some particular resource is limited, an expenditure of it in any amount, even the total, does nothing to demote or diminish the one who makes that expenditure. That individual's attributes and identity remain intact regardless of the generosity he or she might display.

God's relinquishing of time dimensions (or the equivalent) to atone for sin, if he actually did do so, would be incomparable to our giving up a dimension. For us humans to lose the capacity to operate in one of our four dimensions would be catastrophic. It would limit our functionality and either tremendously diminish the meaning of our personhood or eradicate it altogether. But, for God, the case is radically different. He can, as he has already demonstrated, create dimensions of time and space at will. While humanity is subject to whatever time and space dimensions God places us in, time and space are subject to him. Although Christ did make an enormous expenditure of his resources in atoning for our sins, he could do so without depleting or diminishing his supply of power and resources and without altering his identity.

A brief review of the concept of infinity may help clarify this point. Infinity minus one still equals infinity. The psalmist declares that God owns "the cattle on a thousand hills."[33] Making a gift of all those cattle does not make God poor or poorer. His resources are infinite. Infinite wealth minus the cattle on a thousand hills still adds up to infinite wealth.

Does God's infinite wealth mean that any gift he gives us counts as nothing to him? Can he really be considered "generous" if he experiences no depletion? To answer this question requires a contextual shift from the material realm to the nonmaterial. For example, does the giving of love or kindness or compassion deplete our supply of such things? It may deplete our time or energy or other resources, but not these intangibles. Because we still have more to give after we have given, does this eradicate the value of the giving? Hardly. In the same way, no matter how Christ paid for our sins, the gift amounts to more than we can imagine, and it takes nothing away from the equality he shares with God the Father and God the Holy Spirit.

Does the Atonement Permanently Mar Christ?

When the disciples were visited by the resurrected Christ, they were able to see and feel the wounds of his crucifixion.[34] Christ certainly had the power to eradicate these wounds, but he chose to let them remain. One reason may be that these marks were essential to convince the disciples of the reality of Jesus's bodily resurrection. The wounds identified him as nothing else could have. And no doubt these marks helped remind the disciples of what the Creator willingly endured to atone for their sins and of the permanent effects of that atoning sacrifice. This kind of reminder may be of some benefit to future generations of disciples and even to the hosts of angels and demons.

Whether these marks of the cross will remain for us to see when we enter Christ's presence we do not know. The book of Revelation, which gives more description of the heavenly realm and of our future there than does any other portion of Scripture, gives no clear answer to this question. Yet we can speculate that when the magnificence of the new creation is revealed to us, and when we begin to fathom the loss and the horror that hell represents, we may well be sufficiently reminded of the magnitude of the price Christ paid for our atonement.

Beyond Our Imagining

The incarnation is described in the second chapter of Philippians as Christ's becoming "nothing." Such a statement does not deny the wonder and worth of human beings, but it does express the magnitude of what Christ gave up or put aside in accepting life as a human. The humility he demonstrated in coming to us and dying for us exemplifies the humility we need in coming to him. His example of humility, rather than hinting at any weakness or inferiority, indicates just the opposite—the moral perfection of God alone.

The differences made by that one-dimensional gap between the screen people and us, as vast as they are, seem utterly trivial, "nothing," compared with the differences made by the seven-or more-dimensional gap between us and God. What is more, the incarnation and the atonement show us God's capacity to operate in any dimensional realm, any combination of space and time dimensions (or super- or supra-dimensions) he chooses. He can also manifest different aspects of himself in different dimensional realms. The reality in which he can live and move supersedes by far the limits of human imagination. And yet we know he wants us to try to imagine it, to anticipate our future in it, because he gave us sneak previews—in his Word, in his creation, in his incarnation, and in his atonement.

Chapter 11

Dimensional Capacities
of Created Beings

Thus far our attention has been focused chiefly on the reality and ramifications of God's 11-plus space, time, and super- and supra-dimensions. Because God has the capacity to create and remove dimensions, he lives with no dimensional constraints whatsoever—except, of course, any self-imposed ones he deems appropriate to his purposes. The life-forms he created have been designed for and placed within certain dimensional constraints, and these apparently differ from one life-form to another. An exploration of the dimensional features of the different kinds of creatures may help us develop a deeper understanding and appreciation of how these various life-forms, ourselves included, relate to each other and to God.

The first chapter of Genesis distinguishes four life-forms, and other portions of Scripture identify three more: (1) plants; (2) animals; (3) animals with "soulish" characteristics; (4) humans, endowed with both soulish characteristics and spirit; (5) angels; (6) cherubim; and (7) archangels. The biblical terms and descriptions of these different entities appear below. While the descriptions used for Earth's life-forms harmonize well with both the scientific order and scientific classifications, the categorization system was chosen primarily to fit the purpose of the passage: to show how God prepared the way for his creation of humankind.

1. Plants (Hebrew words *eseb, zera ', 'ēṣ, perî, deshe', yereq;* Greek words *chortos, dendron, phuteia*): organisms rooted to some kind of soil and capable of using nutrients in the soil, water, and air to produce food. Plants exist in the space and time dimensions of the universe and are subject to its natural laws.

2. Animals (Hebrew words *shereṣ, dāgâ;* Greek words *herpeton, ichthus*): organisms devoid of any significant capacity to relate to human beings, except perhaps via the food chain. They have the capacity to move and reproduce, responding to instincts that foster their survival. They are dependent on plants (either directly through eating plants or indirectly through eating other animals) for their energy. These creatures exist in the space and time dimensions of the universe and are subject to its natural laws.

3. Soulish animals (Hebrew words *nepesh, hay, ḥayyâ, behēmâ, remeś, be'îr, bāśār, tannîn, ṣippôr, 'ôp, kānāp*; Greek words *orneon, peteinon, ktēnos, thērion, zōon*): animals endowed with the capacity to nurture and relate to one another at levels beyond mere instinct, with some degree of intelligence, emotion, and will. They also possess the capacity to form relationships with human beings, and each separate kind of soulish animal is designed by God to serve and/or please humans in distinct ways. Soulish animals exist in the space and time dimensions of the universe and are subject to its natural laws.

4. Humans (Hebrew words *ādām, 'ĕnôsh, 'îsh*; Greek word *anthrōpos*): soulish creatures endowed with self-awareness and God-awareness, innate moral and ethical standards, and a proclivity for religious expression and exploration. We humans exist in the space and time dimensions of the universe and in a spiritual reality beyond those dimensions. We are subject to natural laws, social laws, and spiritual laws, and we bear responsibility for managing animal and plant life, as well as our own behavior. We were created to serve and please God.

5. Angels (Hebrew word *mal'āk*; Greek word *angelos*): intelligent beings that are dimensionally limited but capable of existing beyond the space and time dimensions of the universe, subject to spiritual laws but not necessarily to natural laws. One third, the fallen angels or demons, are in rebellion against God.[1] The remaining two-thirds bear responsibility for service to God and can, at his bidding, make contact with humans in the space and time dimensions of the universe.

5. Cherubim (Hebrew word *kerûb*, singular, *kerûbim*, plural; Greek word *cheroubin*): a special order of angelic beings with a unique role in directing and expressing worship toward God.

6. Archangels (Greek word *archangelos*): angels of exalted rank and power, sent by God to carry out special assignments.

The Plants

Plants are foundational to God's layering of life on Earth. Only plants can gain food from inorganic matter. While they differ from animals, they possess certain similarities, such as the capacity to respire and reproduce. Because plants are never referred to as "creatures" anywhere in the Bible, some Bible interpreters hold that plants are not alive and do not experience death.[2] However, Job contrasts a tree's vitality with a man's: "Its stump [may] die in the soil, yet at the scent of water it will bud. . . . But a man dies and is laid low."[3] King David makes this comparison: "Like green plants they will soon die away."[4] The Hebrew words for "death" used by Moses and Job denote the physical death of living things.[5]

While the Bible unmistakably refers to plants as living and dying organisms, it offers no support for the concept common to many Eastern religions that plants share in a "cosmic consciousness." Scientific and biblical evidences establish that plants do respond to their environment for survival's sake, sending branches toward sunlight and roots toward water and nutrients. But nowhere in Scripture does God endow them with soul or spirit.

Jesus's curse on the fig tree may not be used to establish any conscious nature in plants.[6] As the Creator of the universe, Jesus has complete command over both the organic and inorganic world. His calming of the storm on the Sea of Galilee provides convincing evidence of such authoritative capacity.[7] Plants are strictly confined to the matter, energy, and the four space-time dimensions of the universe. They cannot form relationships with animals or humans. They manifest none of the attributes identified with the soul or the spirit.

The Animals

Animal life manifests enormous diversity of size, form, mobility, food-getting mechanisms, reproductive processes, respiration, adaptability, longevity, etc. Bible authors categorize them in the general terms appropriate to the text's focus on relationships, responsibilities, and redemption, and not always in the precise terms of scientific methodology. Sometimes wild animals are distinguished from those humans easily make pets of or domesticate. Sometimes animals that do not communicate or interact with humans in any relational way are distinguished from those that do. Mollusks, fish, amphibians, and insects, for example, tend to be grouped (among others) in the non-relational category, if and when the biblical context indicates that such a distinction is being made.

Just as with plants, the Bible refers to these non-relational animals as experiencing life and death. The Lord instructed Moses to tell pharaoh, "The fish in the Nile will die."[8] Later, Moses records the death of fish[9] and, later still, the death of frogs.[10] Solomon describes the laudable behavior and other characteristics of ants[11] and refers to the death of flies.[12]

Animals differ from plants in that they possess the capacity to obtain and digest food rather than to manufacture it. Since they are not typically rooted to the soil or to other vegetation as plants are, most can freely roam the environs of their land or ocean habitat (and in some cases, both). However, they share with plants the following characteristics: (1) confinement to the matter, energy, and four space-time dimensions of the universe; and (2) incapacity (of most species) to display emotion or to respond to the emotions of other creatures.

The Soulish Animals

The Bible singles out certain animal species, or kinds, from others. The distinction first becomes apparent in the Genesis creation accounts. In referring to some creatures, ones we might call "higher animals," the author uses the Hebrew noun *nepesh*. This word singles out soulish creatures from other animals by their capacity to form what may be described as emotional attachments to other animals and to human beings.[13] God created certain species with capacities for interaction at levels involving intelligence, choice, and emotions. Their special characteristics inspire humans to tame, domesticate, train, and make enjoyable pets of various types of birds, mammals, and the few reptile species that are capable of nurturing one another and forming bonds. Humans make pets of other creatures, too, such as frogs, turtles, and snakes, for example, but the relationship possibilities with such pets are essentially one-way.

In recording the account of God's creation of these soulish animals, Moses uses the Hebrew verbs *'āśâ* and *bārā'*. According to Hebrew lexicons, *'āśâ* means "manufacture" or "fabricate," and its sense implies God's action in fashioning the creature.[14] *Bārā'* carries the strong sense of "create," of bringing into existence something new, something that has not previously existed.[15] The biblical text suggests that God personally designed the bodies of these advanced creatures and placed within them some capacity no other earthly creature had possessed previously—a capacity that the Old Testament writers using Hebrew could call a "soul." But this Hebrew "soul" must not be confused with the New Testament Greek concept of "soul," which in many biblical contexts encompasses what the Hebrew would identify as "spirit."[16]

Scripture suggests that the soulishness of birds and mammals gives them the capacity not only to relate to human beings and to serve and/or please them in specific ways but also to detect the presence of extradimensional beings if and when those beings influence the physical or emotional realm they enter. Balaam's donkey, for example, was aware of an angelic visitor even when Balaam was not.[17] Individuals who have observed occult practices, which often involve encounters with demons (fallen angels), report that a bird or a mammal may react visibly or audibly to the demonic visitation, while other animals, such as amphibians, make no response. The most likely explanation for soulish animals' sensitivity to the presence of demons arises from their sensitivity to people's physical cues, to changes of movement, expression, or even odor, however subtle. Both angels and demons are described in Scripture as capable of impacting our dimensional realm, becoming visible, audible, or tangible in some other way. Soulish animals' ability to detect these spiritual beings says more, perhaps, about the abilities of angels and demons to communicate with soulish creatures than about soulish creatures' detection capacity.

Whatever the case, soulish creatures cannot be said to possess spiritual capacities. None of these animal species has ever been observed to engage in worship or to practice any form of religion. Grieving the loss of a life partner, burying the dead, or decorating a nest with trinkets expresses emotional capacity, not a spiritual capacity, within these creatures. Their behavior gives no indication of any awareness of a conscience or of a moral code. Neither do they display any concern over the existence of a Creator or of life beyond physical death. By all indications, when soulish animals die, they return to the dust. They do not possess ongoing spiritual or extradimensional life. This statement does not necessarily mean that none of these wonderful animal species will exist in the new creation to come. The Bible is silent on this issue. But it does suggest that if such creatures are present, they will not be the ones that lived with us here on Earth. Nevertheless, we have solid evidence that God cares for these creatures. The psalmist says,

> All creatures look to you to give them their food at the proper time.
> When you give it to them, they gather it up; when you open your
> hand, they are satisfied with good things.[18]

Jesus indirectly admonishes people to care for their animals on the Sabbath, as on any other day,[19] and he addresses the disciples' fears about evil befalling them with reference to God's awareness of a tiny bird: "Are not two sparrows sold for a penny? Yet not one of them will fall to the ground outside your Father's care."[20] Through Job, God exhorts us not to miss out on the important life lessons that birds and mammals can teach us. Job declares,

> But ask the animals, and they will teach you, or the birds in the sky,
> and they will tell you.[21]

Soulish animals can teach us three important life lessons. First, just as it takes a higher being to tame the soulish animals, so also it takes a higher Being to tame a proud human.[22] Second, as the soulish animals were created to serve and please higher beings, namely us, so also we were created to serve and please a higher Being, namely God. Third, as human sin damages humanity's relationships with soulish animals, so also it damages humanity's relationship with God.

The Spirit Beings

According to Genesis, God created only one species of life on Earth with a capacity called "spirit." Just as with the soulish animals, the wording of the passage indicates the introduction of some new and unique life-form. For God's final work of creation, the narrator chooses the Hebrew noun *'ādām*, and again he uses the Hebrew verbs *'āśâ* and *bārā'* to depict the creative act. "*'Ādām*" refers exclusively to the earthly creature (both male and female) God endowed with a special capacity to communicate with and relate to him.[23] The use of *'āśâ* and *bārā'* again implies that God personally designed the physical and soulish characteristics of the first human and that he did something entirely new in endowing that human with spirit.

The human spirit manifests itself, at least in part, by humans' unique consciousness. While no reputable scholar disputes that human beings are uniquely conscious beings, many scholars hesitate or refuse to give God credit for that conscious nature. Some of this generation's most brilliant researchers have tried valiantly to find within matter, energy, and the natural biochemical processes of our space and time dimensions a hypothesis for the origin and operation of human consciousness, but none of their efforts has come close to succeeding.[24] In fact, their findings only help build the case for a supernatural origin.

Spirit beings, whatever their level of intelligence, manifest a capacity that not even the most highly intelligent soulish animals possess, the ability to discern dimensions beyond the ones we physically experience. We may even interact and dialogue, knowingly or not, with spiritual beings from beyond our physically experienced dimensions. According to the Bible, human beings may sometimes be allowed to see, hear, interact, and dialogue with angels, mistaking them for humans. In the book of Hebrews we are exhorted, "Do not forget to show hospitality to strangers, for by so doing some people have shown hospitality to angels without knowing it."[25] Sometimes people know, or come to recognize, angels as messengers from the spiritual, or extradimensional realm, as we see in accounts of Abraham's, Lot's, and Daniel's interactions with angels.[26]

Because we are spiritual beings, we humans can pray. Through prayer we can cross the space-time manifold of the cosmos and converse with God in his transdimensional/extradimensional realm. Because prayer is transdimensional/extradimensional in its reach, it must be considered the most powerful capacity God has made available to us in our current dimensional context. Prayer is so powerful, it comes with special cautions and restrictions on its use.[27]

Again, because we are spirit beings, we humans, alone among all earthly creatures, possess the capacity to experience life beyond physical death, life that survives outside the physical body we now occupy. God says we will witness his eventual creation of a new universe to replace this one. The new one will function with different physical laws and occupy different space-time dimensions (see chapter 17). Because we humans are spirit beings, we can make this transition to life beyond our earthly body and earthly dimensions, either life without end in the new creation (see chapter 17) or death without end in the lake of fire (see chapter 16).

All human beings—men, women, and children, in all geographical and historical contexts—possess innate knowledge not instilled by human instruction but by our Creator. Whether our family and culture affirm or deny these beliefs, humans gradually become aware of these things:

1. Truth exists and does not change.[28]
2. Life continues forever after death.[29]
3. God deserves our worship, for his standard and his law are perfection.[30]
4. We cannot live up to God's perfect standard.[31]
5. God knows our heart, the core of our being, and will judge (evaluate) us after our earthly life is over.[32]

Those of us who invite God's Spirit to live in the core of our being and to express Christ through us—body, soul, and spirit—become linked forever with God. We experience a change as dramatic as birth, and it is called a spiritual birth. God's character and capacities become available to us as never before, despite the necessary limits of our physical context. From the time this spiritual birth takes place, we begin a never-ending process of growth in love, joy, peace, patience, kindness, goodness, faithfulness, gentleness, and self-control, among other Christlike qualities.[33]

We still need to nourish and maintain our body and soul. Our human bodies keep us subject to the laws of thermodynamics and gravity, for example. We need food, rest, exercise, work, relationships, and recreation. To take care of ourselves is tantamount to caring for "the temple of the living God."[34] Such a comment should inspire us to do a good job. Personal neglect does not please him. Meanwhile, God provides the nourishment that sustains our spirit. We have constant access to it, and it is just as important to our spiritual health as breathing oxygen or drinking water is to our physical sustenance. Elihu reminds us in the book of Job, "If it were his intention and he withdrew his spirit and breath, all humanity would perish together and mankind would return to the dust."[35]

God wants to provide so much more than physical and spiritual vitality. For those who commit their lives to him and invite his Spirit to live within, he supplies both the desire and the power to fulfill his purposes here on Earth,[36] an assignment that yields for each of us what he describes as "life to the full."[37] Jesus spoke to his disciples about this life:

> Truly I tell you, if you have faith as small as a mustard seed, you can say to this mountain, "Move from here to there" and it will move. Nothing will be impossible for you.[38]

> Truly I tell you, if you have faith and do not doubt, not only can you do what was done to the fig tree, but also you can say to this mountain, "Go, throw yourself into the sea," and it will be done. If you believe, you will receive whatever you ask for in prayer.[39]

> Very truly I tell you, whoever believes in me will do the works I have been doing, and they will do even greater things than these, because I am going to the Father. And I will do whatever you ask in my name, so that the Father may be glorified in the Son. You may ask me for anything in my name, and I will do it. If you love me, keep my commands.[40]

Learning to use our extradimensional capacities takes time, for it takes growth in faith, with accompanying wisdom and purity. In asking for "anything," that "anything" must be identified by a heart attuned to God's purposes and plans.[41] How often are we inclined to ask for the removal of trouble from our path? And yet he told us clearly that trouble is a constant companion, a tool for character growth, during our earthly life:

> In this world you will have trouble. But take heart! I have overcome the world.[42]

Knowing what to ask in the face of trouble comes through knowing him better and better. Building any relationship takes effort and attention, and the same is true of our relationship with God. The attention is always fully available on his part; our part is up to us. The apostle Paul tells us that our developing relationship with the Lord can bring such daily renewal and radiance that it overshadows the troubles and even the aging process in our lives.

> And we all, who with unveiled faces contemplate the Lord's glory, are being transformed into his image with ever-increasing glory, which comes from the Lord, who is the Spirit.[43]

> Therefore we do not lose heart. Though outwardly we are wasting away, yet inwardly we are being renewed day by day. For our light and momentary troubles are achieving for us an eternal glory that far outweighs them all. So we fix our eyes not on what is seen, but on what is unseen, since what is seen is temporary, but what is unseen is eternal.[44]

Angels

The angels we see in paintings and sculptures typically have feminine or child-like features, golden halos, and wings ranging from tiny to grandiose. Many artistic portrayals more closely resemble the traditional image of Cupid than they do the biblical description of angels. The Bible tells us they are mighty[45] and holy.[46] It says they are mightier than we humans are.[47] They are so swift as to defy the laws of physics.[48] They are subject neither to decay nor to death. They can be visible or invisible to humans.[49] In most biblically recorded cases of their appearance on Earth, the people who saw and heard them responded with terror. The following account by Daniel illustrates an angel's impact:

> As I was standing on the bank of the great river, the Tigris, I looked up and there before me was a man dressed in linen, with a belt of fine gold from Uphaz around his waist. His body was like topaz, his face like lightning, his eyes like flaming torches, his arms and legs like the gleam of burnished bronze, and his voice like the sound of a multitude.

> I, Daniel, was the only one who saw the vision; those who were with me did not see it, but such terror overwhelmed them that they fled and hid themselves. So I was left alone, gazing at this great vision; I had no strength left, my face turned deathly pale and I was helpless.[50]

Daniel then explains that when the angel started speaking, he (Daniel) passed out, and the angel had to help him to his feet. The angel's purpose in coming to Daniel was to give him a message about the future, to let him know what is written in "the Book of Truth," as the angel called it. The angel also reported his intense conflict with a fallen angel, specifically with the demon who held some measure of authority over Persia. This demon had the power to detain the angel for 21 days.

From these biblical accounts and others, we learn that angels' capacities reflect their existence in at least some of God's dimensions outside the four of the universe. Compared to God, however, angels are limited. The Bible indicates that God alone is omnipotent, omniscient, and omnipresent.[51] Angels are not. Though they have access to more dimensions than we humans do, they occupy a limited dimensionality, as we do. Though they have the ability to exercise extraordinary power,[52] they are created beings, as we are, incapable of creating any other beings.[53] Unlike humans, they do not marry or procreate,[54] though some Bible scholars interpret a few passages of Scripture as suggesting that fallen angels in one way or another, and for a limited time, demonstrated the capacity to produce "mutant" offspring through sexual relations with human women.[55]

Cherubim, Seraphim, and Archangels

God apparently endowed certain angelic beings with power and authority above others. Though many "ranks" of angels may exist,[56] the Bible mentions but three.

The highest order appears to be the *cherubim*. Satan, identified as the most powerful and exalted of all the angels—before his rebellion—was a cherub.[57] No beings in all Scripture, other than God himself, give observers a more difficult descriptive task. Depictions by the prophet Ezekiel[58] and the apostle John[59] represent valiant attempts to portray extradimensional features that far surpass what we humans can comprehend or imagine and far surpass the capacities and attributes shared by the lower ranks of angels. The cherubim alone are entrusted with certain tasks in protecting God's glory and holiness and in proclaiming his grace. What all these tasks entail we cannot yet begin to imagine.

Seraphim is a Hebrew term for "burning ones."[60] This title probably refers neither to fire as we know it nor to the consuming judgment. Rather, it expresses the passionate devotion of a particular order of angelic beings to praise God and proclaim to all creation God's holiness and majesty. Though these angels, too, are awesome to behold, they pose at least a little less difficulty for humans to describe than do the cherubim.[61]

It is possible that God created more than one *archangel*.[62] However, only one, Michael, is mentioned by name in the Bible.[63] His specific role is perhaps most comparable to that of a military leader. He is the commander who leads the angelic host against Satan's demonic forces. Michael's ultimate victory over Satan[64] suggests that his powers and abilities may at least approximate Satan's.

Roles Now and Later

When we read of the amazing powers and attributes angels possess, we may wonder why God would describe us as "a little lower than the heavenly beings" or "angels."[65] Though the dimensionality and capacities of the angels supersede ours by what seems a vast margin, we have the opportunity and capacity to comprehend certain spiritual realities that mystify angels.[66] In the life that continues past our physical death, we humans who choose to worship Christ will be assigned as "judges" (leaders) and teachers of the angels.[67]

For now, one of the roles God has assigned to angels is to help provide for our protection. The more we need, due to age, other dependency factors, and spiritual circumstances, the more protection we receive.[68] God also deploys angels to perform supernatural acts of service on behalf of those individuals who devote their lives fully to spreading the gospel (the good news of what Jesus has offered to humanity) and equipping others to do the same.[69]

Chapter 12

God's Omnipotence vs. Displayed Power

Anyone who has ever taken a philosophy class has probably heard this co-nundrum: Can God create a rock so massive he cannot lift it? If we answer that he *can* create such a rock, we admit God's inability to lift or move the rock and thus imply he is less than all-powerful. If we say he *cannot* create such a rock, then we declare him limited in his creative abilities. If we identify the impasse as a contradiction we must live with, a knot that cannot be untangled, we imply that God may not be logically consistent and/or totally truthful. With this little puzzle, many a nontheist has excused his or her denial or dismissal of God's existence, and many a Christian student has grown a little less confident about his or her faith.

This "proof" against God takes various forms. One that virtually all believers have faced at one time or another is the argument that God must not care or must not be adequately powerful or he would put a stop to evil and suffering. A later chapter will address this particular argument, but we can lay a foundation for that discussion by considering the core fallacy in such challenges to God's omnipotence.

Cannot vs. Will Not
The solution arises in part from addressing a semantic issue, a misuse of the little word *can*, and in part from adjusting our perspective. It seems far more appropriate to ask questions about what God *will* do than about what he *can* do, especially given the "can do" he demonstrated so vividly in creating the universe.

Some things God will not do. In one sense, he cannot do these things, but the reason has nothing to do with a power limitation. Rather, he cannot do certain things because he is powerful enough and righteous enough to choose not to do them, ever. God cannot lie or distort the truth.[1] He cannot do evil.[2]

He cannot accept evil.[3] Nor can he ever overlook evil.[4]

Why can he not do these things? He cannot because he is perfectly consistent. His character is immutable; it simply does not change.[5] His perfection, holiness, love, truthfulness, goodness, and faithfulness (among many other attributes) remain unchanged and unchangeable. They do not begin and end because he does not begin and end. His unchanging character reveals his power, a power that we do not possess, to maintain complete character consistency. He is not subject to the immaturity, ignorance, lack of love, shortsightedness, or genetic and chemical factors that influence our judgments, decisions, and actions and so often render them inconsistent. We could say he has the power to maintain his perfection with perfect self-control.

God's Freedom to Refrain

Time and again, we humans are tempted by our own impatience to question God's inaction. We cannot fathom why he does not frequently intervene in miraculous, dramatic ways in the affairs of humans, preventing or overruling their wrong choices with a display of his extradimensional powers. The irony of our question might be humorous if it were not so terribly immature and arrogant. It is immature in that we fail to appreciate the character development and preparation for our future roles in the new creation that we can accrue from our brief exposure to suffering and evil.[6] It is arrogant in that it is pure folly for us humans to stand in judgment over what God will or will not do and when he will or will not do it, given the immeasurable differences between his moral character and ours, his power and ours, his dimensional perspective and ours, his love and ours.

The Benefit of Moral Perfection

How often have we heard skeptics say, "If God is good, why did he . . ." or "Why didn't he . . ."? In asking this question, the inquirer has either knowingly or unwittingly exalted his or her judgment of what is good and what is warranted over God's knowledge of such things. The questioner in this case implies that God's goodness cannot be believed or trusted.

Jesus set the record straight on this matter when approached by a self-righteous religious leader who flatteringly addressed him as "good teacher."[7] With penetrating insight into the man's puffed up self-evaluation, Jesus replied, "Why do you call me good?" Then he added, "No one is good—except God alone."[8] Jesus's statement affirms a truth revealed throughout Scripture, as well as throughout nature: God is the one and only source and essence of goodness. What he created he declared "good," and he encourages us to do "good" to both our friends and enemies; but goodness emanates from, and is ultimately defined by, him alone.

From a mathematical and dimensional perspective, the Creator's goodness may be described as infinite. Though we humans have the capacity as spirit beings to recognize and express to some degree his goodness, we have no capacity for goodness apart from him. If God did not exist, or if God were not good, we would not even know such a quality were possible.

The Benefit of Power

How often have we heard skeptics say, "If God is good, then he must be weak, otherwise he would . . . "? Again, some fundamentally fallacious assumptions lie behind the challenge.

One of the fallacies is the expressed certainty that we can discern the absolute best course of action in a particular situation. All we can really know of absolutes is that they must exist, for God exists. While God has absolute knowledge of everything, we humans possess absolute knowledge of nothing because of our finite limits (see chapter 4).

A second fallacy lies in our mistaking the exercise of power as the measure of available power. A limited expression of power or a restraint of action cannot be used to indicate what power is possible and available. It cannot be used to infer weakness or lack of power. If we see a well-muscled man carrying a 20-pound backpack along the trail, we would not reasonably conclude that 20 pounds is the maximum load he has the strength to carry. We would demonstrate better logic in concluding that for today's outing, he needs only 20 pounds' worth of supplies. And what if he were to put down his pack for a while as he stops to take pictures or to do a little fishing? Could we reasonably assume that he has lost his strength to carry the pack, that it has suddenly become too heavy for him? A better guess says he does not have reason to carry it right now, but he can and will pick it up again when the time is right.

If God chooses to refrain from exercising a power that he showed he possesses in creating the space and time dimensions, the matter and energy, and the physical laws of the universe, we have no basis for assuming he no longer possesses that immeasurable power or is no longer willing to exercise it. We can only infer that his exercise of that power is subject to his choice. He can and will use it however, wherever, and whenever his goodness and other character attributes direct.

The Benefit of Perspective

"Timing is everything" may exaggerate the case, but the point of this familiar expression merits attention. Who of us has not learned the hard way that right actions at the wrong time thwart our efforts and our purposes? If a man decides to help his wife by making dinner for her, he has done a good thing—assuming he knows how to cook and what she likes. But if he does this right and good thing on an evening when she has plans to eat out, his efforts will probably fail to accomplish the purpose for which they were intended. Perhaps he did not ask, or perhaps she did not tell him when he did ask, but in either case, he lacks the ability to read her mind. He needs tangible clues.

Because God provably possesses the equivalent of at least one more time dimension than we human beings do, and because his space or other dimensions give him a complete view of us, inside and out, we can be confident of his timing in exercising his powers and capacities. He has not only the goodness and the power but also the knowledge and perspective to time his actions perfectly. As the apostle Peter wrote, "The Lord is not slow in keeping his promise, as some understand slowness."[9] His timing will be based not only on what he knows about us individually in any given moment but also on what he knows about the entire human race and all the angelic hosts for all time(s) in our current dimensions and beyond.

A swift and loving resolution to the problem of evil and suffering, thus, must certainly be within God's grasp and must be part of his plan. So far, however, we have said nothing about God's specific strategies and means for eradicating evil and suffering. That topic is addressed in chapter 15.

The Ultimate Goal

Scripture tells us that "God is love,"[10] and the creation testifies to that truth. As with *goodness*, God himself gives meaning to the word. He is love's source and essence. Humanity's hunger for a higher love than we can know in any human relationship—as wonderful as human love can be—reflects a universal hunger for God. The more love we experience in this life, the keener our anticipation for the love that awaits us in his domain, in his tangible presence.

Whatever love is, we know we want more of it to give and to receive. But our dimensional boundaries hem us in. Loving takes time, because loving takes knowing; and knowing, for us, takes time. Our three-dimensional bodies for now contain, and in some ways conceal, a more-dimensional or extradimensional being, a spiritual being. When we transition to the more-dimensional or extradimensional realm, we will gain new capacities for knowing and thus new capacities for loving.

Whatever love is, both here in these dimensions and there in our future home with God, we know it involves choice. Love cannot be coerced and still be love. It cannot be programmed and still be love. If it is not given freely by choice, it is something else, such as duty, and we yearn to give and receive so much more than obligatory care.

Since love involves choice, it also involves risks. In the chapter ahead, we will consider the paradox of an omniscient, omnipotent God who risks giving humanity, and the angels too, real freedom of choice so that real love is possible. And yet he never relinquishes or compromises his sovereign control. This statement of the two truths side by side strikes our minds as a contradiction, or perhaps as an inscrutable mystery, because it is a mysterious contradiction—in four space-time dimensions. But remember, we have discovered that there are more than just those four and more to reality than just the 10 space-time dimensions that physics reveals.

Because we know that God's reality encompasses more than 10 space-time dimensions, we can rejoice that God has something better than Eden in store for us. As beautiful and pleasant as Eden must have been for Adam and Eve before they turned from God's way to their own, God's goal for humanity far surpasses an earthly paradise. He anticipates the moment when he will escort us, all who choose to be his, into the new creation. Building and maintaining the new creation involves more of God's extradimensional capacities than did Eden. It involves much more than just our dimensions, too. The new creation is majestic, rewarding, and enduring beyond anything we can think or imagine. When we read the Bible writers' attempts to describe it, we know that the wonders of the place can never be exaggerated.

We will consider some of the specifics of the new creation in chapter 17. However, an appropriate appreciation of those specifics is only possible given a satisfactory (though not complete) resolution of such paradoxes as these: our free-will choices versus God's plans and control; the security or insecurity of our commitment to God; evil and suffering in light of God's love and power; and how God's love can allow eternal torment in hell. Before considering the glory, majesty, and rewards of the new creation, we must give attention to each of these perplexing issues.

Chapter 13

Extradimensionality and the Battle of Wills

Christians would be hard pressed to identify a doctrine that has caused more difficulty and division in the church through the centuries than the one declaring whose will—human beings' or God's—holds sway in our lives. Many Scripture verses either imply or declare that we humans have the freedom to make choices for our lives, including the choice of whether to worship and serve God, and that we bear responsibility for our choices. Many other verses imply or declare God has control over all things that occur in this dimensional realm and beyond, and that he has predetermined from before the universe was created every aspect of human existence (all of our actions, words, and thoughts) to fit his overarching plan for eternity. In some cases, both sides of this seemingly contradictory message appear together in a single passage. A list of these verses appears in table 13.1.

One of the most widely quoted passages emphasizing the power of human choice occurs in Joshua's final and memorable speech. After entering and occupying the Promised Land, Joshua exhorts his people to make the most important of all choices:

> Now fear the Lord and serve him with all faithfulness. Throw away the gods your ancestors worshiped beyond the Euphrates River and in Egypt, and serve the Lord. But if serving the Lord seems undesirable to you, then choose for yourselves this day whom you will serve, whether the gods your ancestors served beyond the Euphrates, or the gods of the Amorites, in whose land you are living. But as for me and my household, we will serve the Lord.[1]

When the people declare their choice to serve God, Joshua (strangely) warns them, "You are not able to serve the Lord."[2] Then a few moments later he tells them they will be held accountable for their choice to serve him.[3] How can this be?

Even before this moment, the mystery had been introduced. In a dialogue with Moses, God says that his presence will go with the Hebrews in their journey, as Moses requests. Why? Perhaps he has always planned to go, but the reason he gives centers on Moses. He is going in answer to Moses's request because he knows Moses and is pleased with him. Then the focus turns to the Lord's sovereign decision and plan. The Lord says, "I will have mercy on whom I will have mercy, and I will have compassion on whom I will have compassion."[4] Human decision and action seem irrelevant in this declaration. But how can they be if we humans bear accountability for our choices?

Other puzzling statements appear in the New Testament. One of the briefest comes from Luke in his account of the church's earliest days. When Gentiles respond to the message of salvation preached by Paul and Barnabas, he writes, "All who were appointed for eternal life believed."[5] Did these people believe because they were chosen to do so, or were they appointed to eternal life because God knew ahead of time that they would choose to believe?

Most believers and churches will answer that question with an emphasis on either the human decision-maker or the divine one. Acknowledging that actual contradictions cannot exist because God and his Word speak truth and only truth, we respond to these apparently incompatible statements by selecting to put on a pair of interpretive glasses that help us "adjust" the troubling texts one way or another as we encounter them.

Especially since the great debates between John Calvin's and Jacobus Arminius's disciples, these glasses have been available in two colors. One color highlights humanity's freedom of choice; the other, God's sovereign choice. And that is how Christians have typically dealt with the issue ever since. Arguments, even leading to bloodshed, ensued. In these slightly more civilized times, we simply agree to disagree and divide ourselves among the free-will congregations and the election, or pre-determinist, congregations. Rarely are the two willing to meet for dialogue or for worship side by side.

As the laws of nature and of the Spirit dictate, a distorted message will yield further distortion down the line. Any distortion of God's truth about personal choice and responsibility will influence a person's and a church's walk of faith, as well as their approach to spiritual growth and to making disciples in families, workplaces, neighborhoods, and the nations.

Individuals and churches highlighting the free-will side of the issue tend to emphasize what they may refer to as "holy living," or "separation from evil." Those on the other side of the issue may term such a perspective "legalism," or

Table 13.1: Bible Verses Teaching Human Free Will (F) and God's Predestination (P)

Genesis 13:11 (F)	Isaiah 61:10–62:2 (P)	1 Corinthians 4:7 (P)
Exodus 9:16 (P)	Jeremiah 1:4–10 (P)	1 Corinthians 6:19–20 (P&F)
Exodus 33:19 (P)	Jeremiah 8:4–12 (F)	2 Corinthians 3:4–6 (P)
Exodus 34:24 (P)	Jeremiah 17:5–10 (P&F)	2 Corinthians 13:9 (P)
Deuteronomy 10:15 (P)	Ezekiel 18:1–32 (F)	Galatians 1:1 (P)
Deuteronomy 30:19 (F)	Daniel 4:4–37 (P)	Ephesians 1:4–5 (P)
Joshua 11:20 (P)	Hosea 4:4–9 (F)	Ephesians 1:11 (P)
Joshua 24:14–27 (F)	Hosea 5:3–7 (P&F)	Ephesians 2:10 (P)
Judges 5:8 (F)	Hosea 11:4 (P)	Philippians 2:12–13 (P&F)
Judges 21:25 (F)	Joel 2:32 (P&F)	2 Thessalonians 2:7–12 (P&F)
1 Kings 12:15 (P)	Matthew 10:22 (P&F)	2 Thessalonians 2:13–15 (P&F)
2 Chronicles 6:3–6 (P)	Matthew 10:28–30 (P)	2 Thessalonians 3:3 (P)
Job 1:21–22 (P&F)	Matthew 11:25 (P)	1 Timothy 6:19 (F)
Job 7:15 (F)	Matthew 21:21–22 (F)	2 Timothy 1:9 (P)
Job 9:1–35 (P&F)	Matthew 24:24–25 (P)	2 Timothy 1:12 (P&F)
Job 23:10–16 (P&F)	Matthew 24:36 (P)	2 Timothy 2:19–26 (P&F)
Job 36:21 (F)	Mark 13:20–22 (P)	Titus 1:1–3 (P)
Job 38:36 (P&F)	Luke 8:10 (P)	Titus 2:11–14 (P)
Psalms 14:1–3 (F)	Luke 10:42 (F)	Hebrews 3:4 (P)
Psalm 25:12 (P&F)	Luke 12:4–5 (P)	Hebrews 3:12–14 (F)
Psalm 31:15 (P)	Luke 18:27 (P)	Hebrews 4:11 (F)
Psalms 32:5–11 (P&F)	Luke 22:21–22 (P&F)	Hebrews 6:4–12 (F)
Psalms 33:8–22 (P&F)	Luke 22:31–34 (P)	Hebrews 6:17–19 (P&F)
Psalm 58:3 (P)	John 6:44–65 (P&F)	Hebrews 10:35 (P&F)
Psalm 119:30 (F)	John 7:17 (F)	Hebrews 11:25 (F)
Psalm 119:173 (F)	John 8:31–47 (P&F)	Hebrews 13:21 (P)
Proverbs 1:29–30 (F)	John 10:26–29 (P&F)	James 1:13–25 (P&F)
Proverbs 8:10–19 (F)	John 15:5 (P)	James 4:7 (F)
Proverbs 16:4 (P)	John 15:16 (P)	James 4:13–17 (P)
Proverbs 16:9 (P&F)	John 17:6 (P&F)	1 Peter 1:4–5 (P)
Proverbs 21:1 (P)	Acts 2:21 (F)	1 Peter 1:15–16 (P&F)
Ecclesiastes 3:10–17 (P&F)	Acts 4:28 (P)	1 Peter 2:21 (F)
Ecclesiastes 9:1 (P)	Acts 13:48 (P&F)	1 Peter 5:5–10 (P&F)
Isaiah 1:29 (F)	Acts 17:24–28 (P&F)	2 Peter 1:10 (P&F)
Isaiah 7:15–16 (F)	Romans 4:11 (P)	1 John 2:5–6 (F)
Isaiah 40:20 (F)	Romans 8:19–33 (P)	1 John 3:9 (P)
Isaiah 40:23 (P)	Romans 9:10–26 (P)	1 John 4:7–19 (P&F)
Isaiah 41:24 (P)	Romans 10:12–18 (P&F)	1 John 5:18–20 (P)
Isaiah 46:10 (P)	Romans 11:7–8 (P)	Jude 1–4 (P&F)
Isaiah 55:3 (F)	Romans 11:25–12:2 (P&F)	Revelation 13:8–10 (P)
Isaiah 55:6–11 (P&F)	1 Corinthians 1:2 (P)	Revelation 20:11–15 (F)
Isaiah 56:4 (F)	1 Corinthians 1:26–29 (P)	Revelation 22:11–17 (F)

"living by the rules." Individuals and churches highlighting God's sovereign choice tend to emphasize what they might call "freedom in Christ" or "grace living." Those on the other side of the issue might term this approach "license" or "loose living."

Table 13.2: Symptoms of Overemphasis on Free Will

Typically, when a person or fellowship emphasizes the role of human will more than God's will in the spiritual birth and growth processes, the results include (a) working to please God or justify ourselves before him by being good and doing good; and (b) viewing sin as so dangerously and powerfully enticing as to need policing by rigid, external, manmade restraints. Specific ways these distortions manifest themselves include the following, among others:

1. Life seems increasingly exhausting and draining rather than joyous and fulfilling.
2. Fear nags—fear that one has not done enough good things or fear that one has done too many bad things, or both.
3. Doubt nags—especially doubt about whether one is truly saved, or will stay saved.
4. Supernatural gifts of the Spirit seem more important than the fruit of the Spirit because they appear to attest more dramatically to the Spirit's indwelling presence and to God's approval.
5. Conformity to certain behavior patterns, nonessential scriptural interpretations, or rules of conduct and spiritual expression become important validations of salvation.
6. Teaching focuses more on God's standards and justice than on his mercy. Assurance of salvation seems a dangerous door to temptation.
7. The distinction between justification and sanctification appears blurred.
8. Emotional expression, whether the glum extreme or the happy extreme, is taken as a sign of spirituality.
9. Prayers implore instant deliverance from immorality, addictions, and other long-term problems and ailments.
10. Shame lingers and seeks some form of anesthetic.
11. Weaknesses and struggles must be hidden from self and others or attributed to Satan's attacks.
12. The letter of the law receives more attention than the spirit of the law.
13. "Perfect" obedience rather than daily spiritual growth becomes life's goal.
14. Parents, teachers, and church leaders often seek control and justify it.
15. Fear of wrong choices leads to preference for "signs," strongly enforced prohibitions, and relinquishing choice to others, especially to authority figures.

Over the years, a group of believers from widely diverse church backgrounds has assisted me in compiling two lists. These lists recount some attitudes and perspectives typifying one emphasis or the other. One opinion all these people shared: They have been hampered in their spiritual growth by a subtle one-sidedness. (See tables 13.2 and 13.3. Add to them as you see fit, given that they are personal perspectives.)

Table 13.3: Symptoms of Overemphasis on Predestination

Typically, when a person or fellowship overemphasizes God's will and under-emphasizes humans' will in the spiritual birth and growth processes, the results include (a) mistaking God's "grace" for freedom to do as one pleases; and (b) minimizing temptation's power and sin's consequences.

1. Life in Christ seems much the same as any "good" person's life, but with the benefit of an eternal life insurance policy.
2. The initial step or indication of salvation, such as water baptism, confirmation, or applying for church membership, receives more attention than the ongoing process of growth.
3. Teaching emphasizes the mercy and forgiveness of God over the justice of God and the losses resulting from sin.
4. Sermons focus more on comfort and assurance than on conviction, confession, and change. Hell, or God's justice, is rarely if ever mentioned.
5. The role of the Holy Spirit in empowering and disciplining believers for godly living receives little attention.
6. Distinctions between sanctification and glorification seem blurred.
7. God's plans become more his than ours to fulfill. The need for evangelists, missionaries, and counselors and for good teaching in apologetics and theology is downplayed.
8. Parents and church leaders take a somewhat fatalistic approach toward the spiritual life of family and church members and outsiders.
9. Immorality, addictions, and long-term sin are treated as reminders that we are "just human."
10. Remorse seems a sufficient step of repentance.
11. God's promises and reassurances are applied unconditionally.
12. The fight against evil becomes more a societal than a personal battle, especially in view of God's ultimate victory.
13. Self-examination seems a needless flirtation with guilt.
14. The "judgmental" label thwarts attempts to reprove and correct flagrant sin.
15. The Christian label may be broadly applied to those who serve the community or the church, or who express kindness, generosity, and pleasantness.

During Jesus's final evening with his disciples prior to his arrest and crucifixion, he spoke to them at length about the promise (covenant) that would soon take effect: the coming of the Counselor, the Spirit of truth. The Holy Spirit had been present in the world since its beginning, of course. We read of his "hovering" over the surface of the waters as God prepared the earth to receive and support living beings.[6] God's Spirit had for centuries empowered men and women to believe God's promises, to worship God, to discern truth from error, to accomplish feats of valor—supernatural works at times—and to inspire God's servants and prophets to write down God's words for their own and future generations. However, his role was about to include something new, something better than before. Christ's atonement paved the way for a new era in God's relationship with humanity, a new stage in his unfolding plans, and the Holy Spirit was to play a central role in this new interaction.

One aspect of the Spirit's multifaceted role in this new covenant was to remind the disciples of all Jesus's words and to lead and guide them (as well as all disciples to come after them) into greater understanding of truth, "all" truth. Jesus must have anticipated our difficulty in accepting some truth, truth that bothers us because we cannot see how it fits together in our familiar patterns of reasoning and problem solving. He anticipated our temptation to pick and choose pieces of truth to overlap other pieces when the puzzle's picture makes no sense to us. At such times, the Spirit can and will give us courage to face the whole truth squarely and to ask, as James says, for wisdom.

To understand and accept any key doctrine of the Christian faith requires an appeal to God's higher ways and higher thoughts. Through the centuries Christians have struggled to force-fit the truth into a four-dimensional frame. Only by God's Spirit can we resist this compulsion that, as history and our own experience reveal, leads to strife, distortion, and division. Having seen the results of treating the dilemma of "Whose will holds sway?" as a contradiction, or as an antinomy, perhaps we are ready to discover what can be accomplished by approaching it as a paradox, or at least by putting it to the paradox test. We may still end up with truth we cannot picture in our mind's eye. And yet if we end up with a picture that makes sense, we will receive the benefits of embracing the whole truth rather than a lopsided portion of it.

Differing Frames of Reference

Chapter 6 lists steps that can be applied, singly or in combination, to identify and resolve paradoxes. If the approach works, we know we are dealing with a paradox rather than a contradiction. We have nothing to lose in applying these steps to the battle over wills.

The first step is to identify the frame of reference for each of the truths under investigation. Differences here may cause or contribute to the clash. In the case of free will versus predetermination, this step proves productive.

A review of the many Bible passages (see table 13.1) stating the truth of human free choice and the truth of divine predestination reveals a crucial distinction. Human (four-dimensional) perspective frames the statements affirming our freedom of choice and responsibility for our choices. Portions affirming God's sovereign control over all things, including human choice, are framed in the divine perspective that supersedes our natural realm, that is, that goes beyond the four space-time dimensions we humans experience.

In some passages, such as Joel 2:32 and 2 Corinthians 8:16–17, the two different perspectives appear together:

> And everyone who calls on the name of the Lord will be saved; for on Mount Zion and in Jerusalem there will be deliverance, as the Lord has said, even among the survivors whom the Lord calls.

> Thanks be to God, who put into the heart of Titus the same concern I have for you. For Titus not only welcomed our appeal, but he is coming to you with much enthusiasm and on his own initiative.

From the divine perspective, God calls or chooses those who will be saved, while from our human perspective we do the calling or choosing. Other verses declare just as clearly that no one receives salvation without choosing to receive it, and that no one receives salvation unless God chooses him or her to receive it. To state the case another way, all humans who choose salvation will receive it, and all humans whom God chooses to receive salvation will receive it. In four-dimensional thinking, God's choosing makes us puppets having no real freedom. Free choice for humans would be illusory in light of this truth. But Scripture says otherwise. Somehow, transferring from one frame of reference to the other must help make everything compatible. One does not cancel out the other.

Some churches tend to emphasize that predestination pertains only to salvation, specifically to that moment when an individual becomes "born again." Thus, the tension of the paradox of human free will and divine predestination is minimized, even marginalized, by insisting on applying it only to a one-time experience that is humanly intangible and abstract. However, the Scripture list in table 13.1 reveals that predestination extends beyond the justification component of salvation to include sanctification, glorification, and even our experiences before justification.

Predestination subsumes everything in our lives, including the circumstances of our birth, our education, our careers, the growth and development of our families, the people we meet, all the thoughts, words, and events that take place in our life, and the timing, location, and circumstances of our death. As Psalm 139 declares, God determines the day of our birth, the day of our death, and all the situations that take place in between. He is in total control of our lives.

The next step in paradox resolution calls for defining the system(s) operating on each side of the question. The frame of reference suggests that on the human choice side, the system is defined partly by humanity's space and time dimensions, but most importantly by the unidirectional, single time dimension in which cause and effect always proceed in that order. Further, it is defined by limited freedom. Human life begins and unfolds with a number of "givens" over which individuals have no choice. We cannot choose to whom we are born, or when, or where, or how we will be treated at different times by others. We cannot choose the characteristics of body, mind, and personality

Table 13.4: Varying Constraints on Human Choices

No Control (Inheritance Issues)
birthplace
relatives
genetics
aptitudes

Some Control (Circumstantial Issues)
workplace
associates
physique
skills

Considerable Control (Moral Issues)
dwelling
friends
diet and exercise
responsibility, integrity, diligence, and other character qualities and values

that are genetically determined. Absolute freedom of choice does not exist for human beings. For other factors in our lives, we face varying constraints on our capacities to choose and control (see some examples in table 13.4). God's freedom of choice has limits, too, though his limits are self-imposed, as described in chapter 12.

On the divine choice side, the system is defined by God's dimensions, or their equivalent, which we know add up to at least 11 of the space-time type, including more than one time dimension or its functional equivalent. Considering what this extradimensionality makes possible, we begin to see several ways the problem may be resolved. It does fit the definition of a paradox. The system these verses reveal apparently allows human will and God's will to operate independently in some contexts and interdependently in other contexts.

Schematic illustrations, as limited and oversimplified as they may be, help us grasp how such a system *could* operate. The system must include, of course, the influence of our fallen human nature. As God draws us toward himself, toward accepting his truth, life, and love, our rebellious, autonomous impulse, the rebellion instigated by Satan, draws us away from God, tempting us to reject God's truth, life, and love. In such a system, every step we take toward God or away from him has at least these three components: human choice, God's will, and the adversary's will. How God blends all three factors to carry out his plan we cannot definitively say, but a few of the options are presented at the end of this chapter.

Two of these components are predictable, at least in direction and in opposition to one another: God draws us to himself, and our sin nature draws us away from him. One component remains unpredictable from a human perspective: our choices to move toward God or away from him. From our perspective, at least initially, our life is our own to do with as we choose, but somewhere along the way we become aware that to go our own way is tantamount to going Satan's way of self-exaltation. Relinquishing ourselves to that destiny amounts to refusing God's offer of everlasting life with him. According to the Bible, by the time our earthly life is over every one of us will either become an adopted child of God[7] or a committed follower of a false god,[8] possibly our self.

Each choice we make to believe and trust God, to bend our will to his, strengthens the influence of his will in our decision-making process.

In fact, we can observe these three effects, among others:

1. Each decision to move toward God (see figure 13.1) strengthens his influence on our next decision.

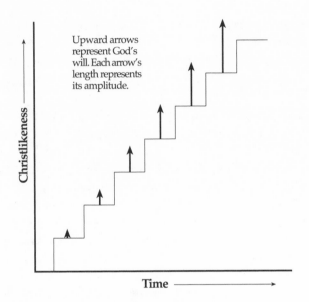

Figure 13.1: Increasing Influence of God's Will in Our Lives
Each step we take toward God, each decision to accept and act upon his light (that is, his love, life, and truth[9]) strengthens God's influence in our lives.

2. Each decision to move toward God weakens the temptation to move away from him (see figure 13.2).
3. With each decision to move toward God, our character becomes more like Christ's[10] (see figures 13.1 and 13.2).

Conversely, as we go against God's will and reject his light, we experience the opposite results:

1. Each decision to reject God's light (see figure 13.3) weakens the tug in God's direction for our next decision.
2. Each decision to reject God's light increases the pull toward darkness (see figure 13.4).
3. With each decision to reject God's light, our character becomes less like Christ's and more like Satan's[11] (see figures 13.3 and 13.4).

The changing amplitude (expressed strength) of God's will, or influence, and of opposition to it by his adversary's will, or influence, seems generally

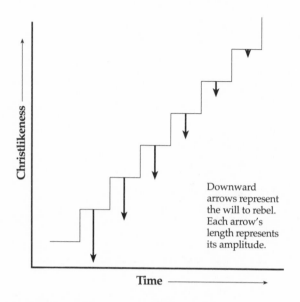

Downward arrows represent the will to rebel. Each arrow's length represents its amplitude.

Figure 13.2: Decreasing Influence of the Will to Rebel
Each step we take toward God, each decision to accept God's light, weakens the influence of God's adversary in our lives.

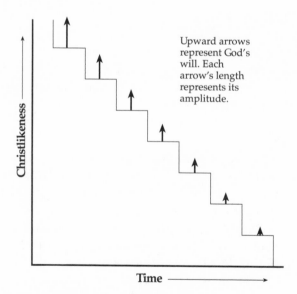

Upward arrows represent God's will. Each arrow's length represents its amplitude.

Figure 13.3: Decreasing Influence of God's Will in Our Lives
Each move we make away from God, each rejection of his light, results in a weakening of the tug in God's direction.

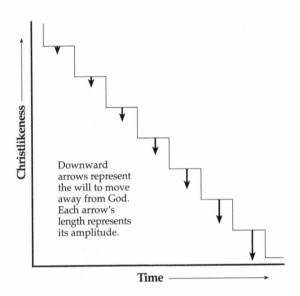

Figure 13.4: Increasing Influence of the Will to Reject God's Truth and Authority
Each move we make in opposition to God's will, each rejection of God's light, strengthens the pull in that direction for our next decision.

predictable, at least in a relative sense, and is consistent. The same cannot be said about the operation of our own will. The strength (or weakness) with which we express our will in either direction is up to us. For as long as we live and for as many decisions as we make to move in God's direction or away, the strength with which we express our will remains variable. We can exercise it strongly or weakly at virtually any point along the way.

As figure 13.5 suggests, a pattern of movement toward God, of accepting his truth and authority, brings a bonus benefit. People whose lives manifest such a pattern can testify that at moments when they faltered in their decision to obey God and even expressed mild resistance, they ended up obeying in spite of themselves. Figure 13.6 suggests that the reverse may also occur. People with a long record of movement away from God can testify that in moments when they are weakly inclined to choose in his direction, they end up rejecting his truth and authority in spite of themselves. Repeated acceptance strengthens God's influence; repeated rejection strengthens the influence of his adversary.

No human being always obeys and accepts God's way or always opposes his way. Each person does some accepting and some rejecting, some trusting

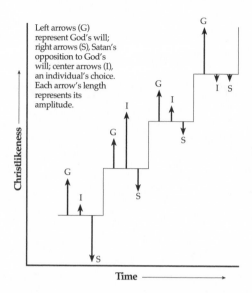

Figure 13.5: Increasing Strength of God's Will Resulting from Choices to Obey
As choices to obey God strengthen the influence of God's will (**G**) in our lives, his will becomes strong enough to overpower ambivalence or a weak expression of rebellion (**I**).

and some distrusting, some obeying and some disobeying. Figure 13.7 depicts the typical choice pattern a person might manifest during and after a period of movement toward Christ. Figures could also be designed to depict a choice pattern after a net movement away from Christ, or a period of wavering back and forth in the middle. In the next chapter we will take a look at where this decision-making process leads: to the unavoidable crossing of the line in God's direction or in the opposite direction during our lifetime—long or short— here on Earth.

What we have done here is expose the dynamics of the seeming clash of truths about our will and God's will. And while an understanding of these dynamics is critical for comprehending the resolution of the paradox, it is not sufficient to complete the resolution. But we already know we need to apply step eight from the list in chapter 6 (see page XX)—namely to calculate or discern the effects of dimensions or realms in which human measurements cannot be made.

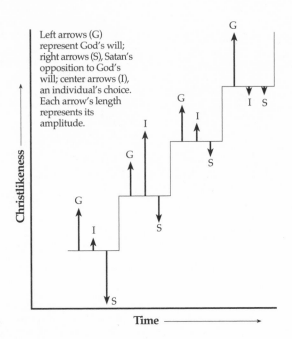

Figure 13.6: Increasing Strength of the Will to Rebel Resulting from Choices to Disobey
As choices to reject God's truth and authority weaken the influence of God's will (**G**) in our lives and strengthen the tug of rebellion, the will to rebel (**I**) becomes strong enough to overpower ambivalence or a weak choice to obey.

God's Cause-and-Effect Capacities

We have looked in previous chapters at God's amazing capacities within two time dimensions or their equivalent. We saw how God's operation in the equivalent of an extra time dimension or two can help make sense of his capacities to hear everyone's prayers simultaneously and to atone for humanity's sin in one sacrificial act. We can also discern that a three-dimensional time domain or its equivalent would enable God to predetermine every action of every human being while sustaining the operation of human choice.

Three-dimensional time could be depicted, for example, as a sphere with lines of time running parallel to the equator (latitudes), perpendicular to the equator (longitudes), and from the center, or other interior points, out to the surface and beyond (radials). The timeline of the universe, with us on it, could be placed along a particular latitude of this time sphere.

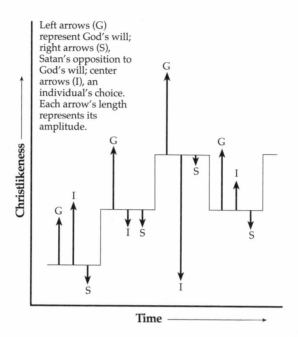

Figure 13.7: Typical Decision-Making Pattern for a Person Who Has Moved Gradually toward God
Strong expression of disobedience or rejection can still move this person away from God. But, because God's influence (**G**) has become so much stronger than what it was and Satan's (**S**) so much weaker, if the person merely expresses his or her individual will (**I**) as before, he or she will be drawn to God much more powerfully than before.

For purposes of demonstration, let's return to the figure of a three-dimensional time sphere introduced in chapter 6. Let's put the universe's timeline along the 30-degree latitude north. While our experience of time would be limited to advancing forward along that latitude, God could operate from anywhere along, within, or exterior to the surface of the time sphere. He can operate along *any* space-time continuum he pleases. He can operate independent of *any and all* space-time continua. He could, for example, position himself at the north pole of this particular time sphere. From that single time point, he could drop a timeline perpendicular to our date of birth, to the moment of our present existence, to the instant of our physical death, to the beginning of the physical universe or before, and to the moment when he replaces this universe with a new one (see figure 13.8). Any and all of these perpendicular timelines meet together at a single point. This convergence implies that God can impact

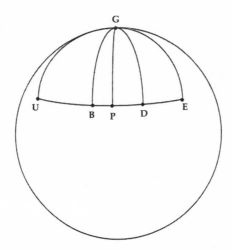

Figure 13.8: God's Operations in a Sphere of Time
In three dimensions of time or the equivalent, God could generate causes anywhere within, on, or outside the sphere. The line segment **UE** represents the time dimension of the universe. At point **U** the universe comes into existence. At point **E** its existence ends. **B** is the birth date for an individual human. **D** is his or her time of death, and **P** the present moment. God, from a single point or instant of time, say **G**, could simultaneously influence points **U**, **B**, **P**, **D**, and **E** along our timeline.

events throughout the history of the universe and the course of our lives (and more) in a single instant of his time.

In two time dimensions, infinite time on our timeline can be shrunk down to less than a trillionth of a second for God (see chapter 7). Adding a third time dimension allows for infinite time to the third power (that is, ∞^3) to be compressed into less than a trillionth of a second. Billions of years in our time dimension and much, much more can be just a single instant for God.

In that single instant, God could see every event in all time, including every event in the lives of every human being who has ever lived, is living, or ever will live. He would see in exquisite detail everything that belongs to our future. The past and future are the present for him. As Jesus said,

> "I am the Alpha and Omega, the First and the Last, the Beginning and the End."[12]

Scripture affirms that he does indeed possess these unique attributes and capacities. His foreknowledge[13] and his identity as "I AM"[14] receive no debate from either Arminians or Calvinists.

Because of God's power and love, his foreknowledge implies much more than mere possession of information. He has the capacity to use that information to influence future events. In his letter to the Romans, Paul says, "For those God foreknew he also predestined to be conformed to the image of his Son."[15] In Romans 9 he adds,

> Yet, before the twins [Jacob and Esau] were born or had done anything good or bad—in order that God's purpose in election might stand: not by works but by him who calls—she [Rebekah, their mother] was told, "The older will serve the younger." Just as it is written: "Jacob I loved, but Esau I hated."[16]

And in Romans 11 we read,

> God did not reject his people, whom he foreknew. . . . At the present time there is a remnant chosen by grace.[17]

Peter begins a letter to fellow believers with these words:

> To God's elect . . . who have been chosen according to the foreknowledge of God the Father, through the sanctifying work of the Spirit, to be obedient to Jesus Christ and sprinkled with his blood.[18]

In three or more dimensions of time or the equivalent, God's foreknowing and predestining can be one and the same. As figure 13.8 illustrates, God has the capacity to view every event along our timeline from a single instant and, from that same instant, to generate cause-and-effect phenomena anywhere along that timeline. God can in a moment of his time cause events to happen before, during, and after the 14-billion-year history of the universe.[19] Literally, before the universe even existed, before our dimension of time even existed, God had access to every event in the history of the cosmos and every action, word, and thought that every human being would ever experience throughout his or her life.

Predestined and Free

The crucial question remains: How does God do the predestining while guaranteeing us the freedom of our will, as the Scriptures and our understanding of love demand? How does God predetermine every choice without infringing on our control over the human choice vectors depicted in the previous figures?

Several workable ways are made possible by the existence of his extradimensional powers. Here are two:

Resolution one: God can see not only what occurs throughout a person's life but also the events and conditions (physically, mentally, emotionally, and spiritually) in which things occur. Each of us expresses our will in response to complex internal and external factors. Knowing all these factors, including the characteristics of our personality, the effects of our experiences and communications with people and even with angels and demons, God anticipates the direction of each choice and how strongly we will express our will in any instance. Thus, God could prescribe the exact conditions to generate the response of our will at any given moment that fits into his total plan. We would remain continuously in control of our will, while God would continuously control the circumstances and conditions in and around us that impact our will.

Resolution two: Let's recall two precepts: (1) Every step we make toward God, every acceptance and trust of his truth, strengthens his influence in our lives and weakens the influence of our innate tendency to reject him; and (2) every step of rejection weakens the influence of God's will while strengthening his adversary's influence on us to rebel against his authority. Then God can determine at each point of decision what amplitude of his will and our rebellious nature brings about the net response that fits into his total plan. In this scenario, we would remain continuously in control of our will while God would remain continuously in control of all the increases and decreases of the effects of his will, as well as of Satan-instigated rebellion, on each one of us.

A slight revision of this resolution scenario would call for God to increase or decrease to whatever degree at whatever time the amplitude of any or all of the three choice vectors. The individual would still be free to exercise his or her will, but whatever influence the individual (or God or the sinful nature) exerts could be amplified or diminished by whatever amount God sees necessary to his total plan.

Given the many, perhaps infinitely, more dimensions or their equivalent available to God, many more resolutions, perhaps infinitely more and better ones, could be offered that preserve the freedom of human choice (control over the central vector in figures 13.5 to 13.7) while acknowledging God's sovereign control over all his creation and beyond.

One reason for proposing these two possible resolutions (plus a variation) centers on the importance of biblical revelation as a reality check. These two scenarios seem consistent, as far as we can tell, with the relevant Scripture passages citing one or both sides of the paradox. The Bible records God's use of natural elements to influence the affairs of humanity.[20] It also attests to God's use of supernatural elements to influence the affairs of humanity.[21] Isaiah, Daniel, and Jude personally experienced dramatic examples of such supernatural occurrences and wrote extensively about their influence in Scripture. The Bible also promises that we will be tempted, but that we will not be tempted above what we are able to bear.[22]

Both scenarios, as well as a combination of the two, seem biblically possible. As to which is more biblically favored, at this point much more theological, philosophical, and scientific research appears necessary to render anything more than an educated guess or preference.

The bottom line is that we cannot expect to be able to form an adequate picture in our minds of how human choice and divine choice can both be fully operational, but if we accept both truths because the Bible teaches them and because God's transdimensional/extradimensional powers demonstrate the possibility of making sense of them, we can experience both the challenge and comfort we need to live as God's children. We need the challenge of responsibility for our choices, and we also need the comfort of comprehending, even to a limited degree, how all things, including our unwise choices and others' choices that impact our lives, can work together for good, for the accomplishment of God's ultimate purpose and plan.[23]

So far, we have examined only the paradox of the freedom of human choice and the sovereignty of God's will from the standpoint of someone not yet fully committed to or against God's camp. Of greater concern to most people is an understanding of the impact of this paradox on the end of their lives here on Earth as compared to the beginning or the middle. Thus, no resolution of this paradox would be complete or humanly satisfying without also looking in to this important corollary.

Chapter 14

Extradimensionality and Salvation's Assurance

The schematic illustrations (presented in the preceding chapter) of the decision-making process leads to yet another challenging question: What basis do we find in Scripture for suggesting there's an ultimate "commitment line," a line of no return, either in God's direction or the opposite direction? The answer to that question is best understood if we first complete the paradox resolution steps as they relate to God's will and humanity's will.

What is the interplay between the two wills in deciding who does or does not become God's child? Because we traditionally have approached the question of wills as something other than a paradox, emphasizing either the prevalence of human choice or the prevalence of God's, further divisions have arisen among individuals and churches over this corollary question: Is our salvation a sure thing, a matter of "once saved, always saved," or can we lose it, either by lack of vigilance or by deliberate choice?

Intents of the Heart

Personal concerns and feelings about family members and friends tend to cloud the issue. Most Christians have known at least one person who professed faith in Jesus Christ, attended church, took communion, read the Bible, was baptized in water, served in the church, perhaps even attended Bible college or seminary and entered the pastorate—and yet who later turned away from Christ and lived as anything but a Christian. Is this individual guaranteed eternal life with God?

What about the millions of people in culturally Christian nations who live for their own pleasure, have no connection with any Christian fellowship, and yet claim they are born again and heaven bound?

We wonder about such things because we resemble, in one sense, the computer screen people. We see each other's outsides, and the outsides do give us some important clues to what goes on inside. But we lack God's extradimensional perspective to look directly upon the "thoughts and intents of the heart." We are fundamentally ignorant. While God can handle such intimate knowledge, evidently we in our present state cannot.

The underlying question we need to consider is this: How is anyone "saved"? According to Scripture, salvation comes by choice—both ours *and* God's, not by one *or* the other. If we emphasize our choice over God's, we may take too much responsibility for our salvation and worry about keeping or losing it. While we do not know our future circumstances, we do know our will is sometimes weak and often changeable. If we emphasize God's choice over ours, we may lean so heavily on his will that we take too little responsibility for our spiritual life, never even bothering to check our hearts to see if we are walking in faith or in presumption.[1]

Initial and Final Conditions

To find and maintain a better balance on this important issue, we can apply step three from the list in chapter 6 to the paradox of the wills: Identify correctly and completely the initial and final conditions of the phenomenon (or set of phenomena) under investigation. Initial and final conditions must be connected to a timeline, in this case the universe's timeline. God, as the Bible explains, is immutable,[2] and thus is unconfined to a single timeline. So his "conditions" remain unchanged.

Initial conditions for humanity, with respect to free choice and salvation, include the following:

1. God placed immortal spirit in an earthly body, male and female, endowed with the freedom to enjoy a relationship of honor and worship toward him. As long as these first humans remained untested, they remained in that wondrous state of innocence; yet not as puppets, but with the real potential to shatter both their innocence and their relationship with God.

2. Satan—once the highest of God's angelic creation, and now the proud adversary—provided the ultimate test of these humans' will. If they had chosen to resist whatever temptation(s) he presented, they would have proven their capacity to withstand any test of their reverence for God and submission to his authority. They would have retained their innocence. However, each of their offspring would face the same test (whether to serve God) by his or her own free choice.

Scripture records how well Adam and Eve did. They eliminated all suspense by falling into the very first (recorded) temptation Satan offered. But their fall is just the beginning of the story. In fact, it is a step in the direction of the final conditions described for us in the book of Revelation, as well as in other parts of Scripture:

1. God will place our spirits in indestructible bodies that can exist in dimensions beyond Earth's four, no longer bound by the laws and limits of cosmic existence.
2. We humans will enjoy a relationship—side by side with the angelic hosts—of honor and worship toward God, freely chosen and tested under the toughest possible conditions and, therefore, no longer subject to shattering. Or, we will receive the outcome of our choice to reject that relationship, despite ample opportunities to accept it, and will share eternity with all those who also have refused it, including Satan and his cohorts, the demons (or fallen angels).

When the universe's timeline ends, we come to a great divide. No longer will believers and nonbelievers, angels and demons, the Prince of Peace and the prince of darkness, interact with one another. Though our will can still be expressed (the angels' too), its direction is fixed like the arrow of a compass, and nothing in us or around us can sway us from our course.

But these final conditions, which we will explore in the context of human beings in chapters 16 and 17, remain for the future. The course of events by which they are attained is still unfolding, as it has been since before the beginning of the world. We read a history of the highlights in the pages of the Bible:

1. God was prepared for the fall in the Garden of Eden. He planned that through the physical death of humans, the extent of their sin could be held in check.
2. He promised to deliver from all sin those who chose to be delivered.
3. He prompted both desperation for and faith in his promised deliverance through the giving of the Law.
4. Through Christ, the sinless "Adam," God paid the death penalty for humanity's sin and graciously provided an inheritance of eternal life in communion with him.
5. Christ sent the Holy Spirit to "seal" the promise, securely grafting all who choose eternal life with God into the vine (see John 15:1–17),

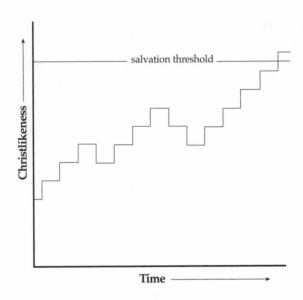

Figure 14.1: Journey toward Salvation
The steps up depict choices to accept God's love, life, and truth, while the steps down depict choices to reject God's love, life, and truth. The process of becoming Christlike is not to be interpreted as the accumulation of good works, but rather the development of humility, submission, and godly character.

giving them both the desire and the power to do his will.

6. The Holy Spirit empowers those in whom he lives to participate in preparing for the new creation, especially by becoming living invitations for other people to join in this new and everlasting life.

We read about the movement from initial conditions to final conditions (on the universe's timeline) in God's Word and in history's annals. The one part of that process we directly observe transpires in our own life spans. For each of us, earthly life begins with sin's penalty over our heads, as well as God's pardon extended to us. No one but God knows what we, or others around us, will do with that pardon—seize it or toss it aside. By life's end, even if no one else knows, God sees what we have done with it.

No one leaves this life in the middle ground between eternal connection with God and eternal separation from him. And no one stumbles into that connection or separation without knowing what he or she is choosing. As Paul declares in Romans 1:20–21, no one has an excuse for worshiping anyone or anything but the Creator of heaven and Earth. Knowledge of his existence, identity, qualities, justice, mercy, and power has been made understandable to all.[3]

Approaching the Salvation Threshold

We humans tend to hear a lot of excuses and see many people whose choices never become clear to us before their deaths. The problem, once again, is that we lack God's extradimensional vision. To find further answers to our questions, we can apply step four from the paradox resolution list: Gather more information on the circumstances surrounding the phenomenon in question.

Figure 14.1 offers another schematic illustration of the decision-making process in the life of a person proceeding toward salvation. As the figure reminds us, the journey toward salvation usually proceeds along a bumpy, up-and-down path. At times we accept and follow God's way, and at times we resist and rebel against it. But the closer we draw to the salvation threshold, the greater the probability that downward dips will decrease in number and magnitude. As figures 13.1 to 13.7 indicate, the more we say yes to God's truth, the more like Christ we become and the stronger the influence of God's will in our lives. At the same time, the propensity for rebellion against God grows weaker.

Changes at the Crossing Point

When we cross over the line by surrendering ourselves—our past, present, and future—to God, exchanging our best and worst efforts for his gracious gift, his Holy Spirit enters our being (see figure 14.2). We gain access to his strength for living in the light, and his "fruit" begins to grow in us.[4]

We do not suddenly begin a life of perfect obedience. We still wrestle with doubt, cowardice, selfishness, and other wrong actions, attitudes, and choices. We still sometimes take detours around God's ways in seeking to meet our needs and wants. When we move in the wrong direction, though, he allows us to experience sometimes painful consequences to guide us back in the right direction. And when we move in his direction, even when doing so proves terribly painful to our body and soul, he rewards us with peace, joy, and affirmation. When trials and tragedies strike, we may be staggered for a while, lost in our hurt, anger, and confusion. When success strikes, we may be staggered for a while, lost in our self-satisfaction and pride. But his influence remains. His faith holds us. We can count on his capacity, not on our own, to keep us from falling below that crucial line.[5]

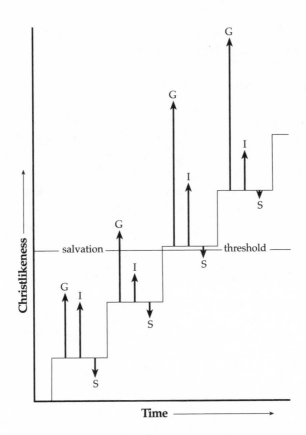

Figure 14.2: God's Will for a Person Gaining Salvation
As one approaches or advances beyond the salvation threshold, God's will (**G**) in one's life gets stronger in small increments. Crossing the threshold, however, results in a substantial increase in God's will in one's life. Meanwhile, Satan's will (**S**) continues to gradually decrease, but the individual retains the freedom to express his or her own will (**I**).

The One-Way Crossing

Or can we? As mentioned previously, Christians hold differing views on whether the salvation line can be crossed *two* ways, both *into* salvation's territory and out again. The confusion arises not only from experience with people, but also from certain portions of Scripture. Table 14.1 provides a fairly comprehensive list of the Bible verses addressing salvation's assurance.

The verses most often cited as proof that salvation can be found and then lost include Hebrews 6:4–6, 10:26–31, and 2 Peter 2:20–22. These three passages may seem to suggest that we human beings have the capacity to cross

Table 14.1: Bible Verses Concerning Whether or Not Believers Can Lose Their Salvation

1 Samuel 2:8–9	John 11:25–26	1 Timothy 1:19
Job 1:8–11	John 14:16	2 Timothy 1:9
Job 17:9	John 15:6	2 Timothy 1:12
Job 23:10	John 17:12	2 Timothy 2:17–19
Psalm 34:19	John 18:9	2 Timothy 4:18
Psalm 37:28	Acts 27:21–44	Hebrews 2:14–15
Psalm 66:9	Romans 5:10	Hebrews 3:6
Psalm 68:18	Romans 6:2–11	Hebrews 3:14–19
Psalms 73:23–28	Romans 6:14	Hebrews 4:11
Psalms 87:5–6	Romans 6:23	Hebrews 6:4–9
Psalms 89:32–33	Romans 7:14–8:17	Hebrews 6:17–19
Psalm 138:8	Romans 8:27–29	Hebrews 7:25
Proverbs 12:3	Romans 8:35–39	Hebrews 8:12
Proverbs 18:10	Romans 11:1–33	Hebrews 9:12
Proverbs 29:1	Romans 13:11	Hebrews 10:14
Ecclesiastes 3:14	1 Corinthians 6:19	Hebrews 10:17
Song of Songs 8:7	1 Corinthians 8:11	Hebrews 10:26–39
Isaiah 14:27	1 Corinthians 9:27	Hebrews 13:5–6
Jeremiah 31:3	1 Corinthians 10:12–14	Hebrews 13:21
Jeremiah 32:40	1 Corinthians 12:13	James 1:22–25
Ezekiel 18:20–32	1 Corinthians 15:2	1 Peter 1:3–9
Ezekiel 34:15–16	1 Corinthians 15:51	1 Peter 5:6–10
Daniel 9:24	2 Corinthians 1:21–22	2 Peter 1:10
Hosea 6:4	2 Corinthians 3:7–11	2 Peter 2:20–22
Hosea 14:1–5	2 Corinthians 5:5	2 Peter 3:17
Malachi 3:6	2 Corinthians 6:1	1 John 1:5–10
Matthew 7:21–23	2 Corinthians 7:1	1 John 2:19
Matthew 12:32–34	2 Corinthians 12:9	1 John 2:27–28
Matthew 13:1–23	Galatians 5:4–6	1 John 3:1–2
Matthew 16:18	Ephesians 1:5	1 John 4:18
Matthew 18:23–35	Ephesians 1:13–14	1 John 5:11–13
Matthew 25:1–13	Ephesians 2:10	1 John 5:18
Mark 13:22	Ephesians 4:30	2 John 8
Luke 8:13	Philippians 1:6	Jude 1
Luke 10:20	Philippians 2:12–13	Jude 12
John 6:39	Colossians 1:22–23	Jude 24
John 6:66	Colossians 2:12–15	Revelation 2:5
John 10:27–29		Revelation 3:11

the line back and forth, into and out of salvation. But a closer study of the text and context reveals a different view. Rather, these verses say that a person who understands what God is offering, including who is offering and what's being offered, and yet still chooses to "trample on" that offer, will never experience a change of heart. Salvation rejected by such an individual remains lost forever. The crucial question is whether this individual can rightly be considered a Christian in the first place. Some argue that the description can apply to a believer.

Here's where we can apply step five from the list of paradox resolution methods: Make more precise measurements. Though we cannot "measure" words as we would typically measure research data, this step toward more precise interpretation accomplishes a similar goal.

The Hebrews 6 passage describes those "who have tasted the heavenly gift, who have shared in the Holy Spirit, who have tasted the goodness of the word of God and the powers of the coming age." Hebrews 10:26 identifies these individuals as sharing in "knowledge of the truth." And 2 Peter 2:20–21 describes them as "knowing our Lord and Savior Jesus Christ" and knowing "the way of righteousness." Each of these descriptive phrases could apply to Christians, but must they, necessarily?

All the qualifying clauses and phrases in Hebrews and 2 Peter seem to constitute the necessary steps for coming to Christ, but they do not clearly imply that the all-important salvation transaction has been made. In other words, the individuals to whom these passages refer have come to understand and acknowledge everything they need to know to enter a relationship with God, but they have not necessarily stepped across salvation's threshold in repentance, acceptance of God's forgiveness, and surrender to God's authority.

The English phrase "have shared in the Holy Spirit" may seem the clearest reference to Christians. Yet theologians Kenneth S. Wuest and Arthur W. Pink, among other scholars, explain that the Greek word translated "shared in" (*metochos*) denotes something less than possession of (or by) the Holy Spirit. More accurately it suggests that these people have received certain benefits and blessings from the Holy Spirit, a *taste* or sampling of what he is like.[6]

The definitive statements identifying the subjects of the Hebrews and 2 Peter passages come after the cautionary words. Many interpreters stop reading before they come to them, but they belong to the context and cannot be overlooked. Hebrews 6:9 says, "Even though we speak like this, dear friends, we are convinced of better things in your case—the things that have to do with salvation." Hebrews 10:39 concludes with this assurance: "But we do not belong to those who shrink back and are destroyed, but to those who have faith and are saved."

Peter finishes with metaphors that no first-century reader would mistake for a reference to a child of God: "A dog returns to its vomit," and "A sow that is washed returns to her wallowing in the mud."[7] To first-century Jews, only God-rejecting nonbelievers could be referred to with such terms as "dogs" and "pigs."

These passages, then, must refer to people who, like the Pharisees, have known who Jesus is and what he offers and yet have decided in their hearts, "We don't want this man [Jesus] to be our king!" (Luke 19:14).

Additional evidence comes from the other side of the question, the side that says a person who is placed in Christ by the Spirit and in whom Christ places the Spirit can never be plucked out, not even by his own words and actions. As Paul declares in Romans:

> For I am convinced that neither death nor life, neither angels nor demons, neither the present nor the future, nor any powers, neither height nor depth, nor anything else in all creation, will be able to separate us from the love of God that is in Christ Jesus our Lord.[8]

This passage seems to leave no loopholes, no qualifying phrase, such as "except a person's decision to reject the love of God." Moreover, three other Bible passages state that when an individual truly makes a commitment of his or her life to Jesus Christ, from that moment onward, he or she receives a guarantee of entry into heaven and of eternal life with God.[9] As the apostle Paul explains, what sustains the believer's commitment to the Savior is not the force of the believer's will but rather Christ himself. Paul declares:

> I know whom I have believed, and am convinced that he is able to guard what I have entrusted to him until that day.[10]

Why Warnings about Loss?

The Hebrews and 2 Peter passages represent just a few of the many Bible verses warning nonbelievers against salvation's loss. Additional warnings, unquestionably aimed at believers, seem unsettling to the case for salvation's security, however strong its supporting Scriptures may appear. Believers are given these exhortations:

> Continue to work out your salvation with fear and trembling.[11]

Be on your guard so that you may not be carried away by the error of the lawless and fall from your secure position.[12]

Watch out that you do not lose what we have worked for, but that you may be rewarded fully.[13]

When we see the words "worked for," we discover an important clue that the passage refers to something other than salvation's free gift, which no "work" of ours can ever possibly merit.[14] The solution to this aspect of the paradox lies in the distinction of salvation's three meanings, or stages. Bible scholars have for centuries recognized that salvation's threshold is "justification"—complete deliverance from sin's penalty, received the moment a person becomes joined to God through Christ. Salvation's ongoing "work" is called "sanctification"— our walk in the light, through which we may discover and express greater and greater freedom from our ungodly ways of thinking and living. "Glorification" can be glimpsed in moments now, as God enables us to experience intense joy, but it remains as our promise of total and permanent freedom from sin as we are received into Christ's glorified presence, the place he is preparing for us.

The apostles' warnings aptly apply to believers who may be tempted to twist God's grace, confusing the freedom not to sin for the freedom to sin without penalty or loss. We can lose ground in our growth toward Christlikeness, and that loss can be painfully serious. According to 1 Corinthians 3, our Christian life can be built with gold, silver, and gems, or it can be built with wood, hay, and straw. Verses 13–15 present this picture:

The fire will test the quality of each person's work. If what has been built survives, the builder will receive a reward. If it is burned up, the builder will suffer loss but yet will be saved—even though only as one escaping through the flames.

The blessing to be gained by cooperating with God, exercising our will in the direction of the upward arrows in the schematic illustration, will be greater by far, both in this life and beyond, than any of us can possibly imagine.

Salvation's Counterpart

As I have mentioned, no one ends earthly life in the middle ground between life and death, connection and separation. We know from Jesus's words and from the Hebrews passages cited on page 159 that a sin can be committed for which no forgiveness remains. We have been instructed to offer no prayers for those

Table 14.2: Bible Verses Concerning Blasphemy against the Holy Spirit

Genesis 6:5	Isaiah 42:20	John 3:18–19
Exodus 7:14	Isaiah 48:6–8, 22	John 5:39–40, 44–47
Deuteronomy 28:20	Isaiah 56:10–12	John 6:36
1 Samuel 15:23	Isaiah 65:12	John 7:32
2 Chronicles 36:16	Jeremiah 6:10, 16–17	John 8:24–27, 33
Psalms 10:3–11	Jeremiah 7:13–28	John 8:37–38, 40, 43–49
Psalm 14:1	Jeremiah 9:5–6	John 9:16–34, 39–41
Psalms 36:1–4	Jeremiah 11:8	John 10:24–26
Psalm 53:1	Jeremiah 17:5, 23	John 11:47–48
Psalms 64:5–6	Jeremiah 18:12	John 12:9–10
Psalms 73:6–12	Jeremiah 44:16–18	John 18:4–9, 38
Psalms 81:11–12	Hosea 4:16–18	Acts 7:42
Psalm 106:24	Amos 5:10	Acts 17:21
Psalm 107:11	Zephaniah 3:5	Acts 24:22–27
Proverbs 1:7	Zechariah 7:11–12	Romans 1:18–32
Proverbs 1:24–31	Malachi 2:17	Romans 8:1
Proverbs 2:12–15	Matthew 2:16	1 Corinthians 1:18
Proverbs 5:12–13	Matthew 5:11	Galatians 1:7–9
Proverbs 9:7	Matthew 9:33–34	Ephesians 4:19
Proverbs 12:15–16	Matthew 10:25	2 Thessalonians 2:8–12
Proverbs 14:6, 9	Matthew 11:16–21	1 Timothy 1:3–7
Proverbs 15:5, 12	Matthew 12:7, 13–14	1 Timothy 4:1–3
Proverbs 17:15, 24	Matthew 12:22–35	2 Timothy 3:1–9
Proverbs 18:2	Matthew 13:14–15	2 Timothy 4:2–5
Proverbs 19:3	Matthew 21:14-16, 32–46	Titus 1:15–16
Proverbs 21:24	Matthew 22:1, 15–17	Titus 3:9–11
Proverbs 23:9	Matthew 23:13–15	Hebrews 6:4–9
Proverbs 26:4–12	Matthew 24:10, 38–39	Hebrews 10:26–31
Proverbs 27:22	Matthew 24:48–51	Hebrews 12:15–17
Proverbs 29:1	Matthew 26:63–68	2 Peter 2:1–22
Proverbs 30:12	Matthew 27:25	2 Peter 3:3–4
Ecclesiastes 10:12–15	Matthew 28:11–14	1 John 5:16–17
Isaiah 1:4	Mark 3:22–30	2 John 10
Isaiah 3:9	Mark 11:18	Jude 4, 8, 10
Isaiah 5:12, 18–24	Luke 6:22	Jude 12–13, 16, 18
Isaiah 6:9–10	Luke 7:30–35	Revelation 2:20
Isaiah 10:13	Luke 12:10	Revelation 3:3, 17
Isaiah 22:12–14	Luke 13:14–16	Revelation 9:20–21
Isaiah 29:13	Luke 16:27–31	Revelation 16:9, 21
Isaiah 30:9–11	Luke 22:67–71	Revelation 22:11

who have crossed that line,[15] a line that may be described as the counterpart to the salvation line. Scripture calls it "blasphemy against the Holy Spirit."

Misunderstanding of this condemnation threshold has caused anguish to many believers. Because it is often termed "the unpardonable sin," people imagine it is a one-time act of defiance for which they will be forever damned. Instead, blasphemy appears to be the result of many choices to reject God's light and rightful authority. The progression toward blasphemy can be seen in biblical narratives, such as the account of Egypt's pharaoh, who repeatedly and knowingly hardened his heart toward the Almighty until he passed a point of no return.[16]

The first use of the specific expression, "blasphemy against the Holy Spirit," appears in the New Testament. Mark quotes Jesus as saying:

> Truly I tell you, people can be forgiven all their sins and every slander they utter, but whoever blasphemes against the Holy Spirit will never be forgiven; they are guilty of an eternal sin.[17]

Table 14.2 gives a comprehensive list of relevant Scripture passages. A study and integration of those verses leads to a composite picture of the blasphemer. This individual knowingly and repeatedly defies God, rejecting his offer of forgiveness and eternal fellowship, rejecting all the Holy Spirit's promptings toward humility and submission to God's truth and grace.

A schematic illustration of an individual's descent toward blasphemy against the Holy Spirit appears in figure 14.3.

Though at times this individual does right and takes steps in the direction of God's will, the closer the rejecter gets to the blasphemy threshold, the greater the probability that rebellion against God's authority and rejection of God's light will become more frequent and more strongly expressed.

As the pattern of ongoing animosity toward God continues, eventually it will drive this person across the blasphemy threshold. There, the will of God in the person's life becomes so weak and the rebellion so strong that the probability of his or her ever rising above the blasphemy threshold drops to zero. This individual has willingly and permanently entered Satan's camp.

Blasphemers cross over when God finally "gives them over" to their own sinfulness and rebellion. In the first chapter of Romans, Paul uses these words to describe what happens to people who purposely "suppress the truth by their wickedness":

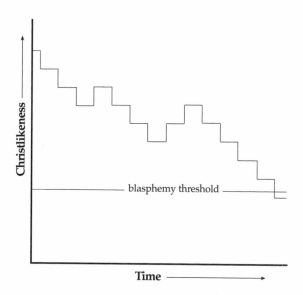

Figure 14.3: Journey toward Blaspheming the Holy Spirit
The steps down depict acts of rebellion against God's authority or acts of rejecting God's love, life, and truth, while the steps up depict acts of obedience or acts of accepting God's love, life, and truth.

> God gave them over in the sinful desires of their hearts to sexual impurity for the degrading of their bodies with one another.[18]

> God gave them over to shameful lusts.[19]

> God gave them over to a depraved mind, so that they do what ought not to be done.[20]

These and other verses indicate that, at the moment anyone drops below the blasphemy threshold, the strength of God's influence in that person's life drops sharply (see figure 14.4). As the rebellion in a person's heart becomes fixed, God gives that individual what he or she has been longing for. He literally gives that person up to his or her own, and by default Satan's, ways.

Disproportionate Numbers

We may wonder why, if this inward progression toward salvation and blasphemy is going on in the lives of people throughout history and all around us

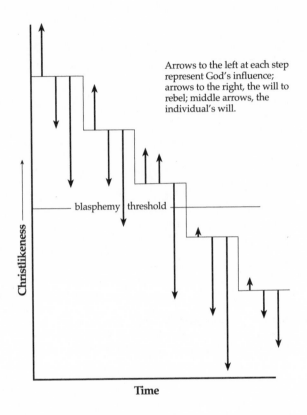

Arrows to the left at each step represent God's influence; arrows to the right, the will to rebel; middle arrows, the individual's will.

blasphemy | threshold

Christlikeness

Time

Figure 14.4: Blasphemy's Effect on God's Influence in a Person's Life
As an individual moves toward the blasphemy threshold, the tug of God lessens. Crossing the threshold results in a substantial decrease, perhaps a total loss. Meanwhile, the tug toward rebellion increases and the individual's freedom to express his or her own will remains the same.

today, the believers seem to far outnumber the committed blasphemers, who are given over to depravity. One explanation may be that God's love works to extend the lives of those who are coming to salvation and to shorten the lives of those guaranteed condemnation.

God's desire is to maximize the eternal rewards of believers. Thus, God's love works to give each believer the necessary time to complete the good works he has prepared in advance for him or her to do.[21] It also works to give them ample time to become mature, to grow in developing the character attributes of Christ.[22]

God's love is at work as well to limit the evil and suffering that the blasphemers will bring about, both to themselves and to others.[23] Typically, the longer God allows such persons to live, the greater judgments they would pile up against themselves.[24] Thus, in many if not most cases, unredeemable reprobates die soon after crossing the blasphemy threshold.

Difficult to Discern

Much of the dispute among Christians over the doctrines of eternal security and blasphemy against the Holy Spirit stems from our human inability to discern exactly when a particular individual crosses either the threshold of salvation or the threshold of blasphemy. Sometimes that crossover seems abundantly clear, but even in such cases we can be wrong.

Few of us have encountered an actual blasphemer, though we may have met many people apparently moving in the direction of blasphemy. Moreover, since Satan's influence is so destructive, the farther below the blasphemy threshold a person goes, the more likely he or she is to self-destruct or to meet death at the hands of evil companions.

Since Christians are more numerous in some populations than are blasphemers against the Holy Spirit, we might assume we could more easily distinguish who has crossed salvation's threshold and who has not. However, that line is blurred, as I mentioned, by our limited perspective and, thus, by our tendency to make hasty and superficial evaluations. Individuals and churches differ widely on what they consider the evidences of the indwelling Holy Spirit, by whom our salvation is secured. Many people who appear to us to be Christians meet about as many of the actual criteria for faith as did the Pharisees and Sadducees—and we know how they, with rare exceptions, responded to Jesus in their hearts. Jesus said that the majority of them never belonged to God.[25]

God alone knows, at any given moment, exactly where each of us stands on the Christlikeness axis. And because our capacity to discern is so limited, we must proceed cautiously in expressing absolute certainty that a person is "in Christ." We know God will keep whatever we commit to him,[26] but justification occurs when we yield to his right to rule our whole being, including the parts we have hidden from ourselves.

Dependent Paradoxes

As this chapter demonstrates, many biblical paradoxes encompass or intersect other paradoxes. Some of these paradoxes cannot be resolved satisfactorily without first resolving or demonstrating the resolvability of more fundamental paradoxes. As we have seen, many questions concerning the security of our salvation and what it rests on could be answered only by a more complete resolution of deeper-level paradoxes, including the question of when and how salvation occurs, how the properties of the Trinity make salvation possible, and the paradox of whose choice determines our eternal salvation or eternal separation. We have but scratched the surface. Much more work remains to be done.

When we who accept the authority of Christ and his Word encounter doctrinal disparity on a particular issue, such as spiritual gifts and the necessity of baptism, we can be assured of the need to delve into the deeper questions and paradoxes on which our conflict rests and work toward resolution at these deeper levels. If we will use our disagreements as opportunities to grow in oneness through doing research and seeking greater depths of wisdom and understanding, we may find more nonbelievers attracted to our faith and interested in our dialogue. (I tend to prefer dialogue over debate because it leads to contemplation more than to conquest.)

The following chapters address the paradoxical nature of some sensitive issues—evil and suffering, the new creation, and the place Scripture calls the "lake of fire." Our struggles with such subjects only indicate that we have much room to learn and grow, and much need to ask help of the Holy Spirit, our Counselor and Guide.

Chapter 15

Extradimensionality and Evil and Suffering

When skeptics ask about any of the controversial topics addressed in preceding chapters, most Christians are ready or at least willing to converse. Some are glad for the chance to discuss our beliefs on these subjects and the basis for these beliefs. Yet there is one issue—the one we are about to explore—that seems to tie our tongues more than any other, even among ourselves. And this is the issue most frequently raised by atheists and other nonbelievers. They view it as our Achilles heel; no other reason has been more widely given for rejecting the God of the Bible. That subject is evil and suffering.

Einstein was neither the first nor the last to discover that the "problem of evil and suffering" is typically treated by Christians and followers of other religions as an unanswerable problem, a mystery we can never—in this life—understand or explain.

Few have been so bold as C. S. Lewis in delivering public lectures on it. Countless books and articles by theologians have addressed it. For the laity, however, their silence is deafening. Reasons for this silence abound. Experience tells us that the person who asks why a loving, all-powerful God would allow evil and suffering to exist may have witnessed or experienced some horrific tragedy. Our hesitancy to respond often comes from recognition that a glib answer will only intensify that individual's anguish and confusion. The person asking may also be seeking an argument or an occasion to embarrass us. Given the emotional charge attached to this issue, it's no wonder even the most learned students of Scripture shy away from addressing it.

A reply affirming that an answer does exist may be the most helpful response when the question comes up, especially when the occasion does not permit a lengthy discussion. At least this reply opens the door for future dialogue and expresses the conviction that God did indeed shed some light on this subject for us. His Word does address it from many angles, including head on, and we're able to see this *if* we step back a bit from the text to take a wide-angle look at God's message. Where does it start? Where does it end?

The challenge we can take up ourselves and pass along to inquirers calls for a reading (or rereading) of the first few and last chapters of the Bible. This review of "initial conditions" and "final conditions" can give us a fresh perspective on what unfolds in between and can help us discover some good and necessary purposes for the evil and suffering God allows in this world. Not that such a view offers a comprehensive response to such a difficult question. But it does provide us with an important context to consider a more complete answer.

First, one great irony must be exposed. Many who argue that the existence of evil and suffering proves the nonexistence of an all-powerful, all-loving Creator have no idea that it proves just the opposite. Naturalistic materialism, the notion that the natural world accounts for itself and needs no outside explanation, cannot account for the evil and cruelty we see among humans. Survival of the fittest does not result in the behavior humans exhibit all over the planet toward the land itself or, worse yet, toward plants, animals, and fellow humans.

Too Much Evil

Though the words sound shocking, one can reasonably say that the quantity of evil expressed on earth exceeds by far what nontheistic evolutionary explanations can account for. Only the real existence of God and of his adversary, Satan, and the biblical account of God's purpose for this life, make sense of the extent and degree of evil and suffering we observe.

Making such a statement may lead to a discussion about the "fact" of evolution, naturalistic or otherwise. That's a significant side trail, and if that's where the conversation heads, one would do well to be prepared with a brief list of some facts that many evolutionary biologists admit (some willingly, others reluctantly) seem to challenge a naturalistic (that is, a materialistic) thesis (see table 15).

Given the complexity of these biochemical and biological issues, a more effective approach to the discussion of evil and suffering may be to stick with the question about the source of the behavior patterns we see among humans. If survival of the fittest were the dominant force shaping humanity, we might see some chaos and randomness, but not the kind and degree of evil and suffering that fills our headlines daily.

We humans are different from all other species. Both anthropology and theology attest to our uniqueness as spiritual creatures.[19] Our spirit component

Table 15: Some Scientific Challenges to a Nontheistic View of Life's Origin and Speciation*

*The scientific literature offers no consensus on the definition of *speciation*. At times the term refers to a breed or a variant of a species in which the individuals cannot (because of controlled breeding) or prefer not to mate with individuals from a different breed or variant. For the purposes of this table, *species* aligns with the biblical term *kind* (*min* in Hebrew), creatures capable of surviving in the wild without human protection and if forced to mate will produce fertile offspring.

1. Regardless of their theological/philosophical preferences, most researchers admit that the universe's age, even if it were closer to 20 billion years, is far from sufficient to explain life's origin as a strictly natural occurrence.[1]

2. The geophysical record establishes that life arose on Earth 3.8 billion years ago in a time span briefer than 10 million years. And it did so without the benefit of a prebiotic soup, or prebiotic mineral substrate, under chemical conditions that would naturally thwart the assembly of life's building-block molecules.[2]

3. RNA and DNA molecules and all their nucleotide building blocks are chemically unstable outside the protective environment of living cells.[3] In other words, these molecules cannot survive under inorganic conditions.

4. Because the nucleotide building blocks for RNA molecules require such radically different chemical conditions (two need freezing environments, while the other two require boiling conditions), it's unreasonable to conclude that all of them formed in the same location.[4]

5. The minimum genome to support independent cell function and reproduction has been determined to be 1,400–1,700 genes (for parasitic cells, at least 256 genes).[5] These minimum genome sizes indicate that the complexity necessary for the simplest possible life-form is far greater than researchers had previously thought.

6. Blue-green unicellular algae fossils dated as 2.5 billion years old are identical in size, shape, structure, and colonization as blue-green unicellular algae alive today, indicating this life-form has been static (non-evolving) for billions of years.[6]

7. Complex multicellular life appeared suddenly about 575 million years ago. This event, called the Avalon explosion, marks the introduction of Ediacaran life. During the subsequent 32 million years, no new phyla appeared, and thereafter the Ediacara phyla experienced serious decline.[7]

8. More than 40 phyla of complex animal life appeared for the first time some 543 million years ago within a time window briefer than 3 million years. These phyla comprised at least 24 of the 30 animal phyla remaining on Earth today, including the most advanced of all phyla—the chordates.[8]

9. Creatures such as horses and whales, which yield the most obvious fossil evidence of transitional forms, are among the least likely to evolve by natural process and the most likely to be driven to extinction by natural processes.[9] Transitional forms, then, are powerful evidence for divine replacement of extinct species.

10. For some mass extinction events in the fossil record, the replacement of extinct species with new and different species occurs far too rapidly to be explained by any known naturalistic cause.[10]

11. Long-term evolution experiments establish severe limits on what changes and rates of change are possible via natural selection, mutations, and gene exchange.[11]

12. Natural selection leads more frequently to stasis than to divergence.[12]

13. Only species with extremely large populations and short generation times can change significantly (and survive) through mutations and natural selection.[13]

14. Speciation of animals since the appearance of humans (when, according to the Bible, God ceased creating) has dropped to a virtual zero by contrast with the abundant speciation before that time.[14]

15. For the majority of animal species, change in the chemical makeup of the genes is so slow that if it does occur, it cannot be observed.[15]

16. While the fossil record indicates that certain genes must have changed very rapidly, chemical experiments document the impossibility of such rapid changes occurring under natural conditions.[16]

17. Chemical differences *within* specific (modern) species are too small—and *between* different species, too great—for these species to be descended by natural processes from a common ancestor.[17]

18. Comparison of the DNA of living humans with that of living primates and bipedal primate fossils contradicts the naturalistic descent-of-man theory.[18]

gives us a powerful capacity both for expressing goodness and for expressing evil. Unlike other species, we can inflict suffering on others for a variety of motives from revenge to perverse pleasure. Unlike other species, we kill for sport, and we tend to kill the best—the trophy animals—rather than the sick, the weak, and the dying. As for killing our own species, Leninist and Stalinist Russia, Nazi Germany, Maoist China, revolutionary France, Inquisitionist Spain, Civil War America, Hussein's Iraq, and countless other modern societies (as well as ancient civilizations) show that we willingly and wantonly slaughter and torture one another.

How do the injurious, deadly, and even disease-promoting behaviors of humans enhance our survival or well-being? A reality check quickly informs us that we cannot chalk up the evil and suffering in our world simply to natural processes and residual survival instincts. Rather than proving the nonexistence of a spiritual realm or of a Creator-God, evil and suffering provide evidence for a good God opposed by some supernatural enemy, a God who for good reasons, some revealed in Scripture, is currently restraining the expression of his almighty wrath against evil. Even in our recognition of the repugnance of such behaviors we see evidence for his existence and holiness.

Return to Eden

How often we hear God's critics boast, "If I were in charge, I could have designed the world in such a way as to eliminate evil and suffering." Whether they admit it or not, such individuals see themselves as wiser and more righteous than God. If we are daring enough to ask for an explanation of what this human-designed, perfect world would be like, we may hear a description that closely resembles Eden: a beautiful and pleasant paradise in which we would be protected from all harm for all time. Evil, if it did arise, would be snuffed out immediately so as to afflict no one but its source.

The Garden of Eden indeed was a wonderful place. Given the parameters of the universe, including its space-time boundaries and its laws of physics, it would be hard to imagine a better environment for the human race. Consider what Genesis says of our original parents' original home:[20]

- The garden, designed and planted by the wisest and most loving of all beings, was beautiful beyond description, well-watered and fertilized, and free of weeds and pests.
- The plants of the garden pleased not only the eye but also the palate.
- Treasures of all kinds, including gold, aromatic resin, and onyx abounded there.
- Adam and Eve had access to optimal health and unlimited longevity.
- Adam and Eve were given the capacity and the freedom to enjoy all the riches that surrounded them.
- They lived in peace, harmony, and fellowship with all the animals.
- Adam and Eve enjoyed peace, harmony, and fellowship with one another.
- They both enjoyed peace, harmony, and fellowship with God.
- There was a complete absence of shame.

The biblical description of Eden reveals a human habitat unexcelled in human comprehension, at least within our current reality's limits. We long for Eden because we long for the best our dimensional experience can suggest to our imagination. But God is not limited. His scope of operation exceeds by far our imaginative capacity. His plans for blessing humanity match his capacity to give—not our current, limited capacity to receive.

How many of us would rather return to Eden, to something good we can visualize, than to move beyond it to the new creation, which God says is better and yet which none of us can visualize? Atheists and agnostics are not the only ones who would rather stick with the familiar realm. Believers and nonbelievers alike share this tendency. Many religious systems, and even some Christians, portray heaven as an Eden-like paradise. Some embellish it with humans' sexual fantasies.

Designed for Removal of Evil and Suffering

In Genesis 1:31 God describes the present creation as "very good." However, only the new creation is described in terms of ultimate perfection. In one respect, though, the present creation is "perfect." That is, it is the optimally designed creation for the fulfillment of God's plan to bring about a rapid, efficient, and permanent conquest and removal of evil and suffering.

In another book, *Why the Universe Is the Way It Is*, I describe how the laws of physics and the cosmic space-time dimensions are designed by God to motivate us human beings to avoid evil, pursue virtue, and seek him.[21] At the same time the physical laws and cosmic space-time dimensions are optimal for the Creator himself to enter into our realm to perform the ultimate redemptive sacrifice so that those humans who are willing can be permanently rescued from the grip of sin and evil. Those same physical laws and cosmic space-time dimensions are optimally designed to provide us with the best possible training ground so that we can be adequately prepared to receive the rewards of the new creation and perform our God-assigned roles in the new creation.

Analogy of the Exodus

An important depiction of the human tendency to prefer the familiar may be seen in the biblical account of the Hebrews' exodus from Egypt. Throughout the books of Exodus and Numbers we read of repeated confrontations between Moses and the migrating Hebrew people. Again and again, because the Promised Land did not become immediately and easily accessible to them, the people begged Moses to forget about the new land and lead them back to Egypt.

There they had all the fish, cucumbers, melons, leeks, onions, and garlic they wanted.[22]

The ancient Hebrews' willingness to exchange their freedom, not to mention a future homeland flowing with milk, honey, fruit, grain, and mineral riches, for an oppressive regime and a few vegetables and fish seems utterly unfathomable. From their perspective, however, the Promised Land remained unfathomable, mere words and dreams. Having never seen it for themselves and having no personal experience of freedom and prosperity, they lacked a vision and hope for what God had promised them. Though they acknowledged that the freedom and the land must be better than slavery in Egypt, they had difficulty recognizing that the difference was great enough to be worth a few months or years of hardship and suffering in the wilderness. Just as importantly, they failed to appreciate that without adequate preparation and training, which their hardship and suffering would provide, their ability to retain the blessings of the Promised Land would be short-lived.

We may be tempted to judge these people harshly, but we dare not because we are so much like them. Our own experience, plus considerable psychological research, reports that in nearly all circumstances, both children and adults will choose something good that is familiar over something better but unfamiliar.

The children of Israel, similar to our own children and ourselves, could not seem to understand that their resistance to God's training program, as difficult as it may have been, only brought them far more difficulty. Their wilderness experience was expected to last 14 and a half months.[23] But their rebellion cost them 40 extra years of desert wandering.[24]

Nearly one-fifth of the Bible is devoted to the exodus story. One reason I see for God giving it so much attention is that it reflects the ongoing journey of the entire human race. As the Hebrews set out from Egypt (a land of onions, garlic, and slavery), the human race set out from Eden (a paradise where humans were slaves to the threat of rebellion and sin). Though Adam and Eve were at first free from sin, they were also free-will beings with the capacity to receive and express love, which meant they or their descendants could choose at any moment to rebel against God's authority and reject his goodness. Just as many Hebrews died in unbelief and rebellion in the wilderness, so too, much of humanity will die without believing or embracing the eternal destiny God has promised. Those people who did follow God into the land were blessed with seeing the glory of God and receiving the bounty of that place.

So, too, those who follow Christ into the new creation will be blessed with seeing his glory face-to-face and with receiving the bountiful rewards of that unimaginable place.

God had the option to lead the Hebrews from Egypt to Canaan along the north coastal road.[25] By that route the journey would have lasted only five to ten days. No one would have suffered. Much less evil would have been expressed and experienced. But, if God had chosen that option, the Hebrews would have been inadequately prepared to handle the many challenges, both physical and spiritual, of conquering and maintaining the new territory.[26] To avoid new forms of evil and suffering, they could have returned to the familiar hardships of Egypt. But the strength they gained from their new trials and troubles helped prepare them to seize and keep the land of their dreams.

The analogy with the human race is that God could take away our current evil and suffering. But if he did, we might lose the capacity to gain and keep access to the new creation. At best, we think we could return to Eden, but not in the same condition as when we left. The Hebrews, too, deceived themselves in thinking they could return to Egypt as it was before the unleashing of the 10 plagues.

We might be tempted to wish that God would take us to the new creation with a little less evil and suffering than we face in this life. Again, the Hebrews' journey through the wilderness suggests why he does not fulfill that wish. In spite of the 41 years of "training" they underwent, and even with the help of all the miracles God showed them both in Egypt and in the Promised Land, they were barely able to gain possession of the land. Eventually they lost their grip on it and have regained it, only partially, in recent years. The history of Israel indicates that God did not overtrain these people.

Likewise, we can be assured that God is not overtraining us. We know how much motivating the Hebrews needed to undertake the exodus out of Egypt. They experienced much evil and suffering and many supernatural proofs of God's power and protection. And we know how much motivating we need of a similar nature to undertake the exodus from sin's captivity. Still more evil and suffering, along with miraculous reassurances, moved the Hebrews along toward possession of the Promised Land. We, too, need more evil and suffering, along with God's miraculous reassurances, to move us along through the process of sanctification so that we will be ready for the splendors of the new creation.

Not all the evil and suffering we endure comes for our benefit alone. Sometimes God allows us to experience evil and suffering so that others may benefit also. Stephen, who was stoned to death by an angry mob of religious leaders, seems to exemplify this point. Holding the coats for that crowd, and seeing the radiant faith and face of the "villain" was a young zealot named Saul, whom God later transformed into the apostle Paul.[27]

If we want to shorten the span of this training program we find ourselves in, we can do it. Just as the Hebrews could have shortened their wanderings by cooperating with God and following Moses's instructions, we can cooperate with God more fully than we have by bending every effort and investing more resources toward completion of Christ's assignment to us. That assignment, which we call the Great Commission, could be carried out in our lifetime. Our struggles with evil and suffering will end when we successfully, by his enabling, bring the gospel to and raise up disciples within every ethnic group on Earth. That goal is within reach of the physical and spiritual resources of Christians, and it has been for some time, as determined by researchers at the United States Center for World Missions. While remarkable progress has been made within the last few decades,[28] we need increased faith and wider involvement among his people to make way for his coming.

Forward to the New Creation
A great boost toward our destination and a greater sense of purpose in enduring evil and suffering will be ours when we turn our focus away from the paradise lost and toward the new creation to be gained. This theme resounds throughout the Bible.[29] Paul states it succinctly in his letter to believers at Philippi:

> Forgetting what is behind and straining toward what is ahead, I press on toward the goal to win the prize for which God has called me heavenward in Christ Jesus.[30]

Because the new creation is extradimensional and thus impossible to visualize, the effort to press toward it seems difficult to sustain at times. I have observed during my years in the classroom on both sides of the lectern that students who look forward to years of exciting research and discovery in physics or astronomy consider a few semesters of "torment" a small price to pay for the thrills that lie ahead. Those who have greatest difficulty in handling the work and for whom the semesters drag lack eager anticipation for such thrills. They are just preparing to support themselves and perhaps a family.

Gaining a clear vision of the reward ahead can be helpful, but we need more than that to spur us onward. Unless we place a high personal value on the reward, we will resent or perhaps seek escape from the pain and difficulty involved in reaching it. To latch onto the Christian faith because someone else thinks the new creation makes a superb travel destination will not get us through the tough times. We must want to go there for our own personal reasons. The author of Hebrews points to Jesus's life as a prime example of anticipation's impact:

> And let us run with perseverance, fixing our eyes on Jesus, the pioneer and perfecter of faith. For the joy set before him he endured the cross, scorning its shame, and sat down at the right hand of the throne of God.
>
> Consider him who endured such opposition from sinners, so that you will not grow weary and lose heart.[31]

We cannot see as clearly and directly as Jesus did the joy he left and that awaited him at the end of his sufferings, but neither are we called upon to suffer as he did. We may endure hardship and persecution at the hands of evildoers, but the people I have met who have suffered most intensely, including Russian and Chinese believers imprisoned for years and tortured horribly, also express emphatically that these sufferings, as awful as they were, "are not worth comparing with the glory that will be revealed."[32] These individuals, even without a perfect view of the reward awaiting them, had enough tangible evidence of its reality and a sufficient taste of its quality, to place a high personal value on it. Therefore, they endured.

We can all do more to enhance our capacity for endurance and enthusiasm for the difficulty of life's training program.[33] Though we cannot in four-dimensional thinking visually picture the physical characteristics of the heavenly realm beyond our earthly existence, we can exercise our spiritual capacity, our eyes of faith, to examine all the clues given in Scripture and develop a composite of its spiritual characteristics. Such an exercise can only (and richly!) increase our hope and anticipation for what soon awaits us.

> Dear friends, now we are children of God, and what we will be has not yet been made known. But we know that when Christ appears, we shall be like him, for we shall see him as he is. All who have this hope in him purify themselves, just as he is pure.[34]

But before we consider what we can now know of the new creation, we have one more hurdle to clear: What can we say in response to the question of a loving God who would consign individuals to eternal torment?

Chapter 16

God's Extradimensional Love in Hell

Comprehending how God can express his love and care through our experience of evil and suffering may be difficult, but that challenge remains orders of magnitude below the struggle—many would say the impossibility—to comprehend how that love is reflected in the Christian doctrine of hell.

Time and space, and physical and spiritual boundaries apply to evil and suffering. God promises that we will never face temptation beyond what we can bear, that he will always provide a "way of escape."[1] But the set of circumstances the Bible refers to as "hell" offers no escape. God also tells us the Holy Spirit acts as a restraining influence in the world right now, holding back the expression of evil. But hell offers none of the dimensional, physical, or spiritual boundaries we know. For God even to tolerate, let alone create, a place or experience such as hell and to consign multitudes of his creatures to it, seems an unthinkable contradiction of his biblically claimed attributes of omnipotence and perfect love.

The doctrine of hell, also called "the lake of fire,"[2] as a place of perpetual torment for those who reject God's offer of salvation has been part of Christian orthodoxy for centuries.[3] Recently, however, especially in the last few decades, the perceived failure of Christian theologians to reconcile eternal torment with an infinitely loving God has led to the erosion or, in some cases, rejection of that doctrine.

To a large degree, this change has resulted from the tendency of many late twentieth- and early twenty-first-century theologians to view God's dealings with humanity in increasingly humanlike terms. An example comes from this excerpt of a published statement from one denomination:

> The most serious problem is that [the doctrine of hell] turns God into a monster. Hitler, at least, was merciful enough to put his

victims out of their misery. But God, we are told, will artificially
sustain human beings, keeping them alive just so they can suffer
throughout eternity—and all this to pay for the misdeeds of a few
short years on this earth.[4]

The statement goes on to explain (1) why hell cannot be located anywhere
in the universe except here on Earth; and (2) why its location on Earth, our "future paradise," must be short-lived indeed. The exegetical flaws in this doctrinal
statement, including its identification of heaven as an earthly paradise, can be
refuted without much difficulty, as the following paragraphs argue.[5]

The charge concerning the monstrous cruelty of a God who would torment people eternally, however, is harder to sweep aside. In fact, this argument
recently persuaded the Church of England to change its doctrinal position.
After 10 years of study, the church's doctrinal committee declared in 1996 that
a fiery eternal hell speaks of a cruel sadistic God and, since the Bible clearly
teaches that God is neither cruel nor sadistic, a correct interpretation of the
Bible would lead to the conclusion that if a person refuses God's offer of salvation, the consequence is "total non-being."[6]

Extradimensionality of Hell

If the doctrine of hell is treated as anything other than a paradox, such either-
or conclusions are unavoidable. Belief that an all-powerful, all-loving God allows people to live in torment infinitely for finite crimes—a four-dimensional,
anthropomorphic contradiction—surely demands "adjustment."

First, the Bible makes clear that the lake of fire exists beyond, not within,
the dimensions of the universe (just as the new creation does). The lake of fire
and the new creation both survive God's "rolling up" of the entire physical
universe, as one rolls up a scroll, and causing it all to disappear in a fiery heat[7]
before replacing the physical universe with something entirely new, including
new (to us) dimensions or realms and new physical and spiritual characteristics.[8]

God's purposes in creating the universe include fulfillment of his plan to
conquer evil once and for all, always.[9] When that plan is fully accomplished,
marked by an event the Bible refers to as the Great White Throne Judgment,[10]
God will then remove the whole physical universe from existence.[11] But the
new creation and the lake of fire are not the only created entities that will remain beyond this dramatic end. Every human who has ever lived and every
angelic being also survives.[12] Apparently, one of the spiritual laws describing

God's reality is that every spirit creature, once created, exists unendingly.

Ultimate non-being describes the fate of the universe, not the fate of unrepentant human beings and fallen angels. In other words, the doctrine of annihilation has been misapplied. God's plan does *not* call for eradication of sin and sinners from the universe, but rather it calls for eradication of the universe while sinners (because they are spirit beings) will never be eradicated. Neither sin nor sinners are anywhere present in the new creation. Twice in the last two chapters of Revelation, John records that those who reject God's authority will continue to exist in what's called the lake of fire after the Great White Throne Judgment—but never inside, always outside, with respect to the new creation.[13]

When the universe's matter, energy, and space-time dimensions no longer exist, the new creation and the lake of fire do still exist. This information indicates that hell occupies a different dimensional realm from the universe. This point may represent a coincidence, but it seems worth mentioning: the biblical references to heaven and hell as somewhere "up" or "down" is completely appropriate from an extradimensional standpoint. Just as the screen people's correct description of a third spatial dimension would be "up" or "down," so, too, for us the proper description for any extra space dimension(s) or realms would be "up" or "down." Thus, when certain Bible verses refer to heaven as "up" and hell as "down," they do not suggest heaven is in the sky and hell is in the earth's core, but rather that heaven and hell reside in some kind of extradimensional realms.

The biblical descriptions of hell also suggest its extradimensionality. Just as the biblical account of the new creation's rewards and blessings presses hard against the limits of human imagination (see chapter 17), so does the account of hell's agonies. In fact, they clearly go beyond anything we can fully comprehend, no matter how graphic the descriptions.

Any solution to the paradox of eternal torment and God's love that can be completely understood in our four space-time dimensions must be incorrect. A satisfactory resolution will require us to look beyond the context of our human experience of love and torment. Such experience provides an inadequate and inappropriate basis for rejecting the reality of hell—and for comprehending how it fits with God's love.

Eternal Rebellion

A temporary sentence to hell for sin might indeed be appropriate if the sinner were merely paying "for the misdeeds of a few short years on this earth." This line of reasoning minimizes the meaning of sin and ignores the eternality of human choice, given the eternality of the human spirit. An individual who knowingly refused to worship God during this earthly life will never change his or her mind. Heaven's "price," worshiping God and God alone, exceeds what this person will ever willingly pay. This individual does not want to be in God's presence and, thus, would find heaven repugnant. As Hebrews says, "no sacrifice for sins is left" for those who knowingly discard God's sacred gift.[14] They may regret their eternal plight but not their rebellion.

Jesus clearly taught that nobody dies without having a clear and adequately understood opportunity to receive or reject his offer of forgiveness from sin and of eternal life with him.[15] No person alive has totally missed "hearing God's call."[16] Ignorance of God and his offer comes from distorting and defying the truth he makes available to each person and, thus, is self-imposed.[17]

Hell is something people choose. While the people experiencing hell will despise their torment, they have demonstrated their preference for anything other than eternal fellowship with God and with all who love the light.[18] For them, the experience of such fellowship would be less tolerable than the torment of hell.

The lake of fire is a place where people and demons get what they want above anything else: freedom from the will and rule of God and freedom from the restraints of conscience (the voice of the Holy Spirit). God yields to the desires of committed rebels by withdrawing forever the influence of his Spirit from their beings.

Scriptures Attesting Eternal Torment

The book of Revelation is the most explicit in declaring that hell is an experience of ongoing agony for its inhabitants:

> There will be no rest day or night for those who worship the beast and its image.[19]

> The two of them [the beast and the false prophet] were thrown alive into the fiery lake of burning sulfur.[20]

> And the devil, who deceived them [the nations], was thrown into the lake of burning sulfur, where the beast and the false prophet had been thrown. They will be tormented day and night for ever and ever.[21]

> Anyone whose name was not found written in the book of life was thrown into the lake of fire.[22]

Some interpreters of Revelation seek to avoid the force of these passages by claiming that we cannot determine which Revelation passages are literal and which are symbolic. However, while Revelation does employ more symbols than do most other books of the Bible, its writer defines each symbol either in the immediate context or by referencing the portion of Scripture in which it has been previously employed and defined. In these particular passages, we do see metaphoric language—but only to underscore the message of enduring torment.

Each of the Gospels also records descriptions of hell. Jesus spoke of it many times in his teaching, sometimes in parables, but usually in direct communication. The following passages record his words:

> He will clear his threshing floor . . . burning up the chaff [nonbelievers] with unquenchable fire.[23]

> It is better for you to enter life maimed or crippled than to have two hands or two feet and be thrown into eternal fire.[24]

> Then he will say to those on his left, "Depart from me, you who are cursed, into the eternal fire prepared for the devil and his angels."[25]

> It is better for you to enter the kingdom of God with one eye than to have two eyes and be thrown into hell, where "the worms that eat them do not die, and the fire is not quenched."[26]

Jesus's quotation of Isaiah's words affirms the metaphoric picture the prophet draws of the contrasts between the place of eternal separation from God and the place of eternal fellowship with him.

In his epistle, Jude made reference to what happened to the people of Sodom and Gomorrah as an example, or warning, of "the punishment of eternal fire."[27] The Bible contains many more verses affirming that hell is real, enduring, and awful. Yet far more of Scripture is devoted to declaring and illustrating God's loving, merciful character. To be consistent with biblical revelation, any resolution of the paradox of God's love and hell's torment must uphold the truth of God's love, hell's existence, and hell's unending experience.

God's Compassion Expressed in Hell

These words may sound strange, but in light of God's character and the character of those sentenced to separation from God, those who inhabit the lake of fire occupy the best possible realm for them. God expresses his love and compassion for hell's inhabitants by afflicting them with sufficient torment to prevent the place from being as bad as its inhabitants have the capacity to make it.

We can only begin to imagine what evil could be expressed by those from whom the restraining influence of God's Spirit has departed. The unleashing of individuals' full potential for cruelty and all manner of evil could make hell vastly more horrible than God designed it to be. The worst thing about hell might be the company its inhabitants must keep. But God will keep in check the horrors these individuals could inflict on one another by immobilizing them to a measured degree, distracting them with a precisely determined amount and kind of pain and/or discomfort.

The measure of immobilization, pain, and discomfort necessary to restrain each person in hell will be different for each person. The book of Revelation speaks of differing levels or degrees of torment for those who choose hell, torment that is commensurate with each person's earthly expressions of sin and rebellion.[28] The measure of wickedness a person practiced on Earth is the measure of that individual's potential to make life more miserable than it already must be for others in hell. One interpretation suggests that God calibrates each person's torment to exactly the level necessary for restraint of his or her potential for expressing evil.

A story might help to illustrate. If the public statements and writings of Adolf Hitler and Albert Camus are indicative of where each of them finished their lives spiritually, then both could be described appropriately as rebels against God's authority. Again, if their public lives offer any reliable indication, Hitler expressed more overt and violent wickedness than Camus. Since both appear to have rejected God's truth and his offer of life in heaven's kingdom, we would assume both will spend eternity apart from fellowship with God. But because Hitler would seem to possess the greater capacity to multiply suffering for his fellow rebels, we can imagine that he would require more torment to keep his capacity for inflicting evil behavior at bay.

The necessity of torment makes us aware that sin is far more grievous than any human can imagine. Because God's Spirit blunts the impact of sin in our world, we tend to underestimate its horror and, in the process, minimize what Christ took upon himself at the cross. If we've ever had dealings with an individual anywhere near blasphemy's threshold, the chill of that encounter should help us more accurately grasp what Christ suffered and what horrors hell's torment prevents.

None of this discussion is meant to imply that the restraint of evil's expression through some kind of torment is *all* that hell is about. My comments here are not intended as a full exposition of the doctrine of hell but simply to demonstrate that hell's torment is not incompatible with God's love.

Is *Torment* the Right Word?

The statements by the Church of England and the Seventh-Day Adventist Church expose what may be, at least partially, a semantic problem. Many who reject the reality of hell do so because they equate the word *torment* with "sadistic cruelty." The concept of a necessarily painful restraining effect—and of its cause—seems to have been overlooked.

While the Greek word for torment (*basanos*) in the early New Testament manuscripts can denote torture, it is also used for "grievous pains" or "distress."[29] (New Testament writers used the same word to refer to the pains of childbirth.) Biblical references to darkness and light provide another helpful illustration of hell's torment. Consider what happens when we walk into bright sunlight from a darkened room. The pain is blinding and excruciating. If it's intense enough, it blocks our ability not only to see but also to function at all. Is the Sun inflicting this torment on us out of malice? Or is the Sun just being what it is in relation to our eyes and the way they are made? Consider what it must be like for a person who chooses a life of spiritual darkness to be exposed to the radiance of God's Being!

Because the torment of hell is an extradimensional phenomenon, Bible writers faced serious limits in their attempt to communicate it. God's love, too, is an extradimensional phenomenon impossible to communicate fully in words. But we humans, even with our limited understanding, can find contexts in which a measured infliction of pain and an expression of love *can* be consistent. At that point we have taken a significant step toward demonstrating that hell's pain and distress do not necessarily contradict God's loving nature and consistent expression of love. And if an example of consistency can be found in our finite realm, surely greater possibility for consistency exists in God's extradimensional realm.

An illustration of the benefit of torment is one used in the preceding chapter: A professor "torments" his students for a semester to help prepare them for future success. A better analogy is that of a mother who inflicts her child with the "torment" of a car seat to protect him or her as they ride. Civilized societies incarcerate criminals to keep their citizens from further harm at the hands of lawbreakers.

A good friend of mine once stumbled into a real-life lesson on the consistency of God's love and his restraint of evildoers. Through the simple error of misreading a map, he was arrested for selling a certain brand of film on the wrong side of the street in the vicinity of Pasadena's Rose Bowl.

Under normal circumstances he would have been driven to the courthouse, cautioned by authorities, and released. But because so many revelers had been arrested the night before, the court system was jammed. All the Pasadena jail cells were full, as were those in the neighboring communities. My friend, who had never even been sent to the principal's office during his school years, was sent to Los Angeles County Jail not just for a few hours but for a whole day and night.

He was placed in a cell with eight other men. While the Los Angeles Police Department do their best to separate violent felons from the rest of the inmate population, their efforts are limited. My friend glanced around to meet eight pairs of eyes staring at this obvious first-timer, each more fearsome than any he had encountered in his life. Eight men watched, waiting for him to fall asleep. He spent that day and night awake and praying, his back glued to the cell wall.

No physical harm came to him during those agonizing hours, but he does remember wishing that an officer would come to handcuff and leg cuff the others so that he could get a moment's rest. Those cuffs would have brought some torment, of course, but certainly no more than the torment my friend endured. From his perspective, the most loving thing the police could have done was to restrain his cell mates with cuffs. But what if some of them didn't really need the cuffs? The most loving scenario for the total group would have been for the police to provide the greatest restraint to the most dangerous inmates, lesser restraint for those less dangerous, and no restraint for those who would likely do no harm to the others. Unfortunately, neither the police nor anyone else can see that clearly into people's hearts. But God can. And since God does see, he would know precisely how dangerous each of hell's inhabitants can be. With this knowledge, he would be able to determine precisely what degree of restraint to apply to each person. And that could be considered an act of love.

How much better, though, to experience his love where it can be fully and freely expressed, in the place he is preparing for our eternal fellowship with him and with one another—the place for which he is now preparing us. We'll obviously need new eyes to see it, and him, in such brilliant splendor.

Chapter 17

Extradimensionality and the New Creation

As far as hell stretches beyond the limits of our imagination, so does heaven, only more so. Many people who talk about going there say they're looking forward to seeing someone, or several people they especially miss or admire. Christians typically express their anticipation for being with "Jesus," or "God," or perhaps "God and all his children." Rarely in my life have I heard anyone express much more than this kind of enthusiasm for the place. Sometimes people's desire to go there reflects more honestly their preference for "pleasantness" and their wish to avoid hell, in case such a place exists.

Because of children's honesty, they are usually the ones to admit their worry that heaven might be boring, a place where we will all resemble the angels (as depicted in Renaissance paintings), ride around on clouds, and play harps or sing praise songs all day (which means all the time since night does not exist in heaven). I cannot help but wonder how many adults harbor this same concern. Seldom do we in our churches and fellowships talk about heaven. Christ's thousand-year reign on earth—for those who accept the doctrine of the millennium—seems to generate more discussion. And that focus makes sense because it seems to resemble the Garden of Eden in some ways. But the biblical descriptions of the new creation sound so strange to us, so far beyond familiar experience—streets paved with gold as clear as glass, for example—that we tend to abandon all earthly images and, thus, all discussion.

Yet the heavenly "prize" is supposed to represent the motivation for pressing on through the challenges of this life. It seems we need to dig a little more deeply into Scripture to gain a clearer view and deeper appreciation for whatever awaits us in the new creation. Because of what we know about God and about the absence of evil there, we can be sure the new creation is better than anything we've seen or experienced in this earthly life. In that case, a game of "Heaven is better than . . ." can be especially helpful to children and beneficial for believers of all ages.

Extradimensionality of the New Creation

Two statements at the beginning of Revelation 21 affirm that the new creation exists in dimensions (or their equivalent) entirely independent of the ones we now experience:

> I saw "a new heaven and a new earth," for the first heaven and the first earth had passed away.[1]

> The old order of things has passed away. He who was seated on the throne said, "I am making everything new!"[2]

According to these verses, God's brand-new creation will be completely different from our familiar universe. This proclamation that the old order of things will pass away and that everything will be made new suggests that no physical entities will be carried over from the old creation into the new creation. "Physical" will have a new meaning. All the forces and laws of physics will be changed.

This brand-newness seems consistent with God's pattern of creative work. Just as God's first creation "week" begins with God's "speaking into existence" something entirely new—a universe of matter and energy, and of space-time dimensions for their distribution and operation (see chapter 5)—so, too, God begins his second creation by introducing a brand-new realm, a new "heaven and earth," denoting the dwelling place of God, of the righteous angels, of redeemed humans, and of the "nations." The new "earth" will have entirely new properties.

Electromagnetism and gravity operate on material objects in three dimensions of space. Stable atom structure and stable planetary and star orbits, for example, are impossible in anything other than three dimensions of space. Evidence that gravity will be different or nonexistent in the new creation comes from the biblical description of the new Jerusalem. The new "city of peace" rests on the new earth and is depicted as some kind of cube or pyramid, 12,000 stadia (1,379 miles or 2,219 kilometers) long, 12,000 stadia wide, and 12,000 stadia high.[3] If the familiar force of gravity were in operation, this cube or pyramid would collapse into a spherical shape, for in our universe, any material object with dimensions exceeding about 300 miles across would be pulled by gravity into a more or less spherical shape.

We cannot assume, however, that the new creation will be devoid of any kind of physicality. If the place were nonphysical in every way, the use of "measuring rods" would make no sense.[4] It is hard to conceive, too, of nonphysical gates, streets, walls, and mountains.[5] More significantly, when Jesus appeared to his disciples after the resurrection, he affirmed both verbally and tangibly that his post-resurrection body had certain physical, though obviously different, characteristics and capacities.[6] Other Scriptures indicate that we who go with Christ into the new creation will receive new bodies, very different from our present ones, but bodies nonetheless.[7]

Further evidence for different physical laws comes from statements about the absence of decay processes in the new creation. Paul tells us that the law of decay is temporary, limited to the present cosmos:

> Our present sufferings are not worth comparing with the glory that will be revealed in us. For the creation waits in eager expectation for the children of God to be revealed. For the creation was subjected to frustration, not by its own choice, but by the will of the one who subjected it, in hope that the creation itself will be liberated from its bondage to decay and brought into the freedom and glory of the children of God.[8]

The apostle John records that death, mourning, crying, and pain will no longer be part of the new creation.[9] Apparently, we will "consume" in some sense without incurring any cost—a further indication of decay's absence.[10] If decay is not in effect there, neither is the second law of thermodynamics. That law states the existence of processes bringing increasing disorder or decay. It's necessary to the operation of the cosmos we know but obviously has no part in the new one. And yet, the texts on the new creation indicate that God, the angels, and we humans will all possess the capacity to perform what could technically be defined as "work." The possibility of work, or activity, without the second law of thermodynamics in effect means that a dimensionality or transdimensionality totally different from ours must exist there.

The most convincing evidence for the transdimensionality/extradimensionality of the new creation comes from the biblical descriptions of our relationships with God and with one another—also from descriptions of our enjoyment of the place.

New Creation Travelogue
While John did actually see some aspects of the new creation, most of what he passed on to us is what one of God's angels told him about its features. Paul

may have been given a glimpse of the new creation,[11] but he was told to keep silent about what he saw. Isaiah offers a description at the close of his prophetic book, while Ezekiel, Joel, and other prophets make several brief mentions in their writings. Jesus in his earthly ministry gave us the most thrilling information about life in his future kingdom.

All these descriptions suggest the enormity of our new habitation. If its population exceeds 10 billion, the new Jerusalem alone would give each person the equivalent of about 40 billion cubic feet of living space (equivalent to a 14-square-mile home with a 100-foot-high ceiling). What we will do with all that space we cannot yet know. We can't even picture what "space" means in the new dimensions of the new creation. However, our habitat will be better than all the splendors of this earth, from ocean depths to mountain grandeur.

Whatever structures Jesus may have meant when he spoke about the "mansions,"[12] they must be magnificent indeed, considering his eye for beauty as seen in this world. Furthermore, no forces in the new creation will cause the wearing down of what he makes—or of what we may make, given the extension of our capacities for creativity. Imagine what our lives would be like if the time and energy we now expend on maintenance and upkeep could be devoted wholly to creative pursuits!

Not only is the new creation free of deterioration, but it is also free of natural and manmade disasters and crime, all the things that so seriously drain our joy and our wealth in this world. In our world, material and relational wealth must be protected, and the costs of such protection increase with the value of what needs protecting. In the new creation, our wealth will not burden us. God can and will bless each of us with an inheritance beyond what we can possibly dream. The Bible says that in the new creation we will inherit everything that Christ inherits.[13]

The new Jerusalem represents just one portion of our new domain. And since the new Jerusalem's size exceeds the earth's largest structures by more than 10 trillion times, the new earth's proportions probably supersede the present earth's by a similar factor. While the new Jerusalem will be roomy enough to serve as "home" for every believer, we will also have full access to the new earth, as well as the new heavens.

The biblical description of the new Jerusalem, the new earth, and the new heavens answers an argument against God's existence posed by particle physicist Victor Stenger in his best-selling book *God: The Failed Hypothesis*. Stenger asserts that if an all-powerful, all-loving God exists, such a God would have blessed humanity with a near limitless habitat space.[14] Because it is now clear to astronomers that the whole universe is hostile to advanced life—except for "this tiny blue speck" of a planet on which humans are confined—Stenger concludes that an all-powerful, all-loving God must not exist.[15]

The fallacy in Stenger's argument against God's existence is his presumption that God intends to confine humans to this tiny blue speck *permanently*. Our present confinement may be likened to parents' placement of their toddler in a playpen for a brief time or in a room with protective "gates." These limits keep the little one safe and secure. As the child matures, the parents can safely release him or her into a much larger habitat. Similarly, from God's perspective humans are too immature to be set loose in a larger living space. But eventually, when God's Spirit brings us to full maturity, we'll be ready to access a living area far greater than anything conceivable in the present universe. The increase in our mobility in the new creation will be dramatic.

Consider the following example. What makes *Star Trek* and other sci-fi films and TV shows difficult for physicists to enjoy are the pervasive violations of physical laws depicted on-screen. We do not know of any way to transport people to distant stars and galaxies without overriding the laws of physics or the physical limitations of our physical bodies.[16] Even visiting the planets in our solar system may be beyond (safe) reach. Researchers have been unable to find a practical means to protect humans in space, long-term, from solar, stellar, and cosmic radiation, meteorites, dust, insanity (due to social and spatial isolation), and other hazards. Such limitations, including the law of gravity, will no longer hamper our travel in the new heavens and the new earth.

Safe from Harm

The absence of pain in the new creation implies that the risks of injury and illness will be gone. Though in Eden pain was reduced, it was still present.[17] Adam and Eve did not possess indestructible bodies. They needed at least some pain sensation to warn them of injury or of impending injury. We who choose life in the new creation will all receive indestructible bodies.[18] Our bodies will experience no injury, sickness, pain, weakness, or weariness.

Hunger and thirst will also be things of the past.[19] No longer will our bodies need food, rest, exercise, repair, or other maintenance. Never again will our bodies let us down. Never again will we have to say, "The spirit is willing but the flesh is weak." Our hunger and thirst for needs other than food and water will be gone, too. We will be completely and continuously "full" and satisfied—physically, emotionally, intellectually, and spiritually. While our lives today bring us moments of satisfaction, the perfect and sustained satisfaction for which we yearn will finally be ours to possess forever in the new creation.

Revelation tells us that sorrow and crying will be past experiences. Their absence suggests that depression, grief, loneliness, and regret will also be past. We will have no cause for sadness in the new creation, for we will never experience loss or injustice or tragedy of any kind. Fellowship will never be broken. Nothing of value to us will ever be diminished. As we recall the former creation, we will have the necessary understanding to recognize that everyone did fulfill the purpose for which he or she was created. Those we knew and loved who chose to reject God's gift of eternal life with him will have been treated with utmost fairness and goodness.

The characteristic of the new creation most frequently emphasized in the biblical passages is the absence of darkness.[20] The light of God's glory illuminates everything, and everything radiates or reflects God's light. Just as the Sun casts no shadow, nothing in the new creation casts shadows. Darkness, even shades of darkness, cannot be found. Again, the Bible speaks of this light without shadows not just in a physical sense but in an emotional, intellectual, and spiritual sense as well.

Relational Wonders

As dramatic as the alterations in our environment and bodies may seem, the relational changes will be more profound. In the new creation no one will fear, hide, or deceive. No one will experience envy or doubt. No one will demean or in any way violate the sanctity of another creature, and no one will exalt anything or anyone above God.[21] Every barrier that prevents or limits intimacy between us will be removed for all eternity. We who have been redeemed by Christ will pass through a fire, not of judgment but of cleansing, a fire that will cleanse us of all that would make us obnoxious to God and one another.[22] Instead, everyone in the new creation will consistently exhibit the character and love of Jesus Christ in all circumstances and for all time.[23]

There will be neither boors nor bores in the new creation. Never again will any of us experience the slightest cringing when we see an individual moving toward us. Because we will be healed of all brokenness and distortions, every person in the new creation will be someone we delight to commune with, much more than we do now with our favorite person on earth.

Each of us in the new creation will be given an assignment for which we are perfectly suited. We will have roles to fulfill as "rulers" over the angels and over whatever God creates in the new kingdom.[24] We will work together in perfect peace and harmony for all of eternity. All of us in the new creation will experience oneness, as God is one.[25] We will be in one accord with God and with each other, and yet each of us will retain some distinct identity and the freedom to choose. Through the training we are now experiencing, we will become adequately convinced of the benefits of choosing what is good and true and will be fully empowered to make those good and true choices (see chapters 13 and 14).

Intimacy without Sexuality (Better Than Sex)

Jesus explicitly stated during his earthly ministry that in the new creation there would be no nuclear families, no marriage as we now experience it, and no sexuality.[26] Many non-Christians, when they hear these truths about heaven, begin to wonder if Christianity is worthwhile. "How can heaven be paradise without sex?" they may ask.

A preliminary answer is that God never takes away anything from us without replacing it with something better. Such an answer, while it is true, typically falls on deaf ears unless we can go on to describe what that "something better" could possibly be. The problem here is that many people can think of no pleasure superior to sex. Outside of Judaism and Christianity, most religions and cults distort and abuse the sexuality God gave us, either in their teachings about the afterlife or in their teachings about earthly relationships and worship practices. Their teachings are either overly restrictive or overly indulgent. In some ironic cases, they are severely restrictive in this earthly life and promise extreme indulgence in the afterlife. These writings reflect the human tendency to exalt the pleasures of sex above all other pleasures. Thus, in its unique perspective on sexuality both in earthly relationships and in heavenly ones, the Bible reflects the inspiration of a transcendent Being.

While much of human thinking and teaching emphasizes the physical side of sex, the Bible focuses on its spiritual and relational aspects. According to the Bible, what heightens the enjoyment of sex and the exploration of its pleasures is not the use of certain physical techniques but the degree of oneness a man and woman have developed in the broad spectrum of their relationship—in their spiritual, emotional, intellectual, and relational values, for example. To build this oneness, a man and a woman must invest generously in their relationship. Because of our current limits in this four-dimensional universe, achieving maximum intimacy requires us to concentrate on one individual to the exclusion of others.

This exclusion principle has application beyond the marriage relationship. Again, because of our space-time context, even our capacity to build friendships is limited. We can choose to have a few close friends and a few dozen casual friends. But time, energy, and other resource limits prevent us from building an unlimited number of close friendships.

We face the frustration of limits continually in this life. Wherever we go, whatever we do, we meet people whose personalities we enjoy and with whom we would like to become better acquainted, possibly building a close and en-riching relationship. We see this potential, and yet we must choose to follow through with only a select few if we wish to maintain our balance and respon-sibilities. In this sense, one thing that made Eden a paradise, and at the same time *not* a paradise, was its population: two.

Intimacy's New Depth and Breadth

The biblical pictures of the new creation suggest the absence of virtually all relationship-limiting factors. Christ often refers to believers in the new cre-ation with singular nouns and pronouns.[27] Specifically, Jesus refers collectively to believers in the new creation as his bride, and he says we all will be one as he, the Father, and the Holy Spirit are one. The oneness of all believers refers to God's presence with all of us simultaneously and to our unity in love and truth. Such oneness dramatically enhances our relationships with each other. But there may be more.

The oneness of the Godhead would be impossible unless the Father, Son, and Spirit are in continuous communication and fellowship with one another. For us to experience that same kind of oneness we, too, would need to be in continuous communication and fellowship with one another. We might gain the capacity to communicate and relate intimately with billions of others all at once—and perfectly enjoy each one.

Our present dimensionality makes such simultaneous communication and fellowship impossible. But with even one extra dimension of time (or its equivalent), we could acquire this capacity. As God can listen and respond to any number of prayers simultaneously in the equivalent of two time dimen-sions (see chapter 7), so we may be able to give our full attention to countless other believers simultaneously—and receive theirs.

That is not to say we will become omnipresent. Just as our current ability to make conference calls to several individuals on different continents does not imply we are everywhere on Earth at once, so too our possible capacity for simultaneous communion with billions of individuals would not necessarily imply that we are present everywhere in the new creation.

With this new capacity for knowing and being known by, loving and being loved by all other human beings in the new creation, our need for marriage and a nuclear family is fully met. We will no longer need to focus our relationship resources on one spouse, our own children, our other family members, and our selected friends. We will continuously enjoy all other members of the heavenly family in a way that's far superior to the pleasures of the very best of times in our earthly relationships, including marriage.

We will all personally commune with those individuals of all ages we have admired most and longed to know. Think of the crowds surrounding Jesus as he traveled and taught on Earth. People had to wait their turn to see him and talk to him, and many who were less patient than Anna and Simeon,[28] less persistent than Zacchaeus,[29] and less resourceful than the men who lowered their friend through a roof[30] never did get that privilege. Such difficulties and disappointments will vanish in the new creation. We will all be able to fellowship with God and with one another as we please, and with greater intimacy and continuity than any of our earthly relationships yet allow.

The people who most fear the loss of sexual relationships in the new creation are most likely those who abuse such relationships. When people feel the pain of disconnection in one or more key relationships, they may tend to ease that pain with sex rather than deal with the pain and brokenness. They hope a sexual union will restore or perhaps replace the love bond they lack. As alcoholics use alcohol to dull the pain and sorrow in their lives, many people use sexual encounters to do the same. But, in the new creation, perfect love and understanding will be fully available to us. The gnawing pain caused by love deficits will be healed, and no anesthesia for that pain will be sought.

Marriage will not be missed because our earthly marriages will be replaced by one unimaginably superior marriage. All believers in the new creation will experience such relational pleasure and one accord with each other and with Christ that we will all relate as one bride to one groom.

Right now we are engaged to Christ,[31] and our engagement gives us the potential to experience a wonderful, growing, personal relationship with him. That relationship takes nothing away from our earthly marriages. In fact, it enhances them. When we become the bride of Christ, the joy and fulfillment of our relationship with him will be multiplied far beyond the best it can be now. Yet that multiplication will take nothing away from the relationships we have with our earthly marriage partners—nor will it detract from any other relationship.

The new creation is a place where none of us will ever need to say goodbye to anyone. We will all be together forever. But our desire for privacy will be taken care of as well. Given that we may possess something like the equivalent of two time dimensions, we would have a near infinite number of timelines for maintaining relationships. After we subtract 10 billion or so to accommodate all the people in the new creation, another hundred million plus for the angels,[32] billions more for whatever new creatures God may create, we will still have a near infinite number of timelines for solitary reflection, projects, hobbies, and pastimes *if* we were to want them.

While our human capacity will be vastly expanded in the new creation, we will not become God or gods. We will never become omnipresent, omniscient, or omnipotent. We will never gain the ability to create something from nothing. Nor will we necessarily gain a power advantage over angels. Our role as judges over them has more to do with direction and authority than with power.

Multiplication of God's Glory and Love

We human beings are created to give glory to God and to reflect his love. Our participation in God's plan to conquer evil totally and permanently fits into these purposes.[33] This is true, too, for developing a Christlike character. In the new creation we will be liberated and empowered to glorify God many times beyond what we can conceive of now. Having been delivered permanently from sin and suffering, we will be free to love as we have never loved before. Given the new capacities God will endow us with, we finally will know through direct experience just how magnificent his love is. We also will have the capacity to receive love from God and others many times beyond what we can conceive of now and to give love to God and others many times beyond what we can conceive of now.

Our ability to receive honor and love from God and to express this honor and love to others will enable us to join Christ in managing much of the new creation and to participate with God in the fulfillment of his plans beyond those we know.

All that has been revealed to us in Scripture concerning God's future plans extends just into his eighth day of creation. We know only the beginning of the future. If the beginning is so staggeringly magnificent, then the remainder of eternity with him will surely hold blessings that stretch still further beyond our ability to imagine. We can only stand in awe and anticipation of something we comprehend as ultimate goodness, and there find a purifying, perpetually motivating hope. Full satisfaction, happiness, and peace await us in our heavenly home.

Chapter 18

Invitation to Soar Higher Still

Extradimensionality and transdimensionality are simply new terms to describe truths that have been known for as long as God has been revealing himself to humanity. The beauty and benefit of these terms and the recent scientific discoveries undergirding them lies both in their affirmation of what Scripture has always proclaimed about God's transcendence and in their potential to help us explore and make sense of the Bible's transcendent teachings that are being challenged more intensely than ever by the so-called "rationalists" of our time.

This integration of science and theology will be welcomed by some and resisted or repudiated by others. It may be misconstrued by those who think any scientific application to biblical texts and doctrines compels us to walk by sight rather than by faith. Yet the opposite is the case. Many of our traditional approaches to discovering theological truths have suffered from the limitations of a four-dimensional, or "sight," perspective. Extra dimensions and transdimensionality cannot be seen and cannot reflect our human perspective because they exist beyond the physical cosmos. Scientists have found them not by seeing them but by discovering their importance for the universe's existence, attributes, and capability to support life. In other words, they have unwittingly rediscovered the necessity of a God whose characteristics happen to match the capacities needed to explain our existence.

The apostle Paul grasped transdimensional/extradimensional reality long ago, as did the prophet Isaiah, whom Paul quotes in these words to the Corinthian church:

> "What no eye has seen, what no ear has heard, and what no human mind has conceived"—the things God has prepared for those who love him—these are the things God has revealed to us by his Spirit.

> The Spirit searches all things, even the deep things of God. For who knows a person's thoughts except their own spirit within them? In the same way no one knows the thoughts of God except the Spirit of God. What we have received is not the spirit of the world, but the Spirit who is from God, so that we may understand what God has freely given us.[1]

Paul's inspired message expresses the apologetics theme of this book. These verses speak of eternal salvation and blessing, not just the future heaven, which God has prepared for us who love him. Our eyes cannot picture it, our ears cannot catch it on physical sound waves, our four-dimensional thinking could never have given birth to it—and yet God's Spirit has opened our hearts to receive it.

The faith to "see" God both in and beyond the extra dimensions from which our universe began comes not from ourselves, as Paul says, but from the Spirit of God. It is the Spirit who alone can reveal to us a transdimensional/extradimensional God and enable us to understand the extradimensional salvation offered by the Father, transacted by the Son, and imparted by the Holy Spirit.

The amazing discoveries in particle physics and astrophysics highlighted in the opening chapters of this book take none of the mystery away from "the deep things of God." If anything, they distinguish for the skeptics of our day the mysteriousness of divine truth from the imaginativeness of human fantasy. The discoveries indicating the existence of extra dimensions and a Causer beyond them simply attest that God's power and wisdom and all other capacities exceed ours by so many orders of magnitude that they bear little if any resemblance to human, four-dimensional thinking.

- What other God but the God revealed in the Bible promises to be nearer to each of us than we are to ourselves, lives beyond the reach of our physical senses and yet fully within the reach of the spiritual sense he placed within us?
- What other God but the God revealed in the Bible claims to have planned and initiated the physical universe from beyond (and independent of) all cosmic dimensions?
- What other God but the God revealed in the Bible can see and hear everything, including the words, thoughts, and prayers of every living being at every moment?
- What other God but the God revealed in the Bible has come personally

and tangibly, to affirm his existence, power, truth, and love through a human body, seeking no glory for self in that body but for God alone?

- What other God but the God revealed in the Bible claims to be simultaneously singular and plural—Father, Son, and Holy Spirit, not three gods but a triune deity of three Persons and one essence—and demonstrates his capacity to be such?

- What other God but the God revealed in Christ's body could take upon himself the penalty for humanity's waywardness and could wield the power to rise bodily from the dead?

- What other God but the God revealed in the Bible could accurately communicate through human authors the distinctive capacities of his created life-forms, from plants to animals to mammals and birds to humans, in terms that scientific research thousands of years later would prove accurate? And what mind could contrive such creatures as he calls angels, archangels, cherubim, and seraphim?

- What other God but the God revealed in the Bible shows total character consistency in all his messages to and dealings with humans?

- What other God but the God revealed in the Bible finds a way to give humans freedom of choice and yet works within that freedom to fulfill all his divine purposes and plans?

- What other God but the God revealed in the Bible could devise a way to secure our eternal destiny while retaining forever our freedom to choose or reject him?

- What other God but the God revealed in the Bible could design and administer a pass or fail "heart" test for each human being with the exact degree of difficulty and time allowance appropriate for his or her ability to respond? Who but God could simultaneously make full use of that test as preparation for our future career in his new creation?

- What other God but the God revealed in the Bible could find a way to express love toward those who hate him and who choose eternal separation from his authority and glory?

- What other God but the God revealed in the Bible promises his children an inheritance anything like the new creation Revelation describes; a place that makes Eden look paltry and pale by comparison; a place where we will find the perfection of love, joy, and wholeness for which we all have perpetually yearned?

- What other God but the God revealed in the Bible would provide for us, as Boaz provided for Ruth, not just the gleanings from the harvest of scientific and biblical truth, but "six measures of barley"—continually multiplying evidences of his intention to provide for all our faith needs in this increasingly irreverent, arrogant, self-destructing world?

The connections made in this book between scientific data (specifically about six extra dimensions and existence beyond all 10) and scientific methods (specifically the application of paradox resolution steps to traditionally divisive biblical doctrines) represent not a fixed set of conclusions and solutions, but rather a suggestion as to where we can begin a new chapter in our age-old pursuit of spiritual truth and understanding. God knows that our intellectual and technological advances have raised new questions and doubts about our ultimate origin, ultimate destination, and thus our ultimate purpose and responsibility. The pace, complexity, and instability of modern life has crowded and clouded our thinking so that we need extra help in "holding onto that which is good" and holding onto childlike trust in him and his Word.

God invites us to make good use of the new discoveries about extra dimensions (among other aspects of his creative work) for building that trust and for breaking through barriers that hamper our relationships with him, with each other, and with those outside the faith. We can run away from these findings and maintain our current course, or we can embrace them and find fresh vitality in our study and exposition of Scripture. The current course seems a path of growing rigidity, damaging division, or wishy-washiness. The push to separate issues of fact from issues of faith is strong and gaining momentum among those who seem to fear truth more than to love it. But the potential for healing and reconciliation, revitalized faith and zeal for outreach, lies in this new direction God has opened to us.

These discoveries about extradimensionality bear the potential to boost Christians' awareness of the extent of power God has made available to us. As Jesus declared, if we know the resources God has made available to us, we can accomplish great things, the great things he has planned before cosmic time for us to do.[2] Imagine what would happen in this world if we Christians were to vastly enlarge our vision of God's capacity to empower us, protect us, use us in fulfilling his plans and purposes, and reward us!

Such a vision would change us. Our appreciation for his Word would change. Our thoughts would change. Our prayer and worship would change. Our relationships would change. Our effectiveness in reaching the world's nonbelievers would change. The results would be dramatic on all fronts. Perhaps this is part of how Christ's prayer will be answered, that they "may be brought to complete unity. Then the world will know that you sent me and have loved them even as you have loved me."[3]

The end of this book is in fact a beginning point. God will continue to give us his light to understand truth as we continue to pursue understanding together, as we live and serve together as children of the light. We can rejoice even now that he is preparing us for life in the full light of his glory—sunglasses no longer needed.

Evidence for Strings

Observational and experimental evidences for the existence and operation of strings throughout the physical universe come from the following six areas of research:

1. Observation of partial force unification: Particle accelerator experiments prove that two of the four forces of physics, the weak nuclear force and electromagnetism, are indeed unifiable. These kinds of experiments also give at least partial evidence that the strong nuclear force is unifiable with these other two. A good example is the discovery of all six quarks predicted by the string theory with each of the different quarks at the expected respective masses. Within the next several years, one or both of the world's two largest particle accelerators (the Large Hadron Collider and Fermilab) should detect another of the predicted unification particles, namely, the Higgs boson.

To date we have no experimental evidence to show that gravity is unifiable with the other three forces. However, that situation could soon change. Currently operational gravity wave telescopes hold the potential to affirm at least part of this theory through the direct detection of gravity waves. Similarly, the Planck satellite will measure the polarization in the temperature fluctuations of the cosmic microwave background radiation (the radiation left over from the cosmic creation event) to such a high level of precision that astronomers anticipate being able to discern from the data the means by which gravity waves propagate throughout the universe.

2. Discovery of both **fermions** *and* **bosons:** Particle accelerators provided proof for the existence of quarks and leptons, particles predicted by supersymmetry theory. Supersymmetry also predicts that for every fundamental particle of matter known as a *fermion,* a wavelike particle known as a *boson* must exist. These bosons mediate the fundamental forces of physics. While particle accelerator experiments have detected fermions and bosons in abundance, none has yet detected a matched fermion-boson pair, which supersymmetry calls for. But we know why such a detection has not been made: experiments to date have lacked the power necessary to find a matched pair. The Large Hadron Collider (particle accelerator) possesses the power to make such a discovery, perhaps within the near future.[1]

3. *Prediction of relativity:* Arguably the strongest evidence comes from testing the relativity theory. In order to be viable, string theory must yield the theories of both special and general relativity exactly as Einstein formulated them. If physicists had been able to discover string theory before they knew anything at all about relativity, both special and general relativity theory would have emerged easily and straightforwardly from the analysis of strings. Strings cannot move self-consistently throughout space and time unless relativity is operating. Thus, the experimental proofs that affirm special and general relativity simultaneously serve as evidence for the validity of string theory.

Such proof has become more than adequate; it is staggering. Observations on the double pulsar binary PKS J0737-3039 affirmed general relativity to better than a ten-trillionth of a percent precision, as already noted. And even stronger evidence exists for special relativity. It has been affirmed to a precision of better than a ten-millionth of a trillionth percent.[2]

Because relativity is solidly established, so are the many components of string theory, including the 10 space-time dimensions, linked with relativity.

4. *Reconciliation of quantum mechanics and gravity:* Additional confirmation comes from the unique role string theory plays in solving major mysteries of physics. String theory is a quantum theory that demands the operation of gravity. It is the only theory that permits quantum mechanics and gravity to coexist. It is the only theory that self-consistently explains all the known properties of the known fundamental particles (now numbering 58), as well as all the properties and principles of quantum mechanics, all the properties and principles of both special and general relativity, the operation of all four forces of physics, and all the known details of the creation event.

5. *Solution of the black hole entropy-information problem:* Thanks to sci-fi movies and TV shows, everybody knows that black holes are objects so massive and so compressed that their gravity sucks in anything that comes near. This "anything" includes not only matter, light, and other forms of energy but also entropy and information. However, all viable physics theories, including the 10-dimensional creation theory we have been discussing, rule out the possibility of infinite "sinks." In other words, matter, energy, entropy, and information cannot be infinitely compressed until they permanently vanish.

These things cannot be utterly destroyed or lost. They can only be transported or rearranged.

Stephen Hawking suggested a solution to this problem 20 years ago, but it fell short on one crucial point. Hawking showed how a black hole that has shrunk to quantum dimensions (dimensions below a picometer, or 10^{-12} meters) could turn "white" (radiating rather than sucking in everything).[3] He drew upon theoretically derived, experimentally verified "virtual particle pairs." These particle pairs apparently arise from quantum fluctuations in the space-time fabric of the universe. They are called "virtual" particle pairs because they are so extremely short-lived (lasting less than a picosecond) that they fade out of existence (reverting back to their space-time origin) before a human observer can directly detect them. However, just beyond the event horizon of a black hole (the distance inside which nothing can escape the black hole), the black hole's gravity is powerful enough to split apart a virtual particle pair, converting one of the virtual particles into a single real particle that zooms off into space. Accordingly, once a black hole shrinks enough, it begins to radiate (or "lose") matter and energy.

Hawking and his team could not explain, however, what happens to the entropy and information sucked into a black hole. On this point the solution stumbled. And on this point, the 10-dimensional origin theory came through with an answer.

As an unexpected bonus, Cumrun Vafa and Andrew Strominger's calculations solved the mystery of what happens to the information sucked into an extremal black hole.[4] While some information is retained along the event horizon, much more is hidden along the multiple dimensions—six, in this case. Taking the investigation further, two physicists from the University of Pennsylvania showed that these six dimensions also set up two event horizons around quantum-sized black holes, an outer event horizon and a shrouded inner horizon.[5] The entropy, they determined, is distributed along both horizons.

In other words, information and entropy are retained as a black hole shrinks to an extremely small volume. Although hidden temporarily, information and entropy eventually escape along with the ejected ("real") particles when the virtual particles split in two.

6. Observations of the spin rate of black holes: The 10-D creation theory predicts that as black holes shrink, they should spin up at a certain rate. Three astronomers from MIT and NASA found a way to measure, indirectly, the spin rate of small black holes (those no more massive than a few times the Sun's mass) that have stellar companions.[6] Using telescopes on four different satellites, the team derived the data to calculate that each black hole they observed is spinning at the extremely rapid rate predicted by the theory. One black hole, GRO J1655S-40, was seen to spin at 100,000 times per second!

Notes

Chapter 1: Invitation to Soar
1. 2 Timothy 2:13.
2. Mark 9:24.

Chapter 2: Takeoff from Ground Zero
1. Joseph Silk, *The Big Bang*, rev. and updated ed. (New York: W. H. Freeman, 1989), 90–96, 165.

Chapter 3: Physics Breaks through to New Realms
1. Hugh Ross, *The Fingerprint of God*, commemorative ed. (Covina, CA: RTB Press, 2010), 33–38.
2. Hugh Ross, *The Creator and the Cosmos*, 3rd ed. (Colorado Springs: NavPress, 2001), 31–67.
3. Hugh Ross, "News Report Hypes Cosmic Age Controversy," *Facts & Faith*, Quarter 4 1994, 1–2; Hugh Ross, "Hubble Constant Conflict Update," *Facts & Faith*, Quarter 1 1995, 3–4.
4. J. C. Mather et al., "Measurement of the Cosmic Microwave Background Spectrum by the COBE FIRAS Instrument," *Astrophysical Journal* 420 (January 1994): 439–44, doi:10.1086/173574; S. Hancock et al., "Direct Observation of Structure in the Cosmic Microwave Background," *Nature* 367 (January 1994): 333–38, doi:10.1038/367333a0; A. C. Clapp et al., "Measurements of Anisotropy in the Cosmic Microwave Background Radiation at Degree Angular Scales Near the Stars Sigma Hercules and Iota Draconis," *Astrophysical Journal Letters* 433 (October 1994): L57–L60, doi:10.1086/187547; A. Songaila et al., "Measurement of the Microwave Background Temperature at a Redshift of 1.776," *Nature* 371 (September 1994): 43–45, doi:10.1038/371043a0; David M. Meyer,

"A Distant Space Thermometer," *Nature* 371 (September 1994): 13, doi:10.1038/371013a0.

5. A. Vibert Douglas, "Forty Minutes with Einstein," *Journal of the Royal Astronomical Society of Canada* 50 (June 1956): 100.

6. Lincoln Barnett, *The Universe and Dr. Einstein* (New York: William Morrow, 1948), 106.

7. Arthur S. Eddington, "The End of the World: From the Standpoint of Mathematical Physics," *Nature* 127 (March 1931): 450, doi:10.1038/127447a0; Arthur S. Eddington, "On the Instability of Einstein's Spherical World," *Monthly Notices of the Royal Astronomical Society* 90 (May 1930): 672; Hermann Bondi, *Cosmology*, 2nd ed. (Cambridge: Cambridge University Press, 1960), 140; Fred Hoyle, "A New Model for the Expanding Universe," *Monthly Notices of the Royal Astronomical Society* 108 (August 1948): 372, doi:10.1093/mnras/108.5.372; Fred Hoyle, *The Nature of the Universe*, 2nd ed. (Oxford, UK: Basil Blackwell, 1952), 109, 111; R. H. Dicke et al., "Cosmic Black-Body Radiation," *Astrophysical Journal* 142 (July 1965): 415, doi:10.1086/148306.

8. Richard C. Tolman and Morgan Ward, "On the Behavior of Non-Static Models of the Universe When the Cosmological Term Is Omitted," *Physical Review* 39 (March 1932): 835, doi:10.1103/PhysRev.39.835.

9. John D. Barrow and Joseph Silk, *The Left Hand of Creation: The Origin and Evolution of the Expanding Universe* (New York: Basic Books, 1983), 32.

10. Roger Penrose, "An Analysis of the Structure of Spacetime," Adams Prize Essay, Cambridge University, 1966; Stephen W. Hawking, "Singularities and the Geometry of Space-time," Adams Prize Essay, Cambridge University, 1966; Stephen W. Hawking and George F. R. Ellis, "The Cosmic Black-Body Radiation and the Existence of Singularities in Our Universe," *Astrophysical Journal* 152 (April 1968): 25–36, doi:10.1086/149520; Stephen W. Hawking and Roger Penrose, "The Singularities of Gravitational Collapse and Cosmology," *Proceedings of the Royal Society of London A* 314 (January 1970): 529–48, doi:10.1098/rspa.1970.0021.

11. Steven Weinberg, *Gravitation and Cosmology: Principles and Applications of the General Theory of Relativity* (New York: Wiley and Sons, 1972), 198; Irwin I. Shapiro et al., "Mercury's Perihelion Advance: Determination by Radar," *Physical Review Letters* 28 (June 1972): 1594–97, doi:10.1103/PhysRevLett.28.1594; R. V. Pound and J. L. Snider, "Effect of

Gravity on Nuclear Resonance," *Physical Review Letters* 13 (November 1964): 539–40, doi:10.1103/PhysRevLett.13.539.

12.   C. Brans and R. H. Dicke, "Mach's Principle and a Relativistic Theory of Gravitation," *Physical Review* 124 (November 1961): 925–35, doi:10.1103/PhysRev.124.925.

13.   R. F. C. Vessot et al., "Test of Relativistic Gravitation with a Space-Borne Hydrogen Maser," *Physical Review Letters* 45 (December 1980): 2081–84, doi:10.1103/PhysRevLett.45.2081.

14.   J. W. Moffat, "Consequences of a New Experimental Determination of the Quadrupole Moment of the Sun for Gravitation Theory," *Physical Review Letters* 50 (March 1983): 709–12, doi:10.1103/PhysRevLett.50.709.

15.   J. H. Taylor et al., "Experimental Constraints on Strong-Field Relativistic Gravity," *Nature* 355 (January 1992): 132–36, doi:10.1038/355132a0; Roger Penrose, *Shadows of the Mind: A Search for the Missing Science of Consciousness* (New York: Oxford University Press, 1994), 229–31.

16.   Penrose, *Shadows of the Mind*, 230.

17.   M. Burgay et al., "An Increased Estimate of the Merger Rate of Double Neutron Stars from Observations of a Highly Relativistic System," *Nature* 426 (December 2003): 531–33.

18.   A. G. Lyne, "A Review of the Double Pulsar—PSR J0737–3039," *Chinese Journal of Astronomy and Astrophysics* 6 (December 2006): 162–68, doi:10.1088/1009-9271/6/S2/30.

19.   I. H. Stairs, "Binary Pulsars and Tests of General Relativity," *Relativity in Fundamental Astronomy* 261 (January 2010): 218–27, doi:10.1017/S1743921309990433.

20.   Nicolas Yunès and David N. Spergel, "Double Binary Pulsar Test of Dynamical Chern-Simons Modified Gravity," *Physical Review D* 80 (August 2009): 042004, doi:10.1103/PhysRevD.80.042004.

21.   J. P. Moreland, "A Philosophical Examination of Hugh Ross' Natural Theology," *Philosophia Christi* 21 (Summer 1998): 33–39.

22.   Ross, *Fingerprint of God*, 35–37; Ross, *Creator and the Cosmos*, 102–7.

23.   Stephen Battersby, "Extragalactic Astronomy: A Ring in Truth," *Nature* 392 (April 1998): 548, doi:10.1038/33281.

24.   Andrew Watson, "Einstein's Theory Rings True," *Science* 280 (April 1998): 205, doi:10.1126/science.280.5361.205.

25.   Ignazio Ciufolini et al., "Test of General Relativity and Measurement of the Lense-Thirring Effect with Two Earth Satellites," *Science* 279 (March

1998): 2100–2103, doi:10.1126/science.279.5359.2100.

26. Ciufolini et al., "Test of General Relativity," 2102; Lorenzo Iorio, "An Assessment of the Systematic Uncertainty in Present and Future Tests of the Lense-Thirring Effect with Satellite Laser Ranging," *Space Science Reviews* 148 (December 2009): 363–81, doi:10.1007/s11214-008-9478-1; Lorenzo Iorio, "Conservative Evaluation of the Uncertainty in the LAGEOS-LAGEOS II Lense-Thirring Test," *Central European Journal of Physics* 8 (February 2010): 25–32, doi:10.24/s11534-009-0060-6.

27. Robert Kahn et al., compilers, "The Gravity Probe B Experiment: Science Results—NASA Final Report," *Gravity Probe B*, December 2008, http://einstein.stanford.edu/content/final_report/GPB_Final_NASA_Report-020509-web.pdf.

28. A. Merloni et al., "On Gravitomagnetic Precession around Black Holes," *Monthly Notices of the Royal Astronomical Society* 304 (March 1999): 155–59, doi:10.1046/j.1365-8711.1999.02307.x. The public announcement was made two years earlier at a meeting of the American Astronomical Society. See Ron Cowen, "Einstein's General Relativity: It's a Drag," *Science News* 152 (November 1997): 308.

29. Eric C. Ford and Michiel van der Klis, "Strong Correlation between Noise Features at Low Frequency and the Kilohertz Quasi-Periodic Oscillations in the X-Ray Binary 4U 1728–34," *Astrophysical Journal Letters* 506 (September 1998): L39–L42, doi:10.1086/311638.

30. Adam Ingram, Chris Done, and P. Chris Fragile, "Low-Frequency Quasi-Periodic Oscillations Spectra and Lense-Thirring Precession," *Monthly Notices of the Royal Astronomical Society Letters* 397 (July 2009): L101–L105, doi:10.1111/j.1745-3933.2009.00693.x; B. Aschenbach, "Evidence for GR Rotational Frame-Dragging in the Light from the Sgr A* Supermassive Black Hole," *Journal of the Italian Astronomical Society* (November 2009): arXiv:0911.2431, http://arxiv.org/pdf/0911.2431v1.pdf; John F. C. Wardle et al., "The Ultra-Fast Quasar PKS 1510-089: Direct Evidence for a Changing Orientation of the Central Engine," *Future Directions in High Resolution Astronomy* 340 (2005): 67, adsabs.harvard.edu/full/2005ASPC..340...67W.

31. Arvind Borde and Alexander Vilenkin, "Eternal Inflation and the Initial Singularity," *Physical Review Letters* 72 (May 1994): 3305–8, doi:10.1103/PhysRevLett.72.3305; Arvind Borde, "Open and Closed Universes, Initial Singularities and Inflation," *Physical Review D* 50 (September 1994): 3692–702, doi:10.1103/PhysRevD.50.3692; Arvind Borde and Alex-

ander Vilenkin, "Singularities in Inflationary Cosmology: A Review," *International Journal of Modern Physics D* 5 (December 1996): 813–24, doi:10.1142/S0218271896000497; Arvind Borde and Alexander Vilenkin, "Violation of the Weak Energy Condition in Inflating Spacetimes," *Physical Review D* 56 (July 1997): 717–23, doi:10.1103/PhysRevD.56.717.

32. Arvind Borde, Alan H. Guth, and Alexander Vilenkin, "Inflationary Spacetimes Are Incomplete in Past Directions," *Physical Review Letters* 90 (April 2003): 151031, doi:10.1103/PhysRevLett.90.151301.

33. Alexander Vilenkin, Many Worlds in One (New York: Hill & Wang, 2006): 176.

34. William Lane Craig, "Hugh Ross's Extradimensional Deity: A Review Article," *Journal of the Evangelical Theological Society* 42 (June 1999): 293–304.

35. Simon van der Meer, "Stochastic Damping of Betatron Oscillations in the ISR," *CERN/ISR-PO/72-31* (August 1972): 1–8; G. Arnison et al., "Experimental Observation of Isolated Large Transverse Energy Electrons with Associated Missing Energy at s=540 GeV," *Physics Letters B* 122 (February 1983): 103–16, doi:10.1016/0370-2693(83)91177-2; M. Banner et al., "Observation of Single Isolated Electrons of High Transverse Momentum in Events with Missing Transverse Energy at the CERN pp Collider," *Physics Letters B* 122 (March 1983): 476–85, doi:10.1016/0370-2693(83)91605-2; G. Arnison et al., "Experimental Observation of Lepton Pairs of Invariant Mass around 95 GeV/$c2$ at the CERN SPS Collider," *Physics Letters B* 126 (July 1983): 398–410, doi:10.1016/0370-2693(83)90188-0.

36. F. Abe et al., "Evidence for Top Quark Production in $\bar{p}\,p$ Collisions at $\sqrt{s}$=1.8 TeV," *Nuclear Physics B* 39 (March 1995): 343–47, doi:10.1016/0920-5632(95)00098-T; F. Abe et al., "Identification of Top Quarks Using Kinematic Variables," *Physical Review D* 52 (September 1995): R2605–R2609, doi:10.1103/PhysRevD.52.R2605.

37. Ross, *Creator and the Cosmos*, 43–44, 151–54; Hugh Ross, "Big Bang Model Refined by Fire," in *Mere Creation*, ed. William Dembski (Downers Grove, IL: InterVarsity, 1998), 363–84.

38. K. C. Cole, "2 Physicists Simplify Study of Four-Dimensional Space," *Los Angeles Times*, November 29, 1994, A1, A29; K. Intriligator, R. G. Leigh, and N. Seiberg, "Exact Superpotentials in Four Dimensions," *Physical Review D* 50 (July 1994): 1092–104, doi:10.1103/Phys.RevD.50.1092.

39. Gary Taubes, "How Black Holes May Get String Theory Out of a Bind,"

Science 268 (June 1995): 1699, doi:10.1126/science.268.5218.1699.

40. Ibid.

41. Ibid.; Gary Taubes, "A Theory of Everything Takes Shape," *Science* 269 (September 1995): 1513, doi:10.1126/science.269.5230.1511; Edward Witten, "The Holes Are Defined by the String," *Nature* 383 (September 19, 1996): 215–16, doi:10.1038/383215a0; Andrew Strominger and Cumrun Vafa, "Microscopic Origin of the Bekenstein-Hawking Entropy," *Physics Letters B* 379 (June 1996): 99–104, doi:10.1016/0370-2693(96)00345-0; Juan M. Maldacena and Andrew Strominger, "Statistical Entropy of Four-Dimensional Extremal Black Holes," *Physical Review Letters* 77 (July 1996): 428–29, doi:10.1103/PhysRevLett.77.428.

42. J. C. Breckenridge et al., "Macroscopic and Microscopic Entropy of Near-Extremal Spinning Black Holes," *Physics Letters B* 381 (July 1996): 423–26, doi:10.1016/0370-2693(96)00553-9; Finn Larsen and Frank Wilezek, "Classical Hair in String Theory II. Explicit Calculations," *Nuclear Physics B* 488 (March 1977): 261–81, doi:10.1016/S0550-3213(96)00700-6; Joseph Polchinski, "Dirichlet Branes and Ramond-Ramond Charges," *Physical Review Letters* 75 (December 1995): 4724–27, doi:10.1103/PhysRevLett.75.4724; Curtis G. Callan Jr. and Juan M. Maldacena, "D-Brane Approach to Black Hole Quantum Mechanics," *Nuclear Physics B* 472 (July 1996): 591–608, doi:10.1016/0550-3213(96)00225-8; Witten, "Holes Are Defined," 216.

43. Yunès and Spergel, "Double Binary Pulsar Test."

44. Ross, *Creator and the Cosmos*, 145–99.

Chapter 4: Science's Tethers

1. Paul Davies, *God and the New Physics* (New York: Simon & Schuster, 1983), vii–8. In Paul Davies' newest and most exhaustive treatment of this subject, he alters his original position to the belief that the complete mind of God is possibly, not probably, within man's grasp. See Paul Davies, *The Mind of God* (New York: Simon & Schuster, 1992), 14–15; Stephen W. Hawking, *A Brief History of Time* (New York: Bantam, 1988), 155–75; Frank J. Tipler, *The Physics of Immortality: Modern Cosmology, God, and the Resurrection of the Dead* (New York: Doubleday, 1994), 2–10.

2. Hugh Ross, *The Fingerprint of God*, commemorative ed. (Covina, CA: RTB Press, 2010), 32–34.

3. Joseph Silk, *The Big Bang*, rev. and updated ed. (New York: W. H.

Freeman, 1989), 90–96, 165.

4.   Edward Harrison, *Masks of the Universe: Changing Ideas on the Nature of the Cosmos* (New York: Collier, 1985), 178–84.

5.   Robert M. Eisberg, *Fundamentals of Modern Physics* (New York: Wiley & Sons, 1961), 146–62, 468–72, 662–64, 695–703.

6.   G. F. R. Ellis, "The Anthropic Principle: Laws and Environments," in *The Anthropic Principle,* ed. F. Bertola and U. Curi (Cambridge: Cambridge University Press, 1993), 30; D. Allan Bromley, "Physics," *Science* 209 (July 1980): 116, doi:10.1126/science.209.4452.110.

7.   Silk, *Big Bang,* 119–24.

8.   Timothy Ferris, "Science and Genesis," in *Cosmic Beginnings and Human Ends: Where Science and Religion Meet,* ed. Clifford N. Matthews and Roy Abraham Varghese (Chicago: Open Court, 1995), 38–39; Edward W. Kolb, "The Big Bang Origin of the Universe," in *Cosmic Beginnings and Human Ends,* 72–74.

9.   Psalm 19:1–4.

10.   Deuteronomy 29:29.

Chapter 5: Extra Dimensions in the Bible

1.   R. Laird Harris, Gleason L. Archer Jr., and Bruce K. Waltke, *Theological Wordbook of the Old Testament* (Chicago: Moody Press, 1980), 1:74–75, 2:935; Bruce K. Waltke, *Creation and Chaos: An Exegetical and Theological Study of Biblical Cosmogony* (Portland: Western Conservative Baptist Seminary, 1974), 20, 25–26.

2.   Harris, Archer, and Waltke, *Theological Wordbook,* 1:127.

3.   Hebrews 11:3.

4.   2 Timothy 1:9.

5.   Titus 1:2.

6.   Proverbs 8:22–23.

7.   John 17:5, 24.

8.   Ephesians 1:4.

9.   1 Peter 1:20.

10.   Harris, Archer, and Waltke, *Theological Wordbook,* 1:74–84; *The New International Dictionary of New Testament Theology,* ed. Colin Brown (Grand Rapids: Zondervan, 1975), 1:524.

11.   John 1:3.

12.   Colossians 1:16–17.

13.   Orville J. Nave, *Nave's Topical Bible* (Chicago: Moody Press, 1974),

434–38.

14. Psalm 90:4.

15. Justin Martyr, "Dialogue With Trypho, a Jew," chapter LXXXI, vol. 1, *The Ante-Nicene Fathers*, ed. Rev. Alexander Roberts and James Donaldson, American ed. (reprint, Grand Rapids, Eerdsmans: 1985), 239–40; Irenaeus, "Against Heresies," book V, chapter XXIII, section 2, in vol. 1, *Ante-Nicene Fathers*, 551–52; Lactantius, "The Divine Institutes," book VII, chapter XIV, in vol. 7, *Ante-Nicene Fathers*, 211–12; Victorinus, "On the Creation of the World," in vol. 7, *Ante-Nicene Fathers*, 341–43; Methodius, "Fragments: Extracts from the Work on Things Created," chapter IX, in vol. 6, *Ante-Nicene Fathers*, 381.

16. 2 Peter 3:8.

17. John 20:19

18. Luke 24:37–43.

19. Luke 24:39–40; 1 John 1:1.

20. Luke 24:42–43; John 21:7–15.

21. Isaiah 37:21–38.

22. 2 Kings 2:1–18.

23. Acts 8:26–40.

24. Luke 9:28–36.

25. Isaiah 38:7–8; 39:1.

26. Hugh Ross, *A Matter of Days: Resolving a Creation Controversy*, 2nd ed. (Covina, CA: RTB Press, 2015), 139–48; Ross, "Fulfilled Prophecy: Evidence for the Reliability of the Bible," *Reasons to Believe*, August 22, 2003, http://www.reasons.org/fulfilled-prophecy-evidence-reliability-bible.

27. Philippians 2:5–11.

Chapter 6: Extradimensional Doctrines

1. J. I. Packer, *Knowing God* (Downers Grove, IL: InterVarsity, 1993), 222–23.

2. Norman Geisler and Thomas Howe, *When Critics Ask: A Popular Handbook on Bible Difficulties* (Wheaton, IL: Victor, 1992); Gleason L. Archer, *Encyclopedia of Bible Difficulties* (Grand Rapids: Zondervan, 1982).

3. John 7–9.

4. Packer, *Knowing God*, 222–23.

5. Hugh Ross, *The Fingerprint of God*, commemorative ed. (Covina, CA: RTB Press, 2010), 33.

Chapter 7: God and Extra Time Dimensions

1. Psalm 139:17–18.
2. Plato, *Parmenides*, 140d–141e; Plato, *Timaeus*, 36e–39e.
3. Aurelius Augustinus, *Saint Augustine, The City of God*, books VIII–XVI, trans. Gerald G. Walsh and Grace Monahan (New York: Fathers of the Church, 1952), 11.5–6, 193–96.
4. Thomas Aquinas, *Summa Theologica* (New York: McGraw-Hill, 1964), Prima Pars 2, Existence and Nature of God, Question 10, The Eternity of God, 2:135–55.

Chapter 8: Extradimensionality and God's Proximity

1. Genesis 16:13.
2. Genesis 28:16.
3. 1 Chronicles 28:9.
4. 2 Chronicles 6:30.
5. Job 23:10.
6. Job 24:23.
7. Job 31:4.
8. Job 34:21–23, 25.
9. Psalm 33:13–15.
10. Psalm 34:18.
11. Psalm 44:21.
12. Psalm 94:11.
13. Psalm 119:151, 168.
14. Psalm 139:1–4, 7–10.
15. Psalm 145:18.
16. Proverbs 5:21.
17. Jeremiah 23:24.
18. Jeremiah 32:19.
19. Matthew 10:30–31.
20. Matthew 28:20.
21. Acts 17:27.
22. Hebrews 13:5.
23. John 4:24.
24. Genesis 28:16.
25. Exodus 33:20.
26. Job 9:11.
27. Job 23:8–9.

28. Job 37:23.
29. Isaiah 45:15.
30. 1 Timothy 1:15–16a.
31. 1 Timothy 6:16a.
32. John 1:18.
33. John 5:37.
34. John 6:46.
35. John 13:33.
36. John 13:36.
37. John 13:37.
38. Since the payment for Peter's sins against God and others had not yet been paid and Jesus had not yet been raised from the dead, the Holy Spirit could not yet permanently indwell Peter. Peter himself explains this in 1 Peter 3:21.
39. John 14:2–3.
40. John 16:6–7.
41. John 16:20–22.
42. John 20:19; 21:1–22; Acts 1:6–12.
43. The Hebrew words conveying faith in the Old Testament are *'ĕmûnâ* and *'ĕmet,* whereas the Greek word used for faith in the New Testament is *pistis. 'Ĕmûnâ, 'ĕmet,* and *pistis* all basically mean acting upon what one has established to be true and trustworthy. *Evangelical Dictionary of Theology,* ed. Walter A. Elwell (Grand Rapids: Baker, 1984), s.v. "faith," by J. I. Packer; R. Laird Harris, Gleason L. Archer Jr., and Bruce K. Waltke, *Theological Wordbook of the Old Testament* (Chicago: Moody, 1980), 1:52–53; W. E. Vine, *An Expository Dictionary of New Testament Words* (Old Tappan, NJ: Revell, 1940), 2:71.
44. 1 Chronicles 28:9.
45. James 4:8.
46. Psalm 145:18.
47. Psalm 34:18.
48. Isaiah 57:15.
49. Hebrews 11:6.
50. 1 Corinthians 15:50.
51. 1 Corinthians 15:52–53.
52. 1 Corinthians 15:42–44.
53. 1 John 3:2.

Chapter 9: Extradimensionality and God's Triunity

1. James Montgomery Boice, *The Sovereign God*, vol. 1 of *Foundations of the Christian Faith* (Downers Grove, IL: InterVarsity, 1978), 147.
2. Genesis 1:26.
3. Genesis 1:27.
4. Genesis 3:22–24; 11:7–8; Isaiah 6:8.
5. R. Laird Harris, Gleason L. Archer, and Bruce K. Waltke, *Theological Wordbook of the Old Testament* (Chicago: Moody, 1980), 1:44–45.
6. Ibid.; G. T. Manley, *The New Bible Dictionary*, ed. J. D. Douglas et al. (Grand Rapids: Eerdmans, 1962), "Names of God."
7. Isaiah 43:11–12; 45:21–22; Hosea 13:4.
8. Isaiah 44:24; 45:18; Colossians 1:16–17; Revelation 4:9–11.
9. Job 19:25; Isaiah 47:4; 49:6–7, 26; 54:5; 59:15–20.
10. Acts 1:22; 2:24, 31; 4:33; 17:31–32; Romans 1:4; 6:5; Philippians 3:10; 1 Peter 1:3; 3:21.
11. Isaiah 63:16; Romans 8:11–15; 2 Thessalonians 2:13; 1 Timothy 1:1; 2 Timothy 1:10; Titus 1:4.
12. Genesis 1:2; Job 33:4; John 1:3; Colossians 1:13–17; James 1:17–18.
13. Matthew 28:6–7; John 2:19–21; 10:17–18; Acts 2:32; Romans 1:4; 6:4; 8:11; Galatians 1:1.
14. Jeremiah 23:5–6.
15. Matthew 28:19.
16. Boice, *Sovereign God*, 141–42.
17. *The International Standard Bible Encyclopedia*, ed. James Orr (Grand Rapids: Eerdmans, 1983), s.v. "Trinity," by Benjamin B. Warfield.
18. Christ Reformed Church, *Ecumenical Creeds and Reformed Confessions* (Grand Rapids: CRC Publications, 1987), 8.
19. Leif Grane, *The Augsburg Confession: A Commentary* (Minneapolis: Augsburg Publishing, 1987), 31–32.
20. John Macpherson, *The Westminster Confession of Faith* (Edinburgh, UK: T. & T. Clark, 1881), 44.
21. C. G. M'Crie, *The Confessions of the Church of Scotland: Their Evolution in History* (Edinburgh, UK: MacNiven & Wallace, 1907), 36–63; Egbert Watson Smith, *The Creed of Presbyterians*, rev. and enlarged ed. (Richmond, VA: John Knox, 1941), 29.
22. Boice, *Sovereign God*, 142–45.
23. Ibid., 141.
24. Charles C. Ryrie, *A Survey of Bible Doctrine* (Chicago: Moody, 1972), 33.

25. *Evangelical Dictionary of Theology*, ed. Walter A. Elwell (Grand Rapids: Baker, 1984), s.v. "Trinity," by Geoffrey W. Bromiley, 1112.

26. Ibid., 1112–13.

27. *New Bible Dictionary*, 2nd ed., ed. J. D. Douglas et al. (Wheaton: Tyndale, 1982), s.v. "Trinity," by R. A. Finlayson, 1222–23.

28. Ibid., 1223.

29. Matthew 4:1–11; Luke 4:1–13.

30. Matthew 26:39, 42, 44.

31. Mark 14:33–34; Luke 22:44.

32. John 17:11, 21–22.

33. John 17:23.

34. Ephesians 3:18–19.

Chapter 10: Extradimensionality, the Incarnation, and the Atonement

1. See Hebrews 2:14–18; 4:15.

2. Matthew 11:27; 12:28; 22:41–46; 28:18–20; Luke 10:22; John 5:17–23; 6:27; 8:58; 10:17–18, 30–39; 14:6–11, 16–26; 15:26; 16:7–15; 17:1–11, 21–24; 20:27–29; Of the nine miracles John describes in any detail in his Gospel, all nine are miracles beyond what any prophet had ever performed and all nine were miracles that contemporary rabbis declared could be performed only by God himself.

3. Hebrews 2:14; 4:15.

4. Matthew 1:18–25; Luke 1:30–35.

5. Matthew 4:1–3.

6. Mark 4:39.

7. Hebrews 2:14.

8. Hebrews 2:17.

9. Hebrews 4:15.

10. Hebrews 4:15; John 8:46; 1 John 3:5.

11. Romans 3:9–20.

12. Ephesians 2:8–9.

13. Luke 14:25–33.

14. John 3:16.

15. Romans 5:12–19.

16. Genesis 3:7–24.

17. Hebrews 1:3–14.

18. 2 Corinthians 5:21.

19. Matthew 12:39–40; Fred R. Coulter, *A Harmony of the Gospels in Modern*

English: The Life of Jesus Christ (Los Angeles: York Publishing, 1974), 231–47.

20. John 16:8–11.
21. Romans 1:18–23.
22. Ecclesiastes 3:11.
23. Romans 8:29; 9:10–13; Ephesians 1:4–14.
24. Romans 5:6.
25. Hebrews 2:9.
26. 1 John 2:1–2.
27. Mark 15:25, 34–39.
28. Alex Metherell and Hugh Ross, *Behold the Man*, video documentary (Pasadena, CA: Reasons to Believe, 1995).
29. Hebrews 9:11.
30. Hebrews 9:24–25, 28.
31. Hebrews 9:11–18.
32. Hebrews 2:3.
33. Psalm 50:10.
34. John 20:24–29; 1 John 1:1.

Chapter 11: Dimensional Capacities of Created Beings

1. Revelation 12:4.
2. Carl Wieland, "Is Cruelty Normal?" *Creation*, vol. 16, no. 3, 1994, 19–21; Kenneth Ham, "Adam and Ants," *Back to Genesis*, no. 33, September 1991, a; James S. Stambaugh, "Death before Sin?" *Impact*, no. 191, May 1989, ii.
3. Job 14:8a–9a, 10a.
4. Psalm 37:2.
5. R. Laird Harris, Gleason L. Archer, and Bruce K. Waltke, *Theological Wordbook of the Old Testament* (Chicago: Moody Press, 1980), 1:496–497.
6. Matthew 21:18–22.
7. Mark 4:35–41.
8. Exodus 7:18.
9. Exodus 7:21.
10. Exodus 8:13.
11. Proverbs 30:25.
12. Ecclesiastes 10:1.
13. Harris, Archer, and Waltke, *Theological* Wordbook, 2:587–91.

14. Ibid., 2:701.
15. Ibid., 1:127.
16. *The New International Dictionary of New Testament Theology*, ed. Colin Brown (Grand Rapids: Zondervan, 1978), 3:689.
17. Numbers 22:21–34.
18. Psalm 104:27–28.
19. Luke 14:5.
20. Matthew 10:29.
21. Job 12:7.
22. Job 40:6–14.
23. Harris, Archer, and Waltke, *Theological Wordbook*, 10.
24. Roger Penrose, *Shadows of the Mind: A Search for the Missing Science of Consciousness* (New York: Oxford University Press, 1994); Michael S. Gazzaniga, ed., *The Cognitive Neurosciences* (Cambridge, MA: MIT Press, 1995); Daniel C. Dennett, *Consciousness Explained* (Boston: Little, Brown, 1991).
25. Hebrews 13:2. An example of communication where the form of the angel could not be perceived by the human participant is given in Job 4:12–17.
26. Genesis 18:1–19:29; Daniel 10:1–21.
27. Jeremiah 7:16; 14:10–12; 1 Corinthians 14:1–40; James 5:13–20; 1 John 5:14–17.
28. John 1:9; 3:19–21; Romans 1:18–21.
29. Ecclesiastes 3:11.
30. Romans 2:11–15.
31. Romans 3:9–20.
32. Revelation 20:11–15.
33. Romans 12:1–2; Galatians 5:22–23.
34. 2 Corinthians 6:16.
35. Job 34:14–15.
36. Romans 12:9–21; 1 Corinthians 12:4–31; Ephesians 4:11–16.
37. John 10:10.
38. Matthew 17:20–21.
39. Matthew 21:21–22.
40. John 14:12–15.
41. John 15:7.
42. John 16:33.
43. 2 Corinthians 3:18.

44. 2 Corinthians 4:16–18.
45. Psalm 103:20; 2 Thessalonians 1:7.
46. Revelation 14:10.
47. 2 Peter 2:11.
48. Matthew 26:53.
49. 2 Kings 2:9–12; 6:15–18.
50. Daniel 10:4–8.
51. Isaiah 42:8; 43:10–11; 44:6; 45:5, 22–24.
52. Revelation 7:2–3; 16:8–9.
53. Isaiah 44:24; Colossians 1:16–17; Revelation 4:11.
54. Matthew 22:30.
55. Genesis 6:2–4; Jude 6–8. A fuller exposition on this interpretation is given in my book, *The Genesis Question,* 2nd ed. (Colorado Springs: NavPress, 2001), 127–37, 203–4.
56. Ephesians 3:10; 6:12; Colossians 1:16; 2:15.
57. Ezekiel 28:12–17.
58. Ezekiel 1; 10.
59. Revelation 4:6–8.
60. Harris, Archer, and Waltke, *Theological Wordbook,* 2:884.
61. Isaiah 6:2–7.
62. Daniel 10:13.
63. Daniel 10:21; Jude 9.
64. Revelation 12:7–9.
65. Psalm 8:4–5; Hebrews 2:6–7.
66. Ephesians 1:8–10; 3:10; 1 Peter 1:12.
67. Daniel 7:18–27; 1 Corinthians 6:2–3.
68. Matthew 18:10.
69. Hebrews 1:14.

Chapter 12: God's Omnipotence vs. Displayed Power

1. Numbers 23:19; 1 Samuel 15:29; Psalm 33:4; 100:5; 117:2; 146:6; Daniel 4:37; John 17:17; Titus 1:2; Hebrews 6:18.
2. 2 Chronicles 19:7; Job 34:10; Psalm 5:4; Matthew 19:17; Luke 6:35; Romans 1:23; James 1:13.
3. Psalm 1:5; 5:4–5; 11:4–6; Habakkuk 1:13; Matthew 7:23.
4. Ecclesiastes 3:17; 11:9; 12:14.
5. Malachi 3:6; Romans 11:29; Hebrews 6:17–18; James 1:17.
6. This subject is addressed in much detail in my book *Why the Universe Is*

the Way It Is (Grand Rapids: Baker, 2008), 95–106, 147–91.
7.   Luke 18:18.
8.   Luke 18:19.
9.   2 Peter 3:9.
10.   1 John 4:7–12, 16.

Chapter 13: Extradimensionality and the Battle of Wills

1.   Joshua 24:14–15.
2.   Joshua 24:19.
3.   Joshua 24:20–27.
4.   Exodus 33:19.
5.   Acts 13:48.
6.   Genesis 1:2.
7.   John 1:12; Romans 8:1–17; 13:11; 2 Corinthians 10:4–5; Philippians 2:12–13; Colossians 1:28–29; 2 Thessalonians 3:3–5; 1 John 3:2.
8.   John 8:34–44; Acts 8:20–24; Romans 7:15–25; Colossians 2:8; 2 Timothy 2:22–26.
9.   1 John 1:5–5:20.
10.   Romans 12:1–2; 2 Corinthians 4:14–18; Ephesians 4:22–24; Colossians 3:9–10; 1 Peter 1:3-9.
11.   John 8:34–44; Romans 1:18–32; 2 Thessalonians 2:9–12.
12.   Revelation 22:13.
13.   1 Samuel 23:10–12; Isaiah 42:9; 46:9–11; 48:5–8; Daniel 2:28–29; Romans 8:29; 11:2; 1 Peter 1:2.
14.   Exodus 3:13–14; John 8:58.
15.   Romans 8:29.
16.   Romans 9:11–13.
17.   Romans 11:2, 5.
18.   1 Peter 1:1–2.
19.   Hugh Ross, *A Matter of Days* (Colorado Springs: NavPress, 2004), 149–206.
20.   Job 38:22–30; Psalm 139:13–16; Proverbs 21:1; Ephesians 2:10; 5:15–17; Colossians 4:5–6; 1 Peter 3:13–4:19.
21.   1 Samuel 23:10–12; 1 Kings 22:19–22; Daniel 10:12–11:1; Acts 8:26–40.
22.   1 Corinthians 10:13.
23.   Romans 8:28.

Chapter 14: Extradimensionality and Salvation's Assurance

1. 2 Corinthians 13:5.
2. Psalms 33:11; 119:89; Ecclesiastes 3:14; Malachi 3:6; Romans 11:29; Hebrews 6:17–18; James 1:17.
3. Hugh Ross, *The Fingerprint of God,* commemorative ed. (Covina, CA: RTB Press, 2010), 145–148.
4. Galatians 5:22–23.
5. 2 Corinthians 1:21–22; 5:5; Ephesians 1:13–14; 2 Timothy 1:12.
6. Kenneth S. Wuest, *Wuest's Word Studies from the Greek New Testament* (Grand Rapids: Eerdmans, 1973), 2:113–117; Arthur W. Pink, *Eternal Security* (Grand Rapids: Guardian Press, 1974), 91–93.
7. 2 Peter 2:22.
8. Romans 8:38–39.
9. 2 Corinthians 1:21–22; 5:5; Ephesians 1:13–14.
10. 2 Timothy 1:12.
11. Philippians 2:12.
12. 2 Peter 3:17.
13. 2 John 8.
14. Ephesians 2:8–9.
15. 1 John 5:16–17.
16. Exodus 7:13; 22–23; 8:15; 19, 32; 9:7; Exodus 9:12, 35; 10:20, 27; 14:4 (NASB).
17. Mark 3:28–29.
18. Romans 1:24.
19. Romans 1:26.
20. Romans 1:28.
21. Ephesians 2:10.
22. Romans 12:1–2.
23. Ross, *Fingerprint of God*, 177–78.
24. Revelation 20:11–15.
25. Matthew 7:21–23; 23:1–36; John 8:19, 23–26, 37–47.
26. 2 Timothy 1:12.

Chapter 15: Extradimensionality and Evil and Suffering

1. Fazale Rana and Hugh Ross, *Origins of Life: Biblical and Evolutionary Models Face Off* (Covina, CA: NavPress, 2014), 111–71; Robert Shapiro, *Origins: A Skeptic's Guide to the Creation of Life on Earth* (New York: Summit Books, 1986), 117–31; Hubert P. Yockey, *Information Theory*

and Molecular Biology (Cambridge: Cambridge University Press, 1992), 129–330; Fred Hoyle and N. C. Wickramasinghe, *Evolution from Space: A Theory of Cosmic Creationism* (New York: Simon and Schuster, 1981), 23–33.

2.   Rana and Ross, *Origins of Life*, 65–105; Yockey, *Information Theory*, 221–41; Shapiro, *Origins*, 86–116.

3.   Stanley L. Miller and Jeffrey L. Bada, "Submarine Hot Springs and the Origin of Life," *Nature* 334 (August 1988): 609–11, doi:10.1038/334609a0; Matthew Levy and Stanley L. Miller, "The Stability of the RNA Bases: Implications for the Origin of Life," *Proceedings of the National Academy of Sciences, USA* 95 (July 1998): 7933–38; H. James Cleaves II and Stanley L. Miller, "The Prebiotic Synthesis of Nucleoside Analogues from Mixed Formose Reactions: Implications for the First Genetic Material," abstract in *ISSOL '02 Book of Abstracts*, comp. and ed. Alicia Negron-Mendoza et al. (Oaxaca, MEX: ISSOL, 2002), 102; Rosa Larralde, Michael P. Robertson, and Stanley L. Miller, "Rates of Decomposition of Ribose and Other Sugars: Implications for Chemical Evolution," *Proceedings of the National Academy of Sciences, USA* 92 (August 1995): 8158–60; Robert Irion, "Ocean Scientists Find Life, Warmth in the Seas," *Science* 279 (February 1998): 1302–3, doi:10.1126/science.279.5355.1302; Rana and Ross, *Origins of Life*, 109–33, 171–204.

4.   Michael P. Robertson and Stanley L. Miller, "An Efficient Prebiotic Synthesis of Cytosine and Uracil," *Nature* 375 (June 1995): 772–74.

5.   Colin Patterson, *Evolution*, 2nd ed. (Ithaca: Comstock, 1999), 23; André Goffeau, "Life With 482 Genes," *Science* 270 (October 1995): 445–46, doi:10.1126/science.270.5235.445; Claire M. Fraser et al., "The Minimal Gene Complement of *Mycoplasma genitalium*," *Science* 270 (October 1995): 397–403, doi:10.1126/science.270.5235.397; Arcady R. Mushegian and Eugene V. Koonin, "A Minimal Gene Set for Cellular Life Derived by Comparison of Complete Bacterial Genomes," *Proceedings of the National Academy of Sciences, USA* 93 (September 1996): 10268–73; Rana and Ross, *Origins of Life*, 159–168.

6.   Elizabeth Pennisi, "Static Evolution: Is Pond Scum the Same Now as Billions of Years Ago?" *Science News*, March 12, 1994, 168–69.

7.   Bing Shen et al., "The Avalon Explosion: Evolution of Ediacara Morphospace," *Science* 319 (January 2008): 81–84, doi:10.1126/science.1150279; Hugh Ross, *More Than a Theory: Revealing a Testable Model for Creation* (Grand Rapids: Baker, 2009), 160–63.

8.   Peter D. Ward and Donald Brownlee, *Rare Earth: Why Complex Life Is Uncommon in the Universe* (New York: Copernicus, Springer-Verlag, 2000), 125–56; Paul Chien, interview by Fazale Rana and Hugh Ross, "'Exploding' With Life!" *Facts for Faith*, no. 2, second quarter 2000, 12–17.

9.   Hugh Ross, *More Than a Theory: Revealing a Testable Model for Creation* (Grand Rapids: Baker, 2009), 83–86, 156–60, 164–69, and citations therein; Hugh Ross, "Creation on the 'Firing Line,'" *Facts & Faith*, first quarter 1998, 6–7.

10.   Julio Sepúlveda et al., "Rapid Resurgence of Marine Productivity after the Cretaceous-Paleogene Mass Extinction," *Science* 326 (October 2009): 129–32, doi:10.1126/science.1176233; Paul Bown, "Selective Calcareous Nannoplankton Survivorship at the Cretaceous-Tertiary Boundary," *Geology* 33 (August 2005): 653–56, doi:10.1130/G21566AR.1; Vivi Vajda, J. Ian Raine, and Christopher J. Hollis, "Indication of Global Deforestation at the Cretaceous-Tertiary Boundary by New Zealand Fern Spike," *Science* 294 (November 2001): 1700–2, doi:10.1126/science.1064706; R. D. Norris, B. T. Huber, and J. Self-Trail, "Synchroneity of the K-T Oceanic Mass Extinction and Meteorite Impact: Blake Nose, Western North Atlantic," *Geology* 27 (May 1999): 419–22; Kenneth G. MacLeod et al., "Impact and Extinction in Remarkably Complete Cretaceous-Tertiary Boundary Sections from Demerara Rise, Tropical Western North Atlantic," *Geological Society of America Bulletin* 119 (January 2007): 101–15, doi:10.1130/B25955.1; Richard K. Olsson et al., "Ejecta Layer at the Cretaceous-Tertiary Boundary, Bass River, New Jersey (Ocean Drilling Program Leg 174AX)," *Geology* 25 (August 1997): 759–62, doi:10.1130/0091-7613(1997)025<0759:ELATCT>2.3.CO;2; Richard A. Kerr, "Cores Document Ancient Catastrophe," *Science* 275 (February 1997): 1265, doi:10.1126/science.275.5304.1265.

11.   Zachary D. Blount, Christina D. Borland, and Richard E. Lenski, "Historical Contingency and the Evolution of a Key Innovation in an Experimental Population of *Escherichia coli*," *Proceedings of the National Academy of Sciences, USA* 105 (June 2008): 7899–906, doi:10.1072/pnas.0803151105; Gail W. T. Wilson et al., "Soil Aggregation and Carbon Sequestration Are Tightly Correlated With the Abundance of Arbuscular Mycorrhizal Fungi: Results from Long-Term Field Experiments," *Ecology Letters* 12 (May 2009): 452–61; doi:10.111/j.1461-0248.2009.01303.x; Ross, *More Than a Theory*, 169–71.

12. Art Battson, "On the Origin of Stasis," *Access Research Network*, February 9, 1998, http://www.arn.org/docs/abstasis.htm; Hugh Ross, *A Matter of Days: Resolving a Creation Controversy*, 2nd ed. (Covina, CA: RTB Press, 2004), 120–125; Ross, *More Than a Theory*, 160–63.

13. Graham Bell and Andrew Gonzalez, "Evolutionary Rescue Can Prevent Extinction Following Environmental Change," *Ecology Letters* 12 (September 2009): 942–48, doi:10.111/j.1461-0248.2009.01350.x; Blount, Boland, and Lenski, "Historical Contingency," 7899–906; Ross, *A Matter of Days*, 124–29; Ross, *More Than a Theory*, 164–66.

14. John H. Lawton and Robert M. May, eds., *Extinction Rates* (New York: Oxford University Press, 1995); Roger Lewin, "No Dinosaurs This Time," *Science* 221 (September 1983): 1168–69, doi:10.1126/science.221.4616.1168; Janet Raloff, "Earth Day 1980: The 29th Day?" *Science News* 117 (1980): 270; Paul R. Ehrlich, Anne H. Ehrlich, and J. P. Holdren, *Ecoscience: Population, Resources, Environment* (San Francisco: W. H. Freeman, 1977), 142; Paul R. Ehrlich and Anne Ehrlich, *Extinction: The Causes and Consequences of the Disappearance of Species* (New York: Random House, 1981), 23, 33; Ross, *A Matter of Days*, 81–83.

15. Fazale Rana with Hugh Ross, *Who Was Adam? A Creation Model Approach to the Origin of Man*, 2nd ed. (Covina, CA: RTB Press, 2015), 59–80, 184–247, 263–378.

16. Stephen A. Smith, Jeremy M. Beaulieu, and Michael J. Donoghue, "An Uncorrelated Relaxed-Clock Analysis Suggests an Earlier Origin for Flowering Plants," *Proceedings of the National Academy of Sciences, USA* 107 (March 2010): 5897–902, doi:10.1073/pnas.1001225107; Blount, Borland, and Lenski, "Historical Contingency," 7899–906; Rana with Ross, *Who Was Adam?* 59–80, 184–247, 263-378.

17. Rana with Ross, *Who Was Adam?*, 59–113, 143–247, 263–378 and citations therein.

18. Ibid., 55–75, 179–243 and citations therein.

19. Ross, *More Than a Theory*, 181–93; Ross, *A Matter of Days*, 235–39; Hugh Ross, *Hidden Treasures in the Book of Job: How the Oldest Book in the Bible Answers Today's Scientific Questions* (Grand Rapids: Baker, 2011).

20. Genesis 2:8–3:24.

21. Hugh Ross, *Why the Universe Is the Way It Is* (Grand Rapids: Baker, 2008).

22. Numbers 11:5.

23. Exodus 12:1–50; Numbers 9:1–5; 10:11–12; 13:1–30.

24. Deuteronomy 1:3–4; Joshua 4:19.

25. Exodus 13:17–18.

26. Ibid.

27. Acts 6:5–8:2; 9:1–22.

28. Ralph Winter, "The Diminishing Task: The Field and the Force," *Mission Frontiers*, January–March 1991, 36; "God's Symphony of Effort," *Mission Frontiers*, January–February 1995, 6; Luis Bush, "The Unfinished Task: It Can Be Done by AD 2000" *Mission Frontiers*, March–April 1995, 7–14.

29. Deuteronomy 29:29; Isaiah 64–66; Ephesians 1:11–23; 3:7–20; Philippians 2:12–18; 3:12–4:1; Hebrews 12:1–2; Revelation 1–22.

30. Philippians 3:13–14.

31. Hebrews 12:2–3.

32. Romans 8:18.

33. James 1:2–4.

34. 1 John 3:2–3.

Chapter 16: God's Extradimensional Love in Hell

1.   1 Corinthians 10:13 (NASB).

2.   Revelation 19:20–21; 20:10, 14–15.

3.   *Evangelical Dictionary of Theology*, ed. Walter A. Elwell (Grand Rapids: Baker, 1984), s.v. "Hell," by R. P. Lightner.

4.   Marvin Moore, "Where on Earth Is Hell?" *Signs of the Times*, January 1996, 29.

5.   It will soon (on an astronomical timescale) be impossible for the universe to sustain advanced life anywhere. Furthermore, it is impossible for the universe to provide the promised rewards of the kingdom of heaven. For the reasons why, see Hugh Ross, *Why the Universe Is the Way It Is* (Grand Rapids: Baker, 2008), 43–78, 95–118, 125–206.

6.   Piers Paul Read, "Why We Need to Believe in Hell; As a Report Casts Doubt on Hell Fire and Eternal Damnation," *Daily Mail (London)*, January 12, 1996, https://www.highbeam.com/doc/1G1-111435535.html; Doctrine Commission of the General Synod of the Church of England, *The Mystery of Salvation* (Harrisburg, PA: Morehouse, 1996).

7.   Isaiah 34:4; 2 Peter 3:10–13.

8.   Revelation 20:7–22:15.

9.   Ross, *Why the Universe*, 159–60, 165–81.

10. Revelation 20:11–15.

11. Revelation 21:1–4.
12. Ecclesiastes 3:11; Revelation 20:10–22:15.
13. Revelation 21:8; 22:15.
14. Hebrews 10:26.
15. John 3:15–21.
16. Hugh Ross, *The Fingerprint of God,* commemorative ed. (Covina, CA: RTB Press, 2010), 145–148; Don Richardson, *Eternity in Their Hearts,* 3rd ed. (Ventura, CA: Regal, Gospel Light, 2005).
17. Romans 1:18–25.
18. 2 Timothy 3:1–9; 2 Peter 2; Jude 8–16.
19. Revelation 14:10–11.
20. Revelation 19:20.
21. Revelation 20:10.
22. Revelation 20:15.
23. Matthew 3:12.
24. Matthew 18:8.
25. Matthew 25:41.
26. Mark 9:47–48; Isaiah 66:24.
27. Jude 7.
28. Revelation 20:11–15.
29. *The New International Dictionary of New Testament Theology*, ed. Colin Brown (Grand Rapids: Zondervan, 1978), 3:856.

Chapter 17: Extradimensionality and the New Creation

1. Revelation 21:1.
2. Revelation 21:4–5.
3. Revelation 21:16.
4. Revelation 21:15.
5. Revelation 21:10–21.
6. Luke 24:36–43; John 20:25–28; 1 John 1:1.
7. 1 Corinthians 15:35–57.
8. Romans 8:18–21.
9. Revelation 21:4.
10. Revelation 21:6–7.
11. 2 Corinthians 12:1–6.
12. John 14:1–4 (KJV).
13. Romans 8:17; Ephesians 1:3; Revelation 3:21.
14. Victor J. Stenger, *God: The Failed Hypothesis* (Amherst, NY: Prometheus,

2007), 160–61.

15. Ibid., 154–62.

16. Hugh Ross, *Why the Universe Is the Way It Is* (Grand Rapids: Baker, 2008), 57–78; Hugh Ross, Kenneth Samples, and Mark Clark, *Lights in the Sky and Little Green Men: A Rational Christian Look at UFOs and Extraterrestrials* (Colorado Springs: NavPress, 2002), 55–64.

17. Hugh Ross, *A Matter of Days: Resolving a Creation Controversy,* 2nd ed. (Covina, CA: RTB Press, 2014), 89–104, especially 102–104.

18. 1 Corinthians 15:42–44; 50–54.

19. Psalm 34:9–10; Isaiah 65:13; Revelation 7:16.

20. John 8:12; 2 Corinthians 4:6; 1 John 1:5; Revelation 21:23–25; 22:5.

21. Revelation 21:8, 26–27.

22. 1 Corinthians 3:12–15.

23. 1 John 3:1–3.

24. Romans 8:17; 1 Corinthians 6:2–3; 1 Peter 2:9; Revelation 22:5.

25. John 17:11; Romans 12:5; 15:5–6; Revelation 21:9–27.

26. Matthew 22:29–32; Luke 20:34–39.

27. John 17:11; Romans 12:5; 15:5–6; Revelation 21:9–27.

28. Luke 2:25–38.

29. Luke 19:1–9.

30. Mark 2:1–12.

31. Ephesians 1:13–14.

32. Revelation 5:11.

33. I explore these purposes in my book, *Why the Universe Is the Way It Is.*

Chapter 18: An Invitation to Soar Higher Still

1. 1 Corinthians 2:9–12.

2. John 14:12–14; Ephesians 2:10.

3. John 17:23.

Appendix: Evidence for Strings

1. Alexander Belyaev et al., "LHC Discovery Potential of the Lightest NMS-SM Higgs in the $h_1 \to a_1 a_1 \to 4\mu$ Channel," Physical Review D 81 (April 2010), 075021, doi:10.1103/PhysRevD.81.075021; Alexander Belyaev, "Supersymmetry Status and Phenomenology at the Large Hadron Collider," *Pramana* 72 (January 2009): 143–60; Shaaban Khalil, "Search for Supersymmetry at LHC," *Contemporary Physics* 44 (May 2003): 193–201; Martin Breidenbach, "Zeroing in on the Elusive Higgs Boson," U. S.

Department of Energy (March 2001), http://www.science.doe.gov/Accomplishments_Awards/Decades_Discovery/35.htm.

2. S. K. Lamoreaux et al., "New Limits on Spatial Anisotropy from Optically-Pumped *sup201*Hg and ^{199}Hg," *Physical Review Letters* 57 (December 1986): 3125–28; Michael Edmund Tobar et al., "Testing Local Lorentz and Position Invariance and Variation of Fundamental Constants by Searching the Derivative of the Comparison Frequency between a Cryogenic Sapphire Oscillator and Hydrogen Maser," *Physical Review D* 81 (January 2010): doi: 10.1103/PhysRevD.81.022003, https://arxiv.org/ftp/arxiv/papers/0912/0912.2803.pdf; Holger Müller et al., "Tests of Relativity by Complementary Rotating Michelson-Morley Experiments," *Physical Review Letters* 99 (August 2007), doi:10.1103/PhysRevLett.99.050401, http://prl.aps.org/abstract/PRL/v99/i5/ e050401; P. Antonini et al., "Test of Constancy of Speed of Light with Rotating Cyrogenic Optical Resonators," *Physical Review A* 71 (May 2005): doi:10.1103/PhysRevA.71.050101; Paul L. Stanwix et al., "Improved Test of Lorentz Invariance in Electrodynamics Using Rotating Cryogenic Sapphire Oscillators," *Physical Review D* 74 (October 2006): doi:10.1103/PhysRevD.74.081101.

3. Stephen Hawking's *A Brief History of Time* (New York: Bantam, 1988), 99–113, provides the best lay-friendly explanation of this discovery I've found.

4. Andrew Strominger and Cumrun Vafa, "Microscopic Origin of the Bekenstein-Hawking Entropy," *Physics Letters B* 379 (June 1996): 99–104, doi:10.1016/0370-2693(96)00345-0.

5. James Glanz, "Strings Unknot Problems in Particle Theory," *Science* 276 (June 1997): 1969–70, doi:10.1126/science.276.5321.1969.

6. S. N. Zhang, Wei Cui, and Wan Chen, "Black Hole Spin in X-Ray Binaries: Observational Consequences," *Astrophysical Journal Letters* 482 (June 1997): L155–L158, doi:10.1086/310705.

Index

About the Author

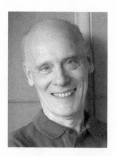

Hugh Ross is founder and president of Reasons to Believe, an organization that researches and communicates how God's revelation in the words of the Bible harmonizes with the facts of nature.

With a degree in physics from the University of British Columbia and a grant from the National Research Council of Canada, Dr. Ross earned a PhD in astronomy from the University of Toronto. For several years he continued his research on quasars and galaxies as a postdoctoral fellow at the California Institute of Technology. His writings include journal and magazine articles and numerous books—*Improbable Planet, Navigating Genesis, Why the Universe Is the Way It Is*, and more. He has spoken on hundreds of university campuses as well as at conferences and churches around the world.

He lives in Southern California with his wife, Kathy.

About Reasons to Believe

Uniquely positioned within the science-faith discussion since 1986, Reasons to Believe (RTB) communicates that science and faith are, and always will be, allies, not enemies. Distinguished for integrating science and faith respectfully and with integrity, RTB welcomes dialogue with both skeptics and believers. Addressing topics such as the origin of the universe, the origin of life, and the history and destiny of humanity, RTB's website offers a vast array of helpful resources. Through their books, blogs, podcasts, and speaking events, RTB scholars present powerful reasons from science to trust in the reliability of the Bible and the message it conveys about creation and redemption.

For more information, contact us via:
www.reasons.org
818 S. Oak Park Rd.
Covina, CA 91724
(855) REASONS | (855) 732-7667
ministrycare@reasons.org

If God made the universe...

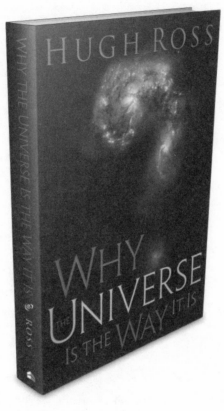